# Praise for *Software Supply Chain Security*

Supply chain security is top of mind for all manufacturing companies; therefore, this book is definitely a reference for those who want to address this systematic risk.

—*Christophe Blassiau, Cybersecurity and Product Security SVP,*
*Global CISO and CPSO, Schneider Electric*

Software touches everything: water, food, electricity, timely patient care. As society increasingly depends upon software, it increasingly depends upon those who produce it. Ready or not, transparency is coming. Where others have made excuses, Cassie has made progress advancing software trust and transparency, and now you can too.

—*Josh Corman, Father of SBOM and Founder of*
*public safety initiative, I Am the Cavalry*

Cassie has been a pioneer in advocating for and advancing SBOM, particularly in critical infrastructure. This volume is a critical contribution that underscores the need for software transparency and highlights paths to implementation.

—*Allan Friedman, PhD in public policy, SBOM champion*

Cassie is a known expert in software supply chain security, and this book provides clear, actionable guidance when the industry is rapidly evolving and in need of wisdom.

—*Christine Gadsby, Vice President, Product Security, Blackberry*

In today's generative AI world, every company is a software company and is impacted by the software supply chain security. This book is a game-changer. This is a must-read guide designed to enlighten CEOs and board members alike.

—*Nikhil Gupta, Founder and CEO, ArmorCode Inc.*

Cassie has written a book that is comprehensive, detailed, technical, and easily readable. It is an excellent overview for beginners but very useful to cybersecurity pros on how the brave new world of software supply chains can be exploited—and defended.

—*Charles Hart, Senior Analyst, Hitachi America, Ltd.*

Cassie Crossley has been in the trenches of supply chain security and understands the real-world operational, legal, and financial challenges in a way that academics and bureaucrats don't always grasp.

—*JC Herz, SVP Exiger Cyber Supply Chain*

Cassie brings a wealth of knowledge to this book, covering relevant attack vectors, emerging frameworks, vulnerability disclosures, products, open source, third-party suppliers and navigating the complex human element, all too often overlooked in software supply chain security.

—*Chris Hughes, President and Cofounder, Aquia;*
*Cyber Innovation Fellow (CIF) at CISA; Coauthor of* Software Transparency

Cassie's book is the most thorough, practical, organized, and actionable supply chain advice I've ever received. Via frameworks and detailed plans, this book lays out exactly what to do to ensure your entire product supply chain (physical or digital) is reliably secure.

—*Tanya Janca (SheHacksPurple), Head of Community and*
*Education, Semgrep; Author of* Alice and Bob Learn Application Security

Securing software supply chains is complex and confusing. Cassie comprehensively addresses this with an experienced practitioner's eye. This is a phenomenal resource for understanding the risks and how to address them. Technology and business leaders alike will benefit from this!

—*Kent Landfield, Chief Standards and*
*Technology Policy Strategist, Trellix*

Software supply chain management requires more than an SBOM. Regulations, legislation, development models, and deployment decisions make the real world complex. Cassie does a fantastic job simplifying this complexity and providing actionable guidance to address your supply chain risks.

—*Tim Mackey, Head of Software Supply Chain*
*Risk Strategy, Synopsys*

# Software Supply Chain Security

*Securing the End-to-End Supply Chain
for Software, Firmware, and Hardware*

*Cassie Crossley*

Beijing · Boston · Farnham · Sebastopol · Tokyo

**Software Supply Chain Security**

by Cassie Crossley

Copyright © 2024 Cassaundra Crossley. All rights reserved.

Published by O'Reilly Media, Inc., 1005 Gravenstein Highway North, Sebastopol, CA 95472.

O'Reilly books may be purchased for educational, business, or sales promotional use. Online editions are also available for most titles (*http://oreilly.com*). For more information, contact our corporate/institutional sales department: 800-998-9938 or *corporate@oreilly.com*.

**Acquisitions Editor:** Jennifer Pollock
**Development Editor:** Rita Fernando
**Production Editor:** Elizabeth Faerm
**Copyeditor:** nSight, Inc.
**Proofreader:** J.M. Olejarz

**Indexer:** Ellen Troutman-Zaig
**Interior Designer:** Monica Kamsvaag
**Cover Designer:** Karen Montgomery
**Illustrator:** Kate Dullea

February 2024:      First Edition

**Revision History for the First Edition**
2024-02-02:    First Release

See *http://oreilly.com/catalog/errata.csp?isbn=9781098133702* for release details.

978-1-098-13370-2

[LSI]

# Table of Contents

# Foreword

The way we work has changed significantly over recent years with the adoption of cloud technologies that drive business strategy, artificial intelligence that brings data to life in ways we never thought possible, and compute power at everyone's fingertips that allows us to do more.

This change has been made possible by the underlying ecosystem of technology that is embedded in every area of our lives. Every device, vehicle, hospital, school, office, and home is driven by technology. This technology has an inherent supply chain of software, hardware, and firmware components to make it work and connect to our daily lives.

The supply chain is seamless to most, but not to those who are tasked with protecting it. It's a magnificent evolution of technology that has changed how we live. It is therefore no surprise that the way in which we design, develop, and operate these technologies must also evolve. That comes with great responsibility to ensure we keep our technology safe and secure from cyberattacks that could cause anything from data exposure to operational failure to revenue impacts to loss of life.

As with any revolution, the pendulum can sometimes swing too far one way before normalizing over time. The inflection point between innovation and regulation, pulling from opposite ends of the spectrum, is a balance we must get right. The supply chain evolution has seen changes in many laws and regulations over the years, ranging from federal regulations to international laws that govern the software development lifecycle. These kinds of laws are important, yet they cannot hinder our ability to innovate and operate.

We must apply them with a practical lens. As with most aspects of security, there are many frameworks designed to ensure controls are in place to protect us from the array of threats we face. Those developed for software development lifecycles give great guidance to a subject that is often misunderstood. Building them into day-to-day practices and leveraging them as an enabler, rather than a hindrance, is very important to the continuity of business.

Before I went into technology, I was a fraud detective in England for many years. As a young recruit, I remember one of my police trainers telling me to "never forget we are all in the people business." How true that statement has been throughout my career, and how true that is for cybersecurity professionals, who are almost 100% reliant on someone else doing something for them to succeed.

As a former chief information security officer (CISO) of *Fortune* 500 companies with vastly different technology supply chains, from buildings to aircraft to software products, I understand the challenges of bringing the many teams together to align on how to tackle these responsibilities. It is a complex ecosystem that needs dedicated focus at every step. Having continuity, integrity, and transparency across your technology supply chain is critical. And as my former police trainer would be proud to hear me say, the people are critical too.

Security is not the job of one person or team alone; it is the job of everyone.

What Cassie has brought together in this book is a thoughtful, end-to-end guide of all the moving pieces and considerations that technology and security teams must think about as they build out their products or services. It is a practical blueprint for how to design and implement your security programs with modern supply chain risks in mind, whether you are in software development, manufacturing, critical infrastructure, or anything in between.

Cassie is one of the very few experts in her craft and draws from her years of hands-on experience managing these processes for complex organizations. She is skilled in managing the broader scope of supply chain risk that has extended beyond a company's own four walls. Supply chain risk must be considered at all levels of your operation, including who you choose to partner with. Every company is an ecosystem.

The multifaceted responsibility of supply chain security is therefore not just about what we develop, manufacture, or provide, but is also about the integrity and security of the partners that are built into our businesses. Third- and fourth-party risks are our responsibility. Cassie explains the importance of this lens throughout this book.

As a venture capital partner, I now have the privilege of working with some of the brightest minds in the business who are looking to solve emerging cyber challenges. It is where innovation meets operation. While the concept of technology supply chain security is not new, the way we work is. Code is everywhere. Risk is everywhere.

With the right approach to balancing the technical designs and processes, the governance needed for transparency and integrity, and the people aspects of what a successful security program looks like, your chances of success are much higher. Cassie's willingness to impart her expertise and share it with others exemplifies what makes the cybersecurity community so strong. We are stronger together.

Stay safe out there!

*— Emily Heath*
*General Partner, Cyberstarts Venture Capital*
*Board Member, Gen Digital (NASDAQ: GEN)*
*Board Member, Wiz*
*Board Member, Logicgate*

# Preface

Software is everywhere. Trillions of lines of source code are running every part of our lives. A single software vulnerability or ransomware attack can stop entire companies from doing business and cause billions of dollars in revenue loss and business recovery. Now, more than ever, we need to ensure that our software, firmware, and hardware are secure to keep our world up and running, safely and securely.

Malware, security vulnerabilities, application security, and product security are not new to the software industry, but now these topics have reached mainstream news because of the effects they have on everyone. My part in this became very real when I was visiting my family on the US East Coast the week of the Colonial Pipeline attack.[1] I spent two hours waiting in line at the sole gas station within 20 miles that had gas, and then the rest of that afternoon explaining to my family about business continuity and supply chain attacks.

Supply chains are critical to our lives. According to Investopedia, "a supply chain is a network of individuals and companies who are involved in creating a product and delivering it to the consumer."[2] The same is true for software. Software usually is developed by multiple individuals, who are often part of multiple organizations or companies. Over time, thousands of developers may have code inside of a single application. For example, I wrote code for ZSoft's paint.exe, which was sold to Microsoft in the 1980s. I'm certain there are lines of my code still in existence within MS Paint on the Microsoft Windows platform. Nearly 40 years later, an untold number of developers have also contributed their talents to the small, but useful, application.

Ensuring software security within the supply chain is difficult, usually due to the longevity of code that was written before secure development and secure design practices were in place. Combined with the ever-increasing threat actors who are constantly discovering new ways to exploit code and systems, it will always be difficult to guarantee a product or application's security, but that should not prevent us from doing our absolute best to secure the software supply chain.

Despite the complicated nature of the software supply chain, it is our duty as software producers to establish secure supply chains and provide information to our consumers. As consumers, we should use this information to address the risks that the supply chain might present to our own organizations.

The effort to improve a company's software supply chain is not small. And it's not only a software development process problem: software supply chain security requires all parties in the supply chain to participate in order to improve the security posture of software, firmware, and hardware.

In this book, I will show you how to implement a software supply chain security program in an organization of any size, but especially for small companies that don't have dedicated application or supply chain security experts. I will explain why each security control exists, without someone needing a computer science or cybersecurity degree to understand the security risks and the reasons for the controls.

This book is not intended to be an all-encompassing set of controls. You can remove any controls that are not applicable and add the controls you need to the controls framework you already have in place. I have included hundreds of references for those needing to follow mandated frameworks, standards, laws, or regulations. However, I must caution you to not limit yourself to those frameworks. You should always be extending and adapting your controls to meet the current gaps and risks within your organization.

## Who Should Read This Book

This book is for anyone who has been tasked with the security of third parties, the supply chain, the purchase of products and applications for their organization, open source software, or software developed within their organization. You may or may not have "security" in your title. Anyone entrusted with the selection, production, and operation of software can use this book to understand the risks in the software supply chain and to implement controls and frameworks. The book doesn't require a cybersecurity background, though some areas will be technical in explanation, with many references to encourage further learning.

I've created this practical reference to be understood by business and technology leaders, as well as those in the legal, procurement, insurance, and supply chain organizations. This book is also for security program leaders, whether in the role of CISO (chief information security officer), CPSO (chief product security officer), CSO (chief security officer), GRC (governance, risk, and compliance), application security, or product security.

# Why I Wrote This Book

My software development story began with a visit to my dad's work at the IBM manufacturing plant in Rochester, Minnesota, in the mid-1970s. My dad was a programmer, and although I didn't really understand what he did, I knew it had something to do with making machines that produced interesting and complex things. Years later, I still find software development to be interesting, complex, and full of nuance. As someone who has participated as a developer, project manager, and executive leader in over a thousand releases for consumer and business applications, I understand the practical nature of releasing quality products on time and on budget. In my roles as cybersecurity leader and product security leader, I have also held the responsibility for delivering secure applications, products, systems, and infrastructure for a portfolio of over 15,000 intelligent products.

What led me to my passion for supply chain security, however, is a result of my work with the thousands of vendors in our supply chain. For years I have been meeting with suppliers to discuss their secure development lifecycle, secure testing plans, vulnerability management, third-party risk, and more. These suppliers, who contribute source code, software libraries, components, products, and services, usually do not have the resources of a large, multinational corporation. Identifying the key controls and practices for their specific situation requires an understanding of priorities, risk, and impacts. It's a collaboration that is extremely important to me, and I've written this book specifically for organizations that are eager to improve software supply chain security.

Software supply chain security changes rapidly. No doubt there will be new and changed frameworks, documents, regulations, ideas, and links before this book is even published. It is my intention to keep this information as current as possible, so please feel free to sign up for my newsletter (*https://www.supplychainsecurity.pro/sign-up*). You can also contact me at *cassie@supplychainsecurity.pro* to send updates, feedback, and corrections; schedule a meeting; or request me as a speaker or guest.

# Navigating This Book

This book is organized as follows:

- Chapters 1 and 2 provide an introduction to the concepts of software supply chain security and explanations of the various frameworks and references in supply chain risk management.

- Chapter 3 summarizes the various infrastructure security controls that need special attention for software supply chain security.

- Chapter 4 explores the key practices within a secure development lifecycle and the various frameworks available.

- Chapters 5 and 6 describe the various types of source code and how to maintain their integrity during development, build, deployment, and operations for software, products, infrastructure, and cloud applications.
- Chapter 7 presents the security risks regarding intellectual property of source code and any data used in the supply chain.
- Chapter 8 discusses the transparency of the products and services through a software bill of materials and vulnerability disclosures.
- Chapter 9 prepares organizations to perform assessments for and manage cyber agreements with third-party suppliers.
- Chapter 10 specifies risks and controls for products that navigate through upstream processes such as manufacturing, logistics, or customer projects before reaching the consumer.
- Chapter 11 focuses on the risks introduced by people in the supply chain, and how to address those risks with awareness and training.

Within most chapters of this book and compiled in an appendix at the end, I also provide nearly 80 controls specifically focused on software supply chain security. You can add, remove, modify, or align these controls to the needs of your organization. The controls are available for download when you sign up for my newsletter (*https://supplychainsecurity.pro/sign-up*).

## Conventions Used in This Book

The following typographical conventions are used in this book:

*Italic*
Indicates new terms, URLs, email addresses, filenames, and file extensions.

`Constant width`
Used for program listings, as well as within paragraphs to refer to program elements such as variable or function names, databases, data types, environment variables, statements, and keywords.

## O'Reilly Online Learning

 For more than 40 years, *O'Reilly Media* has provided technology and business training, knowledge, and insight to help companies succeed.

Our unique network of experts and innovators share their knowledge and expertise through books, articles, and our online learning platform. O'Reilly's online learning platform gives you on-demand access to live training courses, in-depth learning paths, interactive coding environments, and a vast collection of text and video from O'Reilly and 200+ other publishers. For more information, visit *https://oreilly.com*.

## How to Contact Us

Please address comments and questions concerning this book to the publisher:

> O'Reilly Media, Inc.
> 1005 Gravenstein Highway North
> Sebastopol, CA 95472
> 800-889-8969 (in the United States or Canada)
> 707-827-7019 (international or local)
> 707-829-0104 (fax)
> *support@oreilly.com*
> *https://www.oreilly.com/about/contact.html*

We have a web page for this book, where we list errata, examples, and any additional information. You can access this page at *https://oreil.ly/software-supply-chain-security*.

For news and information about our books and courses, visit *https://oreilly.com*.

Find us on LinkedIn: *https://linkedin.com/company/oreilly-media*.

Follow us on Twitter: *https://twitter.com/oreillymedia*.

Watch us on YouTube: *https://youtube.com/oreillymedia*.

## Acknowledgments

I would like to express my sincere gratitude to my wonderful husband Craig and my amazing daughter Emma for providing me time alone to write and edit this book for the past year and a half. I want to thank Craig, Emma, my other amazing daughter Evelyn, my mom Carol, my sister Suzie, my brother Kelly, my best friend Amanda Jackson, as well as all my dear family, friends, and colleagues for their significant support and encouragement. Your excitement to see this book become a reality was very important and uplifting to me.

I would like to thank Charles Hart, Robert Lembree, and Kunal Bhattacharya for their countless hours reviewing and providing excellent suggestions to the chapters. If you ever need anything, I will be there for you.

I am so very grateful to Emily Heath for writing the foreword. She is an incredible inspiration and a rock star in cybersecurity. I'd also like to thank Luc Poulin for the assistance on "ISO/IEC 27034 Application Security" on page 65, Dr. Allan Friedman for all things SBOM, and the many folks in the SBOM communities, including Duncan Sparrell, Tom Alrich, Dmitry Raidman, Chris Blask, Audra Hatch, and Josh Corman.

I would like to thank my incredible current and past colleagues for their support, including Klaus Jaeckle, Christophe Blassiau, Sheila Casserly, Patrick Ford, Trevor Rudolph, Anne Marie van den Hurk, Mansur Abilkasimov, Megan Samford, Paul Forney, Matthieu Adam, Hussain Mujtaba, Dwaraka Atri, Paula Berger, and so many others. I'd also like to thank the Purple Book community members, who are the greatest application security leaders in technology, led by Nikhil Gupta and Lingraj Patil. Without the Purple Book, I would not have met so many brilliant people, including Mike Barlow, who introduced me to the editors at O'Reilly Media.

And my final thank you is to everyone at O'Reilly Media and to the greatest cheerleader and editor, Rita Fernando. She was so professional and understanding about the timelines and writing process. Her smile always gave me comfort, even when I was stressed.

I dedicate this book to my dad, James Forrest Crossley. He was a pioneer and patent holder in technology, but to me he was just a nerdy geek who believed his children could do anything.

## References

1   Charlie Osborne, "Colonial Pipeline Attack: Everything You Need to Know" (*https://www.zdnet.com/article/colonial-pipeline-ransomware-attack-everything-you-need-to-know*), ZDNET, May 13, 2021.

2   Adam Hayes, "The Supply Chain: From Raw Materials to Order Fulfillment" (*https://www.investopedia.com/terms/s/supplychain.asp*), Investopedia, March 28, 2023.

# CHAPTER 1

# Supply Chain Security

When you purchase something, the product you purchase usually has had a long journey from its original idea to the moment of delivery, as shown in Figure 1-1. You may recognize that the supply chain involves many participants in the item's journey, but you may not realize how many opportunities exist for something to happen as that item moves along the path. Supply chain security has been part of our existence for thousands of years, such as when spices were carried from East to West, when ships moved goods between continents during colonization, or when military troops transported food and weapons during world wars. In all those situations, people prepared for attacks and defended their supplies so the items could make it to their intended destination.

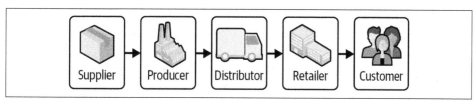

*Figure 1-1. Traditional supply chain*

After all this time, supply chain attacks have evolved and defense mechanisms must adapt to these changes. These attacks can be on individual products, as was the case when seven people were murdered in 1982 from poisoned Tylenol medicine capsules.[1] The follow-on regulations mandating tamper-evident packaging for medicine, food, and drinks in the United States has been repeated throughout the world. Organizations have taken great care in defending their logistics from distribution attacks, but now the attackers have moved earlier in the supply chain by attacking the design, development, and manufacturing processes or by attacking an organization's operations through ransomware attacks, data breaches, and theft of intellectual property. Regardless of the method of attack, when an organization cannot distribute products or services to customers, the supply chain is disrupted. Supply chain attacks have now become global, general-interest media stories after the ransomware attack on Colonial Pipeline disrupted travel and shipping in the eastern US for several days.[2] The impact that ransomware and other malicious attacks have on the supply chains of our products and services every day leads me to the reason for writing this book on supply chain security for software, firmware, and hardware.

The goal of this chapter is to provide you with a foundation to build upon as you read the rest of the book. I start with defining common supply chain concepts so you have an understanding of the terminology that I use throughout the book. I then describe the impacts of supply chain security on organizations and finish by referencing the many worldwide regulations, laws, and guidelines that focus on supply chain security.

# Supply Chain Definitions

When I speak with people about supply chain security, they often do not recognize themselves as part of a supply chain because they think it's only about suppliers or manufacturing. If your organization provides products or services to others, your organization is part of the supply chain. To provide clarity, the following are definitions for the core terminology that I will be using throughout this book:

*Supply chain*
> The people, processes, materials, and technologies used in the creation, production, and distribution of physical or digital products. Thousands of individuals, hundreds of components, and dozens of organizations may be part of the supply chain to create, produce, and deliver a single product (physical or nonphysical), such as a mobile phone or a mobile phone application.

*Supply chain risk*
> "The risk that an adversary may sabotage, maliciously introduce unwanted function, or otherwise subvert the design, integrity, manufacturing, production, distribution, installation, operation, or maintenance of an item of supply or a system so as to surveil, deny, disrupt, or otherwise degrade the function, use, or operation of a system."[3] This definition demonstrates the many opportunities to introduce risk to a product's lifecycle and will be discussed throughout this book.

*Supply chain risk management (SCRM)*
> "A systematic process for managing supply chain risk by identifying susceptibilities, vulnerabilities, and threats throughout the supply chain and developing mitigation strategies to combat those threats whether presented by the supplier, the supplied product and its subelements, or the supply chain (e.g., initial production, packaging, handling, storage, transport, mission operation, and disposal)."[4] The security controls provided in this book should be part of your organization's supply chain risk management program.

*Software supply chain*

The people, processes, software libraries, software or firmware components, as well as technologies used in the creation, development, publication, production, and distribution of digital products, including intelligent physical products such as Internet of Things (IoT), Industrial IoT (IIoT), and operational technology (OT).[5] The primary difference to general supply chain security is the software or firmware development and distribution processes.

*Software supply chain security*

A systematic process for managing software supply chain risk by identifying susceptibilities, vulnerabilities, and threats throughout the software supply chain and developing mitigation strategies to combat those threats, whether presented by the supplier, software libraries, software or firmware components, the supplied product and its subelements, or the supply chain (e.g., initial production, packaging, handling, storage, transport, mission operation, and disposal). The primary addition to the supply chain risk management definition is the risk of software or firmware compromise.

*Third-party risk*

A risk from external sources such as suppliers, organizations, groups, or individuals in your supply chain, infrastructure, systems, or processes. This can include commercial engagements where you purchase items, or free and open source software (FOSS) and tools.[6]

Several of the previous definitions come from the National Institute of Standards and Technology (NIST), which has an extensive glossary in its Computer Security Resource Center (CSRC).[7] Although NIST is a US agency in the Department of Commerce, its mission is to advance measurement science, standards, and technology, which benefits a global. Many of the references and publications mentioned in this book come from NIST and its collaboration with industry, other organizations, and people. I have personally collaborated with NIST on several of the software supply chain topics discussed in this book.

## Software Supply Chain Security Impacts

When I describe supply chain security to people, I always hold up my cell phone and explain to them there were hundreds, maybe thousands, of opportunities for a malicious actor to compromise the phone before I purchased it from the store. As shown in Figure 1-2, the phone is made up of hardware, firmware, and software, and anyone who created my phone or came in contact with it could have put a compromised chip or software into it. I trust my cell phone manufacturer and the operating system publisher, but imagine if malicious software (malware) went unnoticed and millions of phones were impacted before it was discovered. This compromise in the supply chain would be detrimental not only to the company but also to millions of customers. A severe enough event could destroy a company of almost any size.

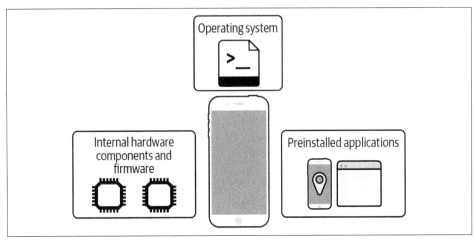

*Figure 1-2. Cell phone hardware, firmware, and software*

Now imagine that your organization was one of the upstream suppliers that wrote the operating system software, or designed the Bluetooth antenna hardware chip, or assembled the phone's components. As a supplier to the cell phone manufacturer, your organization may be found at fault if you don't have strong supply chain security. It could result in a severe financial impact to the organization and its employees, possibly leading to the organization's closure.

You may be on the other end of the supply chain as a downstream customer who purchased thousands of these cell phones for your organization. Were you familiar enough with software supply chain security to have evaluated the manufacturer, set internal policies as to how your employees used the cell phones, and monitored the software security for potential compromises? Understanding the risks of software supply chain security will allow you to prepare yourself and your organization for when, not if, the supply chain will be compromised.

When the infamous software compromise affected the SolarWinds Orion platform (a widely used IP network management tool), it raised awareness of *software* supply chain security, just as the Colonial Pipeline event previously raised awareness of supply chain security. Technical details on the SolarWinds attack will be discussed in Chapter 5, but in summary, the supply chain compromise began in October 2019 and remained undetected until December 2020, by then placing 18,000 customers at risk, with Microsoft confirming 40 customers were breached, including a number of US government agencies.[8,9] The SolarWinds organization settled a $26 million lawsuit with its investors due to the financial losses stemming from the supply chain attack.[10] This loss does not include the millions spent by SolarWinds and its customers on incident response, threat investigations, downtime, remediations, and loss of revenue when customers' systems were unavailable.

Third-party risks from commercially purchased or open source software libraries can also cause significant impacts worldwide. Two software vulnerabilities (security weaknesses that can be exploited by a malicious actor or software) announced in December 2021 in the Apache Log4j logging framework can be found in hundreds of thousands of open source packages, according to an article published by SC Media.[11] The math indicates there are millions of applications using the Log4j open source libraries, and many of these applications have not yet upgraded the software libraries to a version where the vulnerabilities have been patched. In the SC Media article, the author, Menghan Xiao, noted cost estimates to locate Log4j vulnerabilities range between $33,000 and $90,000. Multiplied by millions of applications, the financial impact is quite high, especially since this does not yet include any breach or legal costs for applications that do not patch Log4j. A user may not even be aware these vulnerabilities exist in their software applications if the software publisher has not disclosed (announced) the vulnerabilities or provided a list of software components using a software bill of materials (SBOM), as I will discuss in Chapter 8.

Impacts to an organization from supply chain attacks may result in reputational damage, loss of customer confidence, lawsuits, government penalties, and a reduction of future business after the event. An attack also can cause disruptions or downtime to an organization's business operations, which could cause loss of revenue. If something doesn't work, it can't make money. Also, as a result of the attack, there will need to be incident response, threat investigations, and remediations, which take up time and use resources. Software supply chain security attacks affect not only the company and its direct customers but also those at the nth degree of separation.

# Requirements, Laws, Regulations, and Directives

The risks and impacts to users, organizations, national infrastructure, and global economies have triggered governments around the world to release requirements, laws, regulations, directives, and guidance for organizations to follow in regard to software supply chain security. Many of these requirements pertain to third-party risk, supply chain risk management, and software development. Table 1-1 contains a summary of supply chain security references in worldwide laws, regulations, guidance, and directives at the time of this book's publication. The documents referenced in this table are the basis for the software supply chain risks and controls throughout this book.

*Table 1-1. Government mentions relevant for supply chain security*

| Location | Document | Supply chain security mentions |
|---|---|---|
| Australia | Guidance: Cyber Supply Chain Risk Management[12] | • Identify the cyber supply chain, understand the risk, set expectations, audit for compliance, monitor and improve. |
| Australia | Guidance: Identifying Cyber Supply Chain Risks[13] | • Foreign control, influence, and interference.<br>• Cyber supply chain risks.<br>• Security practices, transparency, access, and privileges. |
| Australia | Critical Technology Supply Chain Principles[14] | • Ten principles grouped into three pillars: security-by-design, transparency, and autonomy and integrity.<br>• Know your suppliers, what needs to be protected, and your transparency requirements. |
| Australia | Security of Critical Infrastructure Act 2018[15] | • Vulnerability assessments and incident management. |
| China | GB/T 36637—2018 (Information Security Technology ICT Supply Chain Security Risk Management Guidelines)[16] | • Chinese technical standard on supply chain security for Information and Communication Technology (ICT). |
| China | New Measures for Cybersecurity Review[17] | • Cybersecurity reviews of data processing, network products, or services for critical infrastructure information and network platform operators. |
| China | National Standard on Information Security Technology Software Supply Chain Security Requirements (proposed)[18] | • Security requirements, security testing, and evaluation for the software supply chain.<br>• Organizational management and supply activity management requirements, including personnel, intellectual property, and delivery.<br>• Derived from GB/T 36637—2018 (Information Security Technology ICT Supply Chain Security Risk Management Guidelines). |
| EU | GDPR: General Data Protection Regulation[19] | • Parties to ensure data rights are enforced.<br>• Compliance to security standards.<br>• Liability for data processing leaks. |
| EU | Cybersecurity Act[20] | • Mutual Recognition Agreements between governments for conformity assessments, conformity marks, certificates, and test reports by conformity assessment bodies. |
| EU | Cyber Resilience Act[21] | • Digital elements are developed in a secure manner and have timely security updates.<br>• Manufacturers should include software bills of materials (SBOMs) and ensure their products do not contain vulnerable components developed by third parties.<br>• The supply of incorrect, incomplete, or misleading information can lead to administrative fines. |

| Location | Document | Supply chain security mentions |
| --- | --- | --- |
| EU | Council conclusions on ICT supply chain security[22] | • Strengthen resilience and security of supply chains.<br>• Continuous assessment, analysis, and monitoring.<br>• Diversify suppliers.<br>• Certification schemes that include requirements on supply chain security.<br>• Supply chain risk management.<br>• Development of an Information and Communication Technologies (ICT) Supply Chain Toolbox. |
| EU | Network and Information Systems Directive 2 (NIS2)[23] | • Member states to designate Computer Security Incident Response Teams (CSIRTS) to monitor for supply chain compromises.<br>• Member states' cybersecurity strategies should help small and medium-sized enterprises with supply chain challenges.<br>• Align to industry standards and best practices including supply chain assessments.<br>• Supplier's secure development procedures.<br>• Coordinated security risk assessments on critical supply chains. |
| EU | Chips Act (proposed)[24] | • Building and reinforcing Europe's capacity (including resiliency) to innovate in the design, manufacturing, and packaging of advanced chips.<br>• Developing an in-depth understanding of global semiconductor supply chains. |
| Ireland | Electronic Communications Security Measures (ECSM) 009: Supply Chain Security[25] | • Implement supply chain security measures such as risk profiles, incident management, and monitoring.<br>• Security requirements between parties must be in place.<br>• Minimize data sharing to only what is necessary.<br>• Host data natively instead of through a third party when possible. |
| New Zealand | NCSC Cyber Security Framework[26] | • Knowing where security responsibilities lie between an organization and its suppliers. |
| New Zealand | Supply Chain Cyber Security[27] | • Introduction to understanding and managing supply chain cyber risk.<br>• Three phases (identify, assess, and manage) to guide organizations. |
| United Kingdom | Supply Chain Security Guidance[28] | • Twelve principles, including risk management, controls, and continuous improvement.<br>• Know your suppliers, security risks, and requirements.<br>• Security awareness, incidents, assurance, and measurements. |
| UK | Supplier Assurance Framework: Good Practice Guide[29] | • Consistent proportionate baseline, implementable in stages, for managing information risk in supplier contracts.<br>• Risk levels and visibility.<br>• Physical security, business continuity, cyber, personnel and information security.<br>• Common Criteria for Assessing Risk (CCfAR) assessment—set of outline criteria according to risk levels.<br>• Statement of Assurance (SoA) tool—assessment criteria aligned to ISO 27001:2005 information security. |

| Location | Document | Supply chain security mentions |
|---|---|---|
| UK | Secure development and deployment guidance[30] | • Guidance for developers on producing clean and maintainable code; securing the development environment, code repository, build pipeline, and deployment pipeline; and continuous testing.<br>• Contains implementation actions and self-assessments. |
| UK | Supply Chain Guidance[31] | • Guidance for business leaders, practitioners, and suppliers.<br>• Governance, culture, expectations, security levels, and risk management.<br>• Questionnaires, assessments, contracts, performance, and termination.<br>• Threats, exposure, incident management. |
| UK | How to Assess and Gain Confidence in Your Supply Chain Cybersecurity[32] | • Supplier relationships and the ways organizations are exposed to vulnerabilities and attacks.<br>• Cybersecurity in supplier assessments and contracts.<br>• Continuous improvement for supply chain security.<br>• Expected outcomes and steps for supplier cyber assessments. |
| US | NIST Cybersecurity Framework (CSF): Framework for Improving Critical Infrastructure Cybersecurity[33] | • Identifies four tiers of supply chain risk management maturity.<br>• Requirements to communicate with stakeholders.<br>• Outlines cyber supply chain relationships.<br>• Framework core includes the Supply Chain Risk Management category. |
| US | NIST SP 800-53: Security and Privacy Controls for Information Systems and Organizations[34] | • Supply chain risk management controls, processes, strategies, and planning.<br>• Supply chain incident management.<br>• Supply chain risk assessments. |
| US | Executive Order 14017: America's Supply Chains[35] | • Supply chains for semiconductor manufacturing and advanced packaging, information and communications technology (ICT), energy sector, transportation, digital products.<br>• Third-party risks (nation-states).<br>• Location of key manufacturing and production assets.<br>• Alternative and redundant sources for critical goods and materials.<br>• Workforce skills and best practices.<br>• Addressing software vulnerabilities.<br>• Supply chain monitoring. |
| US | Executive Order 14028: Improving the Nation's Cybersecurity[36] | • Remove contractual barriers that prevent sharing of threats, incidents, and risks.<br>• Service providers collect, preserve, and share information relevant to cybersecurity events.<br>• Publish software supply chain security guidelines for secure software development environments and tools, software origins, and software bills of materials. |
| US | The Minimum Elements for a Software Bill of Materials (SBOM)[37] | • An SBOM is a formal record containing details and supply chain relationships of various components used in building software.<br>• Minimum elements for data fields, data formats, practices, and processes. |

| Location | Document | Supply chain security mentions |
|----------|----------|-------------------------------|
| US | Memo M-22-18: Enhancing the Security of the Software Supply Chain through Secure Software Development Practices[38] | • US federal agencies must only use software that meets NIST guidance (e.g., NIST 800-218).<br>• Self-attestation forms and SBOMs must be obtained from software publishers. |
| US | NIST SP 800-161: Cybersecurity Supply Chain Risk Management for Systems and Organizations[39] | • Cybersecurity Supply Chain Risk Management (C-SCRM) is a process for managing exposure to cybersecurity risks throughout the supply chain and developing response strategies, policies, processes, and procedures.<br>• Guidance to enterprises on how to identify, assess, select, and implement risk management processes and mitigating controls.<br>• C-SCRM security controls including access control, training, configuration management, identification and authentication, incident response, physical and environmental protection, personnel security, risk assessments, system and information integrity, and supply chain risk management. |
| US | NIST SP 800-218: Secure Software Development Framework (SSDF)[40] | • Identifies secure software development practices: protect the organization, protect the software, produce well-secured software, and respond to vulnerabilities.<br>• Communicating requirements to third parties.<br>• Third-party attestation and provenance. |
| US | Chips and Science Act[41] | • Funding for security, innovation, facilities, equipment, and workforce to support the development, fabrication, assembly, testing, and packaging for semiconductors, telecommunications, and emerging technologies.<br>• Support information security measures for the development and lifecycle of software and the software supply chain. |
| US | National Cybersecurity Strategy[42] | • Secure the federal civilian executive branch (FCEB) through software supply chain risk mitigation.<br>• Strategic objective to secure global supply chains for information, communications, and operational technology products and services. |
| US | Food and Drug Administration (FDA)—Cybersecurity in Medical Devices: Quality System Considerations and Content of Premarket Submissions[43] | • Requires a Secure Product Development Framework (SPDF) and secure design when creating medical devices.<br>• Transparency including SBOMs.<br>• Supply chain security of third-party software components. |

Countries also have certain requirements and regulatory oversight such as the US Food and Drug Administration, as referenced in the previous table, the US Federal Risk and Authorization Management Program (FedRAMP), which we'll mention in Chapter 8, and the Federal Energy Regulatory Commission (FERC). We can expect there to be more requirements and laws as supply chain security risks increase globally.

You should leverage customers, industry associations, and peer networks to maintain awareness of new supply chain requirements, standards, laws, directives, guidance, and regulations. Industry groups, such as technology alliances, may have sector-specific supply chain guidance, as seen in the North American Electric Reliability Corporation's (NERC) Supply Chain Risk Management Program.[44]

# Summary

Supply chain security is an age-old topic, but it has received significant attention over the past few years as malicious actors have taken advantage of vulnerabilities, suppliers, open source, and supply chains. New concepts, such as software having its own supply chain, raise the importance of understanding how supply chains work for physical and digital products. Software supply chains are being attacked daily by malicious actors, thus leading to business impacts such as data loss, operational downtime, lost revenue, decreased customer trust, and potential violation of regulations or laws. It is vital that organizations understand and comply with global supply chain security laws and regulations before implementing the frameworks, standards, or models that I'll introduce in Chapter 2.

# References

1    Marcia Wendorf, "Tamper-Resistant Packaging Began in 1982 with 7 Still Unsolved Murders" (*https://interestingengineering.com/innovation/tamper-resistant-packaging-began-in-1982-with-7-still-unsolved-murders*), Interesting Engineering, December 16, 2019.

2    Katie Balevic, "Colonial Pipeline Ransomware Attack Fuels Gas Price Fears after Russian 'DarkSide' Hack Halts Pipeline Between TX and NJ" (*https://www.thesun.co.uk/news/us-news/14905150/colonial-pipeline-ransomware-attack-gas-price-russian-hack-pipeline*), The Sun, May 10, 2021.

3    "Supply Chain Risk" (*https://csrc.nist.gov/glossary/term/supply_chain_risk*), NIST, accessed December 7, 2023.

4    "Supply Chain Risk Management (SCRM)" (*https://csrc.nist.gov/glossary/term/supply_chain_risk_management*), NIST, accessed December 7, 2023.

5    Firmware is software permanently programmed into hardware, and then the firmware can instruct the hardware to perform functions. Firmware is also known as embedded software, though historically firmware was for lower-level functions and embedded software was for higher-level functions.

6    Free and Open Source Software (FOSS), which includes open software libraries and source code packages (a collection of binaries, scripts, and data), is free to use, copy, study, and change according to its software license. Popular examples of FOSS

are the Linux operating system, MySQL database, OpenSSL secure communication package, and Log4j logging framework.

7   "Computer Security Resource Center" (*https://csrc.nist.gov*), NIST, accessed December 7, 2023.

8   Pam Baker, "The SolarWinds Hack Timeline: Who Knew What, and When?" (*https://www.csoonline.com/article/3613571/the-solarwinds-hack-timeline-who-knew-what-and-when.html*) CSO, June 4, 2021.

9   Catalin Cimpanu, "Microsoft Confirms It Was Also Breached in Recent Solar-Winds Supply Chain Hack" (*https://www.zdnet.com/article/microsoft-was-also-breached-in-recent-solarwinds-supply-chain-hack-report*), ZDNET, December 17, 2020.

10   Eduard Kovacs, "SolarWinds Agrees to Pay $26 Million to Settle Shareholder Lawsuit over Data Breach" (*https://www.securityweek.com/solarwinds-agrees-pay-26-million-settle-shareholder-lawsuit-over-data-breach*), Security Week, November 7, 2022.

11   Menghan Xiao, "Digging into the Numbers One Year after Log4Shell" (*https://www.scmagazine.com/feature/third-party-risk/digging-into-the-numbers-one-year-after-log4shell*), SC Media, December 16, 2022.

12   "Cyber Supply Chain Risk Management" (*https://www.cyber.gov.au/resources-business-and-government/maintaining-devices-and-systems/outsourcing-and-procurement/cyber-supply-chains/cyber-supply-chain-risk-management*), Australian Cyber Security Centre, May 22, 2023.

13   "Identifying Cyber Supply Chain Risks" (*https://www.cyber.gov.au/resources-business-and-government/maintaining-devices-and-systems/outsourcing-and-procurement/cyber-supply-chains/identifying-cyber-supply-chain-risks*), Australian Cyber Security Centre, May 22, 2023.

14   Commonwealth of Australia, *Critical Technology Supply Chain Principles* (*https://www.homeaffairs.gov.au/cyber-security-subsite/files/critical-technology-supply-chain-principles.pdf*), 2021.

15   "Security of Critical Infrastructure Act 2018" (*https://www.legislation.gov.au/Details/C2022C00160*), Australian Government, May 2, 2022.

16   "国家标准" (*https://openstd.samr.gov.cn/bzgk/gb/newGbInfo?hcno=56123482721B1AC3CEDCD3B5C022CAD8*), National Standardization Management Committee, March 9, 2022.

17   "网络安全审查办法_信息产业（含电信）_中国政府网" (*http://www.gov.cn/zhengce/zhengceku/2022-01/04/content_5666430.htm*), Gov.cn, accessed December 7, 2023.

18    "全国信息安全标准化技术委员会" (*https://www.tc260.org.cn/front/bzzqyjDe
tail.html?id=20220930173005&norm_id=20211108000018&recode_id=48921*),
Org.cn, accessed December 7, 2023.

19    "Regulation (EU) 2016/679 of the European Parliament and of the Council of 27
April    2016"    (*https://eur-lex.europa.eu/legal-content/EN/TXT/?uri=CELEX
%3A02016R0679-20160504*), EUR-Lex, accessed December 16, 2023.

20    "Regulation (EU) 2019/881 of the European Parliament and of the Council of 17
April 2019" (*https://eur-lex.europa.eu/eli/reg/2019/881/oj*), EUR-Lex, accessed December 16, 2023.

21    The European Parliament and Council, *Proposal for a Regulation of the European
Parliament and of the Council on Horizontal Cybersecurity Requirements for Products
with Digital Elements and Amending Regulation (EU) 2019/1020* (*https://ec.europa.eu/
newsroom/dae/redirection/document/89543*), September 15, 2022.

22    "Council Conclusions on ICT Supply Chain Security" (*https://data.consi
lium.europa.eu/doc/document/ST-13664-2022-INIT/en/pdf*), Council of the European
Union, October 17, 2022.

23    "Directive (EU) 2022/2555 of the European Parliament and of the Council of 14
December 2022" (*https://eur-lex.europa.eu/eli/dir/2022/2555/oj*), EUR-Lex, accessed
December 16, 2023.

24    "European    Chips    Act"    (*https://commission.europa.eu/strategy-and-policy/
priorities-2019-2024/europe-fit-digital-age/european-chips-act_en*), European Commission, April 18, 2023.

25    Government of Ireland, *Electronic Communications Security Measures 009—Supply    Chain    Security    (https://www.gov.ie/pdf/?file=https://assets.gov.ie/
205231/36cba263-8a62-4777-a314-74d4685741d5.pdf*), 2021.

26    "NCSC Cyber Security Framework" (*https://www.ncsc.govt.nz/resources/ncsc-
cyber-security-framework*), National Cyber Security Centre of New Zealand, accessed
December 7, 2023.

27    National Cyber Security Centre of New Zealand, *Supply Chain Cyber Security. In
Safe Hands* (*https://www.ncsc.govt.nz/assets/NCSC-Documents/NCSC-Supply-Chain-
Cyber-Security.pdf*), accessed December 7, 2023.

28    "Supply Chain Security Guidance" (*https://www.ncsc.gov.uk/collection/supply-
chain-security*), UK National Cyber Security Centre, January 28, 2018.

29    Cabinet Office, *Supplier Assurance Framework: Good Practice Guide* (*https://
assets.publishing.service.gov.uk/government/uploads/system/uploads/attach
ment_data/file/707416/2018-May_Supplier-Assurance-Framework_Good-Practice-
Guide.pdf*), version 1.1, May 2018.

30  UK National Cyber Security Centre, "Secure Development and Deployment Guidance" (*https://www.ncsc.gov.uk/collection/developers-collection*), November 22, 2018.

31  "Supply Chain Guidance" (*https://www.npsa.gov.uk/protected-procurement*), National Protective Security Authority, April 21, 2022.

32  "How to Assess and Gain Confidence in Your Supply Chain Cyber Security" (*https://www.ncsc.gov.uk/collection/assess-supply-chain-cyber-security*), UK National Cyber Security Centre, October 12, 2022.

33  National Institute of Standards and Technology, *Framework for Improving Critical Infrastructure Cybersecurity* (*https://doi.org/10.6028/nist.cswp.04162018*), version 1.1, April 16, 2018.

34  Joint Task Force Interagency Working Group, *NIST 800-53: Security and Privacy Controls for Information Systems and Organizations* (*https://doi.org/10.6028/nist.sp.800-53r5*), National Institute of Standards and Technology, September 2020.

35  "Executive Order on America's Supply Chains" (*https://www.whitehouse.gov/briefing-room/presidential-actions/2021/02/24/executive-order-on-americas-supply-chains*), The White House, February 24, 2021.

36  "Executive Order on Improving the Nation's Cybersecurity" (*https://www.whitehouse.gov/briefing-room/presidential-actions/2021/05/12/executive-order-on-improving-the-nations-cybersecurity*), The White House, February 24, 2021.

37  US Department of Commerce, *The Minimum Elements for a Software Bill of Materials (SBOM)* (*https://www.ntia.doc.gov/files/ntia/publications/sbom_minimum_elements_report.pdf*), July 12, 2021.

38  Shalanda D. Young, "Memo M-22-18: Enhancing the Security of the Software Supply Chain through Secure Software Development Practices" (*https://www.whitehouse.gov/wp-content/uploads/2022/09/M-22-18.pdf*), Executive Office of the President, Office of Management and Budget, September 14, 2022.

39  Jon M. Boyens, Angela Smith, Nadya Barol, Kris Winkler, Alex Holbrook, and Matthew Fallon, *NIST SP 800-161 Rev. 1: Cybersecurity Supply Chain Risk Management for Systems and Organizations* (*https://doi.org/10.6028/nist.sp.800-161r1*), National Institute of Standards and Technology, May 2022.

40  Murugiah Souppaya, Karen Scarfone, and Donna Dodson, *NIST SP 800-218: Secure Software Development Framework (SSDF) Version 1.1* (*https://doi.org/10.6028/nist.sp.800-218*), National Institute of Standards and Technology, February 2022.

41  "H.R.4346—Chips and Science Act: 117th Congress (2021–2022)" (*https://www.congress.gov/bill/117th-congress/house-bill/4346*), Congress.gov, August 9, 2022.

42   The White House, *National Cybersecurity Strategy* (*https://www.whitehouse.gov/wp-content/uploads/2023/03/National-Cybersecurity-Strategy-2023.pdf*),   March   1, 2023.

43   US Food & Drug Administration, *Cybersecurity in Medical Devices: Quality System Considerations and Content of Premarket Submissions: Guidance for Industry and Food and Drug Administration Staff* (*https://www.fda.gov/media/119933/download?attachment*), September 27, 2023.

44   "Supply Chain Risk Mitigation Program" (*https://www.nerc.com/pa/comp/Pages/Supply-Chain-Risk-Mitigation-Program.aspx*), North American Electric Reliability Corporation, accessed December 7, 2023.

# CHAPTER 2

# Supply Chain Frameworks and Standards

Supply chain frameworks are supporting structures for supply chain management systems. These frameworks, combined with supply chain standards created by standards bodies, focus on evaluating the risk introduced by organizations and their third parties in the overall supply chain. In Chapter 1, I provided a high-level summary of the supply chain security topics covered in various worldwide laws, regulations, and guidelines. In this chapter, I describe various risk management and supply chain frameworks and standards that an organization can use to meet the requirements established by governments and customers. Although specific vendors are not mentioned in this book, you can also evaluate several commercial risk assessment tools that use a framework approach, and these may target general supply chains or specific industries (e.g., energy or healthcare).

In order to discuss supply chain frameworks and standards, I will first provide an overview of risk management frameworks most used for technologies and software supply chains. By understanding risk management itself, you will then have the foundation, as shown in Figure 2-1, for the supply chain frameworks and standards that usually fit within an overall risk management framework.

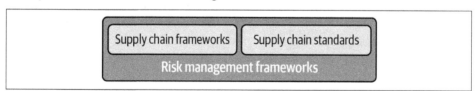

*Figure 2-1. Supply chain risk management*

The NIST IR 8286 series ("Integrating Cybersecurity and Enterprise Risk Management [ERM]") can also help you use cybersecurity risk information as inputs in your organization's risk management processes.[1] After I describe the technology risk management frameworks, supply chain frameworks, and supply chain standards, you can then choose which ones will be the best for your organization and suppliers to follow.

# Technology Risk Management Frameworks

Risk is an element in every business or organization decision, even when it is not labeled specifically as a risk. Whether to work with a supplier or to create something internally is one of the first steps in many of your organizational decisions. Sometimes referred to as a "build versus buy" decision, this process may assess financial and credit risks (e.g., is it more expensive to build it ourselves or to trust a supplier that may go out of business?) or strategic and operational risks (e.g., will the supplier copy our approach and become a competitor?).

A risk management framework (RMF) is a set of guidelines and practices used by organizations to identify, eliminate, mitigate, measure, and monitor risks. A technology RMF includes a number of risk types for evaluation, such as financial, credit, strategic, operational, technical, regulatory, legal, and political. RMFs all provide some core components to consider—identification, assessment, prioritization, mitigation, and governance—which are the basis for supply chain risk management, but are not necessary for you to select an RMF for adoption within your organization. Knowing these frameworks exist, and which RMFs are available, provides a foundation for discussing supply chain risk management frameworks.

## NIST SP 800-37 Risk Management Framework (RMF)

In my experience, the NIST RMF is the most comprehensive of the technology RMFs due to its frequent additions and updates to the suite of documents covering security, privacy, monitoring, information systems, assessments, supply chain, and engineering.[2] There are over 20 documents referenced as part of the NIST RMF, with the primary document being NIST SP 800-37 ("Risk Management Framework for Information Systems and Organizations: A System Life Cycle Approach for Security and Privacy").[3] Although an abundance of documentation can be a good thing, it can also make it difficult to locate what you need. In this book, I hope to provide you with an understanding of not only this set of documents but how hundreds of documents and article references can come together to create a software supply chain security practice for your organization.

NIST is an organization within the US Department of Commerce, and although the RMF was developed for the US federal government, the contributors to the NIST frameworks and documents are from all around the world. International organizations and governments provide feedback and, in turn, reference those documents in their own security and supplier frameworks. For example, Ireland's "Electronic Communications Security Measures (ECSM) 009: Supply Chain Security" references several NIST documents.

The freely available NIST RMF consists of a seven-step process to manage information security and privacy risk, as shown in Figure 2-2:

*Prepare*
Conduct activities to prepare the organization for managing security and privacy risks. This step interacts with every step of the RMF. It helps you identify key roles, set the organization risk management strategy, perform organizational risk assessments, and establish continuous monitoring of risks.

*Categorize*
Identify the adverse impacts for organizational processes and tasks with respect to the loss of confidentiality, integrity, and availability of systems and the information processed, stored, and transmitted by those systems. During this step you will document system characteristics for categorizing the systems from a security viewpoint.

*Select*
Establish the security and privacy controls to protect the systems based on the risk assessments. This step has usually been performed if your organization has an information security program, but you should also include the security controls provided throughout this book if your control set does not include them.

*Implement*
Deploy the required controls to your organization. This step includes setting technology controls such as configurations.

*Assess*
Verify the controls are in place, operating as intended, and producing the desired outcomes. This step requires examining statements, evidence, or reports to confirm the controls have been met and defining remediations for any deficiencies.

*Authorize*
Request leadership approval to validate the security and privacy risks have been met. This step is a formal process to ensure accountability at the top level of the organization.

*Monitor*
Track the implementation of controls and the level of risk on a continuous basis. This step should employ technologies, automation, and repeatable processes to alert you when controls are not being met.

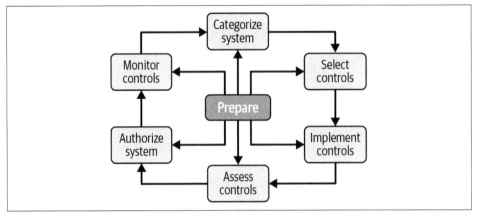

*Figure 2-2. The seven steps of the NIST risk management framework*

For each step, the NIST website includes the outcomes you should receive from each step, resources for implementing the RMF, and the supporting NIST publications you will need to perform each step.[4]

## ISO 31000:2018 Risk Management

For any organization using ISO/IEC standards, the ISO 31000:2018 Risk Management standard provides a solid foundation for risk management.[5] First released in 2009, the ISO 31000 standard replaced the Australia and New Zealand Standard (AS/NZS) 4360:2004. ISO 31000 was updated in 2018 and is also supported by IEC 31010:2019 Risk Management—Risk Assessment Techniques.[6]

The for-purchase ISO 31000 standard manages risks based on principles, framework, and process. It does not have a technology focus, but as an ISO standard, it is easily referenced by other ISO standards. Since this is more of a general risk management standard, you may already have much of this structure in place within your organization.

The risk management principles, as shown in Figure 2-3, are as follows:

*Integrated*
Include risk management in all organizational activities.

*Structured and comprehensive*
Maintain consistency and be thorough in risk management.

*Customized*
Adapt the risk management framework and process to your organization's needs.

*Inclusive*
> Incorporate stakeholders into the risk management process for them to provide input and to improve their awareness of the organizational risks.

*Dynamic*
> Update the risks as the organization's context changes.

*Best available information*
> Use historical and current information as inputs to risk management.

*Human and cultural factors*
> Recognize behavioral and cultural influence in the risk management process.

*Continual improvement*
> Enhance the risk management process through learning and experience.

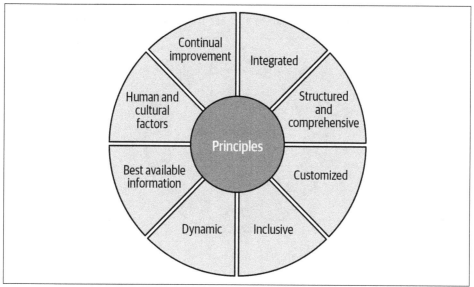

*Figure 2-3. ISO 31000 principles*

Once the principles of risk management are understood, the risk framework can be applied. The framework assists the organization in integrating risk management into significant activities and functions. Risk management should be included in the organization's decision making, and it requires stakeholder support.

The components of the framework, as shown in Figure 2-4, are as follows:

*Leadership and commitment*
> Senior management and the organization's board should provide support and resources to ensure that risk management is integrated into all organizational activities.

*Integration*
> Include risk management in the organization's purpose, governance, leadership, strategy, and operations.

*Design*
> Understand the organization and its mission, communicate the leadership commitment, assign roles, allocate resources, and share risk information.

*Implementation*
> Develop and execute a risk management plan into the organizational activities and decision-making process.

*Evaluation*
> Measure and assess the risk management plan's performance.

*Improvement*
> Adapt the risk management plan to address changes and required improvements.

*Figure 2-4. ISO 31000 framework*

As you put the framework in place, you should build out the risk management processes. These iterative processes include the policies, procedures, and practices for communicating, consulting, scoping, monitoring, reviewing, recording, and reporting, as shown in Figure 2-5 and described as follows:

*Scope, context, and criteria*
> Customize the risk management process for the organization and understand the environment.

*Risk assessment*
> First identify and describe the risks, then analyze and comprehend the nature of the risks, and finally evaluate the risks to support decisions.

*Risk treatment*
  Select and implement options for addressing risk.

*Communication and consultation*
  Assist stakeholders in understanding risk, promote awareness, and obtain feedback.

*Monitoring and review*
  Assure and improve the effectiveness and quality of the process design, implementation, and outcomes.

*Recording and reporting*
  Document and provide the results on the activities and outcomes.

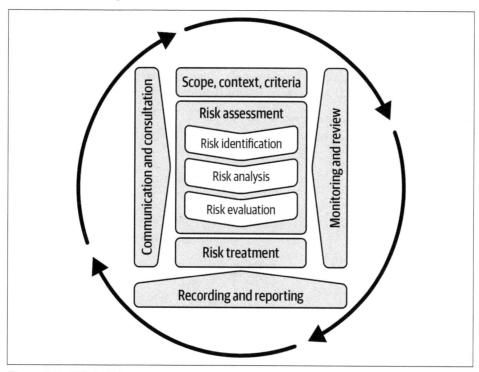

*Figure 2-5. ISO 31000 process*

The ISO 31000 Risk Management standard is a good start for a risk management framework and is adaptable to nontechnology risks. A more IT-focused control framework, such as COBIT 2019, described in "Control Objectives for Information and Related Technologies (COBIT®) 2019" on page 22, may be more suitable for a larger organization that needs to manage many technology risks.

# Control Objectives for Information and Related Technologies (COBIT®) 2019

Originally developed in 1996 by the Information Systems Audit and Controls Association (ISACA) for financial auditing of IT systems, the COBIT IT governance system and framework has expanded and matured through its six versions.[7] Applicable to organizations of all sizes, COBIT 2019 has six principles in its governance system, as shown in Figure 2-6 and described as follows:

*Meet stakeholder needs*
Implement a governance system to generate value from information and technology.

*Holistic approach*
Integrate various components to create the governance system.

*Dynamic governance system*
Consider the impact each time a design factor (areas that influence the governance system such as strategies, risk profiles, and requirements) is changed.

*Distinct governance from management*
Separate management activities and the governance system.

*Tailored to enterprise needs*
Use a set of design factors to customize and prioritize the governance system components.

*End-to-end governance system*
Expand beyond the IT function to all information and technology processing.

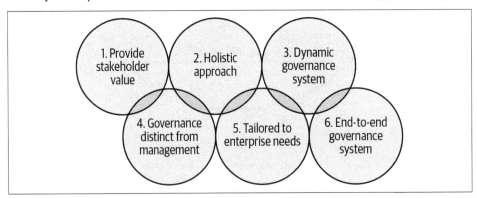

*Figure 2-6. COBIT 2019 governance system principles*

The COBIT 2019 documentation is separated into multiple documents, which, like the NIST RMF, can be overwhelming when considering adoption of the framework.[8] Although the COBIT 2019 Toolkit is free, there are specific publications, for example the "COBIT for Small and Medium Enterprises Using COBIT 2019," that are available for purchase.[9] The documents are free to members who have an ISACA certification, such as a certified information security auditor (CISA).

Inside the COBIT 2019 Toolkit are several spreadsheets that can be used for implementing the 40 COBIT IT objectives in your organization. These controls are grouped into five governance and management objectives, as shown in Figure 2-7 and described as follows:

*Evaluate, direct, and monitor (EDM)*
> These five controls ensure there is a governance framework, business value, risk optimization, and stakeholder engagement.

*Align, plan, and organize (APO)*
> These 14 controls manage the framework, strategy, enterprise architecture, innovation opportunities, IT portfolio, budgets, human resources, stakeholder relationships, service agreements, vendors, quality, technology risk, security, and data.

*Build, acquire, and implement (BAI)*
> These 11 controls establish IT programs, requirements, solutions, availability, organizational changes, IT changes, change acceptance, knowledge bases, asset management, configurations, and projects.

*Deliver, service, and support (DSS)*
> These six controls govern operations, IT services, problems, continuity, security services, and business processes.

*Monitor, evaluate, and assess (MEA)*
> These four controls measure performance, internal controls, compliance to external requirements, and assurance.

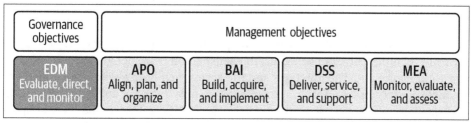

*Figure 2-7. COBIT 2019 objectives*

Although COBIT 2019 is more of an IT controls framework than a risk management framework, COBIT does have risk management practices, which require examination of the business risk for the ownership, operation, and adoption of IT within an organization. By using the COBIT framework guidance, IT and business managers can incorporate IT risk into enterprise risk management.

## NIST Cybersecurity Framework (CSF)

The NIST Cybersecurity Framework (CSF) is a voluntary set of information security measures and controls that can help organizations to identify, assess, and manage cyber risks. There are many similarities with the ISO/IEC 27001 Information Security Management standard, with the most obvious differences being that the NIST CSF is free and does not have a compliance certificate, whereas organizations must purchase ISO/IEC 27001 and they have the option to certify to the standard.[10]

The NIST CSF uses business objectives to guide cybersecurity activities and consider cybersecurity risks as part of the organization's risk management processes. As shown in Figure 2-8, the NIST CSF version 1.1 has five Framework Core functions: Identify, Protect, Detect, Respond, and Recover. At the time this book was published, NIST was in the revision process to create CSF version 2, which may include—based on the drafts—a new Govern function that will reside within the center of the other five functions.

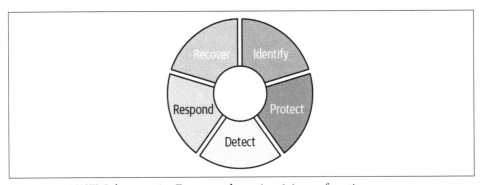

*Figure 2-8. NIST Cybersecurity Framework version 1.1 core functions*

For each function there are categories, subcategories, and informative references (references to other standards, guidelines, and practices for the purpose of achieving the outcomes). In the CSF draft version 2, implementation examples are now included, as shown in Figure 2-9. The functions and categories each have a unique identifier. For example, in version 1.1, ID.SC represents the Identify function and its Supply Chain Risk Management category. In draft version 2, GV.SC represents the Cyber Supply Chain Risk Management category within the new Govern function. When CSF version 2 releases, it will include a change log that describes everything that changed between the two versions.

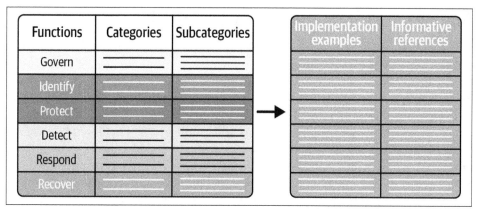

*Figure 2-9. NIST Cybersecurity Framework version 2 draft core functions*

In addition to the Framework Core, the NIST CSF has two other parts: Implementation Tiers and Framework Profiles. The implementation tiers provide context to an organization's view of its cybersecurity risk and risk management processes. The four tiers are similar to those in other maturity models: Partial (tier 1), Risk Informed (tier 2), Repeatable (tier 3), and Adaptive (tier 4). CSF draft version 2 has renamed these to be Framework Tiers and suggests that not all organizations need to be at a particular tier (e.g., tier 3 or 4).

An organization can use the Framework Profiles to align and prioritize its cybersecurity activities using the tiers to define the current profile and the target profile. For example, ID.SC is tier 1 in the current profile, but the organization would like to reach tier 2 within 12 months. The Cyber Risk Institute developed a financial services cybersecurity profile with financial sector references and sector-specific tiers.[11] After the release of CSF version 2, NIST hopes that other groups will create community target profiles, such as original equipment manufacturer (OEM) profiles or startup SaaS provider profiles.

For organizations that do not already have or plan to obtain ISO/IEC 27001 certification, I prefer NIST CSF because it contains a basic supply chain risk management category that any organization can implement. It also has many references and connections to the more comprehensive NIST SP 800-161 Cybersecurity Supply Chain Risk Management document that I discuss in "Supply Chain Frameworks and Standards" on page 26.

There are many risk management frameworks that I did not elaborate on due to their similarity with those already mentioned in this chapter or their concentration on cybersecurity. Two of these frameworks are the Factor Analysis of Information Risk (FAIR) and the Committee of Sponsoring Organizations of the Treadway Commission (COSO) Risk Management Framework.[12,13] The next layer of risk management, beyond enterprise and IT risk management, is found in the supply chain frameworks of the next section.

# Supply Chain Frameworks and Standards

Although this book will provide overall guidance, if you need  a formal way to address software supply chain security, you may want to adopt one of the established supply chain frameworks or standards mentioned in this section. Free government frameworks, such as NIST 800-161 ("Cybersecurity Supply Chain Risk Management for Systems and Organizations"), are developed for their own agencies and organizations to use when managing transactions with commercial suppliers. These frameworks can include special language, procurement rules, and regulations. Standards from organizations such as ISO or IEC, however, must be purchased and, if certification is desired, may be quite costly to deploy and receive accreditation. Table 2-1 summarizes the key attributes of the supply chain frameworks or standards described in this section.

*Table 2-1. Attributes of supply chain frameworks and standards*

| Framework/Standard | Technology | Cybersecurity | Considerations |
| --- | --- | --- | --- |
| NIST 800-161 Cybersecurity Supply Chain Risk Management for Systems and Organizations | Yes | Yes | Free and referenced globally |
| UK Supplier Assurance Framework | Yes | Limited | Assessment tool available |
| MITRE System of Trust™ (SoT) Framework | Yes | Yes | Extensive supplier risks |
| ISO/IEC 20243-1:2023 Open Trusted Technology Provider Standard (O-TTPS) | Yes | Yes | Self-assess certification |
| SCS 9001 Supply Chain Security Standard | Yes | Yes | Updated frequently |
| ISO 28000:2022 Security and Resilience | No | No | General supply chain security |
| ISO/IEC 27036 Information Security for Supplier Relationships | Yes | Yes | Limited supply chain security and product security |

When deciding which frameworks and standards to adopt, you need to consider your organization's industry, products, and services. For example, if your organization works primarily with government agencies, you may choose the US or UK frameworks. For those specifically working with ICT products or services, the standards discussed in this section, such as ISO/IEC 20243, SCS 9001, or ISO/IEC 27036, may be good options.

## NIST SP 800-161 Cybersecurity Supply Chain Risk Management for Systems and Organizations

NIST SP 800-161 ("Cybersecurity Supply Chain Risk Management for Systems and Organizations"), also known as C-SCRM, is the most comprehensive supply chain risk management document available at the time of this book's publication. NIST SP 800-161 has over 300 pages, which makes for a very complete approach but one that can be overwhelming to implement within an organization. I will provide highlights of the NIST SP 800-161 document in this section. However, you'll find key elements of C-SCRM and other supply chain frameworks throughout this book as well.

The first part of NIST SP 800-161 describes the various dimensions within the C-SCRM framework to establish how organizations can positively impact cybersecurity risk in the supply chain. The 12 dimensions of C-SCRM are shown in Figure 2-10 and described as follows:

*Culture and awareness*
Educate the organization on the importance of successfully adopting C-SCRM practices such as supplier risk management and secure development.

*Security*
Maintain the confidentiality, integrity, and availability for supply chain information of the product or service. This information includes the physical and digital supply chain paths, intellectual property, and the participants in the supply chain.

*Suitability*
Find the correct product or service by leveraging information from the supply chain.

*Safety*
Ensure there are no conditions where the product or service may cause illness, injury, damage, or death.

*Reliability*
Ensure the product or service operates for the required time period.

*Usability*
Verify that the product or service satisfies the users' requirements for effectiveness and efficiency.

*Quality*
Achieve performance and meet specifications for the product or service while mitigating weaknesses and vulnerabilities.

*Efficiency*
Verify that the product or service delivers timely results.

*Maintainability*
Assess whether the product or service can accommodate changes and improvements.

*Integrity*
Ensure the products or services have not been tampered with or improperly modified.

*Scalability*

Validate the capacity of the product or service to meet future growth and demand.

*Resilience*

Verify that the product, service, or supply chain can adapt to change conditions and disruptions.

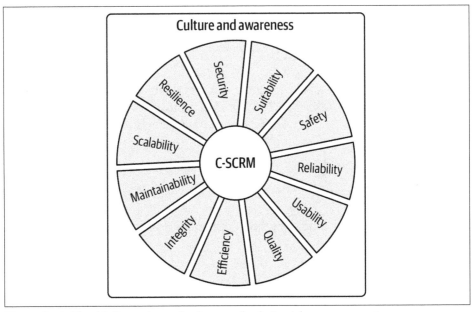

*Figure 2-10. The 12 dimensions of cyber supply chain risk management*

Once the dimensions of the C-SCRM are understood, NIST SP 800-161 then describes critical success factors necessary to successfully address cybersecurity risks in the supply chain. The six critical success factors are designed to reach goals for a successful C-SCRM program and are described as follows:

*Integrating C-SCRM into acquisitions*

Success is when purchasers include C-SCRM requirements, controls, and risk assessments in the purchasing lifecycle. Organizations should also monitor changes to cybersecurity risks in the supply chain that can trigger mitigations or reassessment. The goal is to reduce cybersecurity risk and exposure by implementing C-SCRM in the procurement process.

*Supply chain information sharing*

Success is when organizations have visibility into the cybersecurity risks throughout the supply chain and can share that information with others. Information may include threats, security alerts, vulnerabilities, and potential impacts to systems. The goal is to have the sharing agreements in place before critical situations occur.

*C-SCRM training and awareness*

Success is when C-SCRM education and communication is provided to system owners, human resources, information security, legal, procurement, engineering, software developers, risk managers, IT, management, and engineering. Training should include the required responsibilities, processes, and procedures, as well as how to manage security events. The goal is to have all individuals understand their responsibilities within the C-SCRM framework.

*C-SCRM key practices*

Success is when the foundational C-SCRM practices are in place, such as a dedicated C-SCRM program management office (PMO), senior leadership support, and risk management processes, policies, and procedures. Additional practices include supplier management, governance, and incident management. The goal is to have the C-SCRM practices implemented throughout the organization.

*C-SCRM measurements*

Success is when the C-SCRM program and outcomes can be measured for effectiveness against outcomes, completion, or a framework such as the NIST Cybersecurity Framework. C-SCRM activities can be divided into three levels: foundational, sustaining, and enhancing. The goal is to reach the highest maturity in cybersecurity supply chain practices.

*Dedicated resources*

Success is when resources, both funding and personnel, are provided to create and operate a C-SCRM program. Existing funds and the use of shared services can be redirected toward managing supply chain cybersecurity risk. The goal is to fund the C-SCRM activities and controls in the organizational budget.

As shown in Figure 2-11, a significant portion of NIST SP 800-161 contains supply chain security guidance and controls as an overlay to NIST SP 800-53 ("Security and Privacy Controls for Information Systems and Organizations"). For example, the original definition for provenance, NIST control SR-4, was enhanced to include a software bill of materials (SBOM). To get a complete understanding of NIST control SR-4, you need to read the SR-4 definitions in both NIST SP 800-53 and NIST SP 800-161.

This additional control guidance, found in NIST SP 800-161's Appendices A ("C-SCRM Security Controls") and B ("C-SCRM Security Control Summary"), are grouped into 20 control families dedicated to C-SCRM. Any controls from NIST SP 800-53 not referenced within NIST SP 800-161 are thus not applicable to supply chain security.

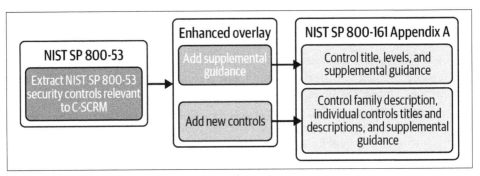

*Figure 2-11. C-SCRM security controls overlay*

As part of the updated security and privacy controls, each definition includes a label called "Levels" to show where the control applies in the organization's risk framework. The three levels range between strategic and tactical risks, as shown in Figure 2-12: on Level 1 are the enterprise-wide risks that are more strategic in nature; on Level 2 are the business process risks; and on Level 3 are the operational risks that are more tactical. Most of the software controls related to supply chain address risks in Levels 2 and 3. Risks associated with Level 1 would be noted in a high-level enterprise supply chain strategy, implementation plan, and policy. Level 2 would provide specific strategies, policies, and implementation plans for the business processes, and Level 3 would be the operational supply chain risk management plans.

*Figure 2-12. C-SCRM risk levels*

NIST SP 800-161 also includes a discussion of valuable scenarios that provide templates and examples of a risk exposure framework in Appendix C, "Risk Exposure Framework." The risk exposure framework is similar to a risk register often used by project managers. Typically a risk register identifies the *impact* if the risk were to materialize and the *likelihood* that the risk would happen. The risk would then be a multiplication of the impact times the likelihood (impact × likelihood).

The risk exposure framework goes beyond the typical risk register, by including threat scenarios before determining the impact, likelihood, and risk. This encourages organizational risk managers to analyze potential threats and plan mitigations for supply chain risks. I highly recommend reviewing the template and the example scenarios in the document's appendix. The risk scenarios you create for your organization can become great tabletop exercises (coordinated events used to practice roles for an emergency scenario) to help prepare your organization for cybersecurity events.

The last section I will call attention to is Appendix D, "C-SCRM Templates." As the name implies, it contains templates for a C-SCRM strategy, policy, plan, and risk assessment. Within the templates are objectives and sample text that you can modify to fit your organization's needs.

Overall, NIST SP 800-161 is a wealth of knowledge for anyone wanting to understand the many layers of cybersecurity supply chain risk management. You can use the practical templates in the appendices to create an excellent supply chain risk management strategy and plan without having to read the entire document.

## UK Supplier Assurance Framework

Other countries have also released supply chain risk management frameworks and best practices. The UK government identified the need for a supplier assurance framework and released a set of guidelines in May 2018.[14,15] These guidelines contain an assessment process named the Common Criteria for Assessing Risk (CCfAR) that had been previously released a few years earlier. Within the CCfAR process is a flexible framework and tool for assessing suppliers, but the questions and risks are limited to only a few topics in asset identification, asset management, and impacts. It does not contain the many topics covered in Chapter 9, but the CCfAR assessment may provide some questions worth asking suppliers, and also aid in the identification of high-risk projects.

As supply chain risk continues to grow globally, governments around the world will release frameworks, best practices, rules, regulations, and more to address the risk for their country and government purchases. If your organization is selling products or services to any type of government, investigate what supply chain security requirements are necessary for risk and compliance.

# MITRE System of Trust™ (SoT) Framework

There are other frameworks for evaluating supply chain risk that organizations may choose to leverage. The MITRE Corporation, known for its Adversarial Tactics, Techniques, and Common Knowledge (ATT&CK®) framework, has designed the System of Trust (SoT) framework for defining, aligning, and addressing the specific concerns and risks of suppliers, supplies, and service providers.[16] The framework offers a comprehensive, consistent, and repeatable methodology for identifying and assessing the risks from a supplier, its products, and its services.

SoT provides a taxonomy and a measurement model for collecting and organizing the supplier, product, and service risks that an organization may need to consider. The organized collection of identified risks can empower organizations to conduct assessments in a practical, timely, and cost-efficient manner that focuses on the needs of the organization and allows for broad adoption, training, and automation. The SoT framework drills down into 14 top-level risk areas, 200 risk subareas, and over 1,200 risk factors and detailed risk measurement questions, as shown in Figure 2-13.

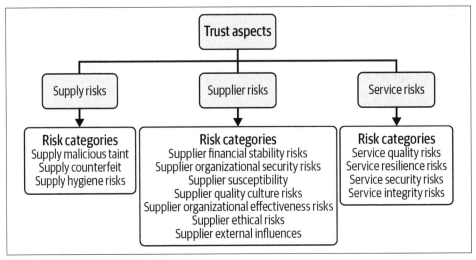

*Figure 2-13. MITRE System of Trust risk categories*

Using the SoT "Risk Model Manager" (RMM) cloud application, users can view, organize, and tailor SoT content to an organization's specific areas of concern. The RMM can be tailored by an organization to create specific profiles, such as ICT product, SaaS provider, or contract development, using the RMM's adjustable questions, measurements, and scoring. The RMM is hosted within your organization, which allows your internal systems to integrate to it, provide data, and generate results.

## ISO/IEC 20243-1:2023 Open Trusted Technology Provider Standard

Standards provide clearly defined, repeatable requirements for organizations to follow, and the ISO/IEC 20243-1:2023 Open Trusted Technology Provider Standard (O-TTPS) is specifically focused on product integrity and supply chain security.[17] Created by The Open Group, O-TTPS was the first certifiable standard that information and communications technology (ICT) providers could follow throughout the full lifecycle of their products in order to mitigate the risk of tainted (e.g., malware-infested) and counterfeit components. The standard focuses on the commercial off-the-shelf (COTS) ICT provider's product lifecycle, including internal design and development, as well as the supply chain through the following phases: design, sourcing, build, fulfillment, distribution, sustainment, and disposal.

The challenge with using standards in your organization is the cost to purchase the standard, the time and resources required to meet the standard's requirements, and, if you choose to obtain certification (for standards which have the option), the additional cost for a third party to assess your organization and maintain the certification. What is unique about O-TTPS is that in addition to certifying through a third-party assessor, The Open Group also provides the option for organizations to self-assess and receive an official O-TTPS certificate.[18]

## SCS 9001 Supply Chain Security Standard

For any organization wanting a certification explicitly for supply chain security, ISO/IEC 20243-1:2023 or the SCS 9001 Supply Chain Security standard are worth considering, but you would need to evaluate both standards to see which is a better fit for your organization. Workgroups in the Telecommunications Industry Association (TIA) designed the SCS 9001 standard on the foundation of the foremost quality management system, ISO 9001.[19] SCS 9001 contains supply chain security requirements and controls such as:

- Asset identification, risk assessment, and mitigation
- Secure design, development, and lifecycle management
- Software, hardware, and component traceability
- Counterfeit parts processes
- Security performance benchmarking
- Incident response

This certifiable, process-based cyber and supply chain security standard was started in 2020 for the ICT industry and issued its second release in 2023. It is well aligned to other standards and government requirements, and it quickly adapts to the rapidly changing supply chain security risks rather than the five-year refresh cycle commonly used by ISO, IEC, and ISA.

## ISO 28000:2022 Security and Resilience

Frequently referenced by other standards as a general supply chain security standard, ISO 28000:2022 is applicable to many types of organizations.[20] Originally released in 2007 for the shipping and maritime industries, this standard focuses on the core functions of a security management system, internal compliance, and conformance to the standard. ISO 28000 is the first standard within a series of security management standards:

- ISO 28000:2022—Security management systems
- ISO 28001:2007—Best practices for implementing supply chain security, assessments, and plans
- ISO 28002:2011—Development of resilience in the supply chain
- ISO 28003:2007—Requirements for bodies providing audit and certification of supply chain security management systems
- ISO 28004—Four-part series of guidelines for the implementation of ISO 28000
- ISO 28005—Two-part series for electronic port clearance

For the purpose of software supply chain security, the ISO 28000 standard does not offer any benefits that cannot be found in other frameworks or standards, but if your organization has already deployed ISO 28000, it can be the foundation for a software supply chain security program.

## ISO/IEC 27036 Information Security for Supplier Relationships

The multipart standard, ISO/IEC 27036, assists organizations in securing their information and information systems within the context of supplier relationships.[21] This standard is part of the ISO 27000 suite of standards and is intended for both purchasers and suppliers. Separated into four documents, it applies to various goods and services such as hardware, software, and ICT services, cloud computing services, and even public services such as power:

- ISO/IEC 27036-1—Overview and concepts
- ISO/IEC 27036-2—Requirements
- ISO/IEC 27036-3—Guidelines for information and communication technology supply chain security
- ISO/IEC 27036-4—Guidelines for security of cloud services

Although it isn't a complete supply chain security or product security standard, it does go beyond the other standards with its focus on services and the commercial relationship. Unlike the ISO 28000 standard, it is not possible to obtain a certification for ISO/IEC 27036.

# Framework and Standards Considerations Summary

Depending on the size of your organization, you may already have in place a technology risk framework such as NIST RMF, ISO 31000, or COBIT. These frameworks aren't required for supply chain security, but they are useful for establishing organizational decision making and risk management.

It's never too late for organizations, such as startups, to establish a supply chain risk management program. In addition to the ones mentioned previously, there are also sector-specific supply chain risk guidelines, such as the Supply Chain Risk Management Guide from the Health Sector Coordinating Council or the energy sector's North American Electric Reliability Corporation (NERC) publications within its Supply Chain Risk Mitigation Program.[22,23]

Although it's not necessary to select a supply chain framework or standard, I highly recommend using the controls in the book as a baseline for software supply chain security and then maturing into a framework or standard. For organizations wanting to keep costs down, using the free NIST and MITRE supply chain security frameworks can expand the teachings of this book. For more ambitious practitioners, the standards available for purchase, such as ISO/IEC 20243 and SCS 9001, can lead to formal compliance and certifications, which may be desirable to your organization and customers.

If you are a supplier to governments, critical infrastructure, healthcare, or segments with strict safety standards, your organization should consider adopting official standards and certifications, even if you are a smaller organization with limited products or services. For example, you may certify to or require certification of the HITRUST CSF as a healthcare organization.[24] If you do select a supply chain standard, be prepared to respond to inquiries on how your organization complies with ISO, IEC, or NIST standards, because companies all over the world have identified those frameworks and standards as a baseline for suppliers.

# Summary

Risk management is the foundation every organization should have in place before embarking on the journey to supply chain security. Regardless of whether your organization has a formal risk management framework such as NIST RMF, or you have established your own version, your organization's decision-making process should account for any number of risks, including cybersecurity risks.

Once an organization has established enterprise risk management, within that framework is where we find the supply chain frameworks and standards. Typically, frameworks are free and standards must be purchased.

Standards for supply chain security are not as well known or used, but as the topic gains momentum, we may see these standards recognized and adopted by larger organizations. Standards such as ISO/IEC 20243 or SCS 9001 are beneficial if an organization wants to have a third-party certification to prove compliance to a standard.

After understanding the various frameworks and standards for risk management and supply chain security, your organization can decide which is best for your situation. The main outcome for all of these frameworks and standards is to lead organizations toward the foundational elements of software supply chain security. In Chapter 3, I'll discuss the risks and controls for infrastructure security that specifically support the end-to-end product or application lifecycle.

## References

1   Kevin Stine, Stephen Quinn, Greg Witte, and R. K. Gardner, "Integrating Cybersecurity and Enterprise Risk Management (ERM)" (*https://csrc.nist.gov/pubs/ir/8286/final*), National Institute of Standards and Technology, October 2020.

2   "NIST Risk Management Framework Publications" (*https://csrc.nist.gov/Projects/risk-management/publications*), National Institute of Standards and Technology, November 8, 2023.

3   National Institute of Standards and Technology, *Risk Management Framework for Information Systems and Organizations: A System Life Cycle Approach for Security and Privacy* (*https://nvlpubs.nist.gov/nistpubs/SpecialPublications/NIST.SP.800-37r2.pdf*), December 2018.

4   "NIST Risk Management Framework" (*https://csrc.nist.gov/Projects/risk-management*), National Institute of Standards and Technology, November 8, 2023.

5   "ISO 31000: Risk Management" (*https://www.iso.org/iso-31000-risk-management.html*), ISO, accessed December 8, 2023.

6   "IEC 31010: 2019 Risk Management—Risk Assessment Techniques" (*https://www.iso.org/standard/72140.html*), International Electrotechnical Commission, accessed December 8, 2023.

7   "COBIT: An ISACA Framework" (*https://www.isaca.org/resources/cobit*), ISACA, accessed December 8, 2023.

8   On the COBIT Resources page within the "Why COBIT" tab is the link for "Access the COBIT Toolkit," which links to a ZIP file containing spreadsheets and

other COBIT 2019 documents. The "Publications" tab contains links to many publications available for purchase or free to ISACA members.

9    "COBIT for Small and Medium Enterprises Using COBIT 2019" (*https://store.isaca.org/s/store#/store/browse/detail/a2S4w000004L2noEAC*), ISACA, accessed December 8, 2023.

10    "ISO/IEC 27001:2022—Information Security, Cybersecurity and Privacy Protection" (*https://www.iso.org/standard/27001*), ISO, accessed December 8, 2023.

11    "CRI Profile v1.2" (*https://cyberriskinstitute.org/the-profile*), Cyber Risk Institute, accessed December 8, 2023.

12    "FAIR Risk Management" (*https://www.fairinstitute.org/fair-risk-management*), FAIR Institute, December 8, 2023.

13    "Guidance" (*https://www.coso.org/guidance-erm*), COSO, accessed December 8, 2023.

14    Supplier assurance is when there is confidence in a supplier. There can be many aspects in assurance, including trust, quality, safety, security, and meeting commitments.

15    Cabinet Office, *Supplier Assurance Framework: Good Practice Guide* (*https://assets.publishing.service.gov.uk/government/uploads/system/uploads/attachment_data/file/707416/2018-May_Supplier-Assurance-Framework_Good-Practice-Guide.pdf*), May 2018.

16    "Supply Chain Security System of Trust" (*https://sot.mitre.org/index.html*), MITRE, accessed December 8, 2023.

17    "ISO/IEC 20243-1:2023 Information Technology—Open Trusted Technology ProviderTM Standard (O-TTPS)" (*https://www.iso.org/standard/86338.html*), ISO, December 8, 2023.

18    "O-TTPS Certification Program" (*https://ottps-cert.opengroup.org/getting-started-organization-certification*), The Open Group, accessed December 8, 2023.

19    "SCS 9001™ Cyber and Supply Chain Security Standard" (*https://tiaonline.org/what-we-do/scs-9001-supply-chain-security-standard*), Telecommunications Industry Association, accessed December 8, 2023.

20    "ISO 28000:2022 Security and Resilience—Security Management Systems—Requirements" (*https://www.iso.org/standard/79612.html*), ISO, accessed December 8, 2023.

21    "ISO/IEC 27036-1:2021 Cybersecurity—Supplier Relationships" (*https://www.iso.org/standard/82905.html*), ISO, accessed December 8, 2023.

22    Health Sector Coordinating Council-Cybersecurity Working Group, *Health Industry Cybersecurity—Supply Chain Risk Management Guide v2.0* (*https://healthsec torcouncil.org/wp-content/uploads/2023/10/HIC-SCRiM_2023-2.pdf*), October 2023.

23    "Supply Chain Risk Mitigation Program" (*https://www.nerc.com/pa/comp/Pages/ Supply-Chain-Risk-Mitigation-Program.aspx*), NERC, accessed December 8, 2023.

24    "HITRUST CSF Framework" (*https://hitrustalliance.net/product-tool/hitrust-csf*), HITRUST Alliance, accessed December 8, 2023.

# CHAPTER 3

# Infrastructure Security in the Product Lifecycle

The security of intellectual property and the final product, including code, data, defect information, scripts, and production files, relies on the various infrastructure, systems, and devices used throughout the product lifecycle. In this chapter, I will highlight the important processes and controls that you should address for infrastructure security in the software supply chain. Infrastructure security doesn't focus only on IT-managed platforms or stop when code is complete—it must extend to all platforms and processes (e.g., digital copies, cloud, mobile app stores, development systems, download centers, manufacturing systems, supply chain logistics, services, and end users).

The core tenets of infrastructure security are represented by the CIA (confidentiality, integrity, and availability) triad. Organizations need to embody these tenets in all aspects of their networks in order to have strong infrastructure security. I have seen organizations with strong infrastructure security in their business environments, but little or no policies, standards, rules, controls, or guidelines in the development, testing, and supply chain environments shown in Figure 3-1. Although not having policies may feel liberating, allowing you to design and build products without constraints, it can lead to security gaps. As a software developer, I fully understand the need for freedom, but there must be a balance between flexibility and security.

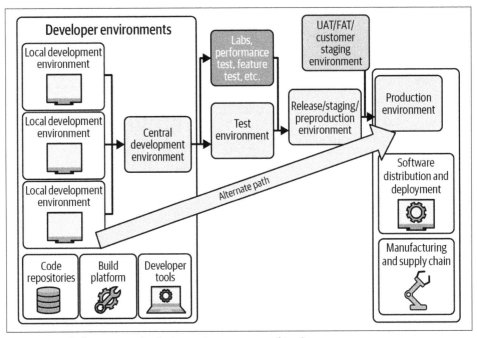

*Figure 3-1. Software supply chain environments and tools*

This chapter will discuss risks and controls necessary for the software supply chain environments and tools. The controls in this chapter provide a specific focus toward the environments and tools that present risk to the software supply chain. You can integrate and expand the controls from this chapter into your existing infrastructure controls (such as the Center for Internet Security's CIS Controls).[1] Due to the specific nature of cloud infrastructure and tools used within the production environments, I address the cloud controls in more detail throughout Chapter 6.

## Developer Environments

In a typical corporate environment, most users have similar devices (usually referred to as endpoints) such as laptops, desktops, tablets, and mobile devices. IT organizations standardize these endpoints to allow for easier endpoint management and maintenance of operating systems, upgrades, patches, and security. Developers, however, usually have the capability to maintain their own developer environments due to the complexity and flexibility required for creating new applications and products. This could include, but is not limited to, virtual machines (VMs), virtual private clouds (VPCs), hypervisors, and dual-boot operating systems (e.g., Linux and Windows). These other environments are often invisible to IT organizations—they're sometimes called shadow IT—and their endpoint management systems.

Developers believe they require the flexibility to spin up a virtual machine, install applications, and manage their environments. They do not want controls that lock down administrator access to their systems, stop their ability to create environments, or require dozens of approvals for modifying environments. The best path forward to secure these environments is to work together with the development teams in establishing policies, processes, controls, and tools specific for your organization. This should include preconfigured environments (e.g., infrastructure as code) that can be created, deployed, configured, and deleted.[2] You should also require that any environment accessible from the internet must have strict controls, rules, and policies to prevent malicious threats reaching into the environments. In situations where the security is not sufficient, you should implement operational, technical, or management controls, also known as compensating controls, to raise the security posture.

Even with preconfigured environments, the standard IT security policies and controls may be unrecognized in developer systems. Additional IT security practices should be specifically created for these environments to detect data loss (e.g., intellectual property, source code, private keys, or project files), intrusion by threat actors, and malware. One proactive way to reduce risk is by requiring highly secured or encrypted communications, protocols, tools, and technologies such as a VPN (virtual private network), jump server (virtual machine to manage other systems), or bastion host (provides access to a private network from external networks). However, encrypted communications can prevent monitoring tools from detecting intellectual property or data loss. For more information on other risks in the development lifecycle, refer to Chapters 7 and 11.

Within organizations, the business applications and infrastructure may be configured for alerts and connected to security operations centers (SOCs). However, the nonstandard environments such as development are often not patched, and they may be ignored by security monitoring tools. Controls, policies, and alerts must exist to maintain the security of the development environments. However, be certain that activities or alerts don't impact production environments.

To reduce security risk, routinely examine the logs of the developer environments and the tools connected to those systems. Monitoring tools should be trained to recognize developer-specific activities to prevent false positives (incorrect results claiming an issue) when issuing alerts or restricting activities. For example, admin-level tasks such as installing applications, elevating access privileges, or running scripts for testing often trigger alerts within security monitoring tools. One type of alert could be due to an unsigned (no digital signature) script file because it had no information regarding the author of the file.[3] By reviewing existing logs, developers and IT security should be able to identify normal and uncharacteristic behaviors, scripts, or programs within the tools and environments in order to flag actual concerns when they arise.

> ## Infrastructure Security Controls 01–02
>
> Control IS-01: Implement policies, processes, and controls required for creating, configuring, updating, and operating environments.
>
> Control IS-02: Log and monitor events such as access control, access elevation, permissions modification, and object execution.

# Code Repositories and Build Platforms

A development team must store code somewhere for daily use and preservation. In today's world, this is usually a cloud-hosted solution, such as GitHub, although some teams may still retain code repositories on premises or in a private data center. Generally, the development teams maintain these applications rather than IT administrators, who manage business applications. In Chapter 5, I describe the risks and source code management (SCM) controls, such as multifactor authentication (MFA), that should be applied to code repositories and build platforms as they should be for all critical applications and confidential data within the organization. Within that chapter, I also discuss the Google SLSA (Supply-Chain Levels for Software Artifacts) framework that organizations are using to secure the source code and build management process.

For the code repositories and build platforms, safeguards and controls must be put in place to restrict access to only approved endpoints and also to carefully log and monitor all activity. You can restrict access to systems using zero-trust technologies and reduce risk by frequently updating access keys. Similar to other high-value systems in your organization, you should conduct penetration tests on the repositories and build environments to identify where a malicious actor or threat can compromise the systems, manipulate code, inject malicious code, or steal intellectual property.

The SolarWinds hack of 2020 is the most noteworthy example of a threat actor inserting malicious code into the software build process and thus compromising the software supply chain.[4] Using the modified SolarWinds Orion software, the attackers compromised hundreds of organizations and then specifically breached dozens of companies and federal agencies through a "back door" that remained hidden for over six months.[5]

Even with awareness of the SolarWinds hack, development and build environments continue to be a significant risk in the software supply chain. Three years after the SolarWinds event, the 3CX Desktop App had both its Windows and Mac software versions compromised when a malicious actor injected malware into the 3CX desktop applications through the build environment.[6] Ironically, the malicious actor entered the 3CX systems using a software supply chain hack of the X_TRADER software package installed in the development environment.

Intellectual property code theft is also a real threat for a business, yet it is very difficult to monitor and control. When a developer needs to modify code, the development tools (e.g., GitHub) download a local copy of the code to the developer's system or VPC. The developer makes changes locally before submitting (committing) new code to the repository. Code repository monitoring and even behavior analytics tools will not be able to identify problems once the code is no longer available in a managed environment, such as a developer system. I recommend informing the development team that, as a preventative measure to intellectual property loss, the code repository will be monitored for downloads and activity. You can even have an internal dashboard or SOC that monitors for patterns in code commits, and therefore any deviation from the pattern can trigger alerts to the SOC for investigation and action. Tools can also generate alerts when certain conditions are met, such as a full download of a code project or a certain volume of data, which could indicate behaviors for intellectual property theft.

Additional security controls you can implement include disabling external mass storage devices and only allowing legitimate systems to access the code repositories. Ultimately, the SCM controls for code repositories need to be as strong as possible due to the potential risk of intellectual property or data loss, which I discuss in Chapter 7. Given the data loss risks that could result in severe business risks if someone grants the wrong person access to the code repository, I would not allow teams to self-manage the identity and access management (IAM) functions of the code repository. The best approach is to connect an IAM or single sign-on (SSO) solutionto the code repository, so the moment someone loses access to the corporate environment, they will also lose their access to the code repository. Even when the code repository is in a cloud environment and not connectable to an IAM or SSO solution, the IT team can include access creation and removal in its standard procedures, which will reduce risk to the organization when access control is managed quickly when all other access is terminated.

When establishing access, use access control techniques that will allow a developer or system to retrieve only the code needed to perform the work ("need-to-know") and limit the code repository functionality to only the necessary capabilities (e.g., read-only, normal, privileged, administrative). For example, an intern can be restricted to only one of the code libraries without the capability to delete code or database tables. Without proper access controls on all the systems, entire code repositories or, worse, an entire production database can be deleted, which is a true story from an intern's first day at work.[7]

# Development Tools

In addition to code repositories, there are many other tools and applications in use by development teams today. The tools include, but are not limited to, code editors, integrated development environments (IDEs), code development frameworks, debugging and testing tools, version control systems, continuous integration/continuous deployment (CI/CD) tools, management systems for Agile or defect tracking, collaboration tools, and cloud management tools.[8] It is important for you to maintain a list of all the tools and applications used in the development process and monitor the technologies for cybersecurity risk. From "Code Repositories and Build Platforms" on page 42, Controls IS-03 and IS-04—which focus on access control and monitoring—are applicable for any multi-user or hosted tool.

An additional risk to consider for all development tools is the authenticity and integrity of the tool itself. If possible the tools and applications should be signed, meaning the author guarantees that the code is not altered, to ensure authenticity. It is common for developers to locate tools, plugins, or scripts in public project repositories. However, these items are often unsigned or they may be signed even though they contain back doors, key loggers, logic bombs, or other malicious code. You must consider all development tools, especially open source and public domain tools, at risk for software supply chain attacks. In 2015, the XcodeGhost malware mimicked Apple's Xcode development environment, affecting over four thousand applications, according to the security research company FireEye.[9] Similar to website typosquatting (malicious actors waiting for you to type appel.com instead of apple.com, for example), malicious actors take advantage of common tool names by replacing them with compromised applications, packages, and code.

For the sake of agility, development organizations may not be following a corporate assessment process to check the security posture of the development tools. This increases software supply chain risk since source code may be in contact with dozens of insecure tools and applications. It also provides opportunities for infected tools to manipulate lines of code or give entry to malicious actors. In 2022, the security team for the Jenkins open source automation server announced 29 zero days (a vulnerability for which no fix was available when the vulnerability became public) in an equal number of plugins.[10] The impacted plugins were identified in more than 22,000 installs, which left them vulnerable to future exploitation. This one situation also highlights the security risk of exposing development tools and environments to the internet.

As supply chain security attacks continue to increase, organizations are now requesting their vendors to provide origin and provenance information. Simply put, provenance (or pedigree) is the history of changes made and who made the changes. For example, if there had been origin and provenance information captured from the beginning of Microsoft paint.exe, there would have been origin records showing ZSoft Inc. as the original development company in Marietta, Georgia, US. The provenance information would have also shown me and colleagues as authors of different components in the software. Current origin information would include Microsoft Inc. in Seattle, Washington, US (and likely other locations). The current provenance information would have hundreds of thousands of changes and developers, potentially also using open source packages, in the decades since the application was created.

Although it is not possible to turn back time and capture provenance for previously created code, software developers should capture this information going forward using development tools. In your organization, review the development tools in use to see what provenance capabilities are present. Many development tools use the W3C provenance specification to provide a consistent model for provenance information.[11] However, not all development tools capture origin information. I discuss software provenance and origin in more detail in Chapter 8.

In summary, every organization should have a process for assessing the authenticity and integrity of tools and applications, regardless of the size of the organization or the tool itself. You can use provenance to validate authenticity for the development tools in your organization and then leverage some of those tools to capture provenance information for the software you build. This lowers the risk to your organization by assessing the upstream software supply chain risk, and it also lowers the risk for any custom-built applications.

## Infrastructure Security Control 05

Control IS-05: Maintain an asset inventory for all tools, scripts, and APIs used by the development organization. Using origin and provenance information, validate the authenticity and integrity of the information in the asset inventory.

# Labs and Test Environments

There are multiple physical, logical, and virtual environments as part of the software supply chain. Although it is less common now for organizations to have on-site data centers with test servers lined up in a network rack, these environments still exist in various forms and need proper security controls. As I previously discussed in "Developer Environments" on page 40, shadow IT practices can happen with labs and test environments. Frequently these environments do not have privileged access controls in place but instead allow users to access all areas of the environment to make their changes. Although I understand the need for environment flexibility, lab and test environments are highly susceptible to software supply chain attacks and must have detailed audit logs and continuous monitoring. Therefore Control IS-02 (access control, logging, and monitoring) is also applicable for every lab or test component, product, system, or environment.

If physical products or components are required for the labs or environments, such as the IoT environment shown in Figure 3-2, these, too, may introduce security risks. IT malware and intrusion detection scanning capabilities do not typically support complex IoT, OT (operational technology), or cyber physical devices, such as drones, which may use real-time operating systems such as Embedded Linux. As mentioned in the previous sections of this chapter, it is critical to have an asset inventory of both the hardware and software in every environment. Using the asset inventory, the development, IT, and security teams must agree on access, logging, monitoring, and security controls.

Security risks increase when there are a number of different environments; a single product team may have dozens of development, lab, and test environments to support specific use cases. These environments may lay dormant or inaccessible for a period of time until needed for specific development or testing purposes. Patch management processes (upgrading the software versions) may not exist, meaning the environments are susceptible to known exploitable vulnerabilities. Although it's not always possible to have fully patched systems due to backward compatibility and interoperability reasons, where possible the environments should be patched and monitored for threats. Periodic reviews and penetration testing of key assets, applications, and infrastructure can help identify the weakest links in the chain, which can then be patched in an effort to reduce the potential attack surface.

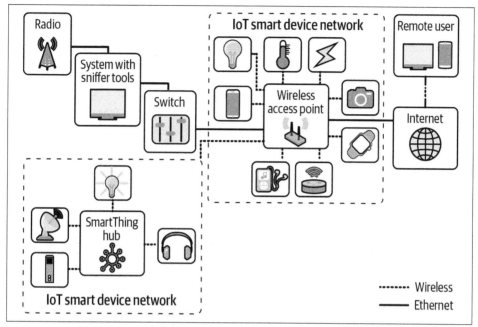

*Figure 3-2. IoT sample test lab environment*

An additional risk is the possibility of a lateral movement attack—an attacker moving between systems, environments, or networks—within these uncontrolled environments on generally unsegmented networks. For example, an attacker may take advantage of the vulnerabilities in an unpatched test environment and move onto an organization's financial accounting platform. In the VMWare Global Incident Response Threat Report for 2022, companies reported that lateral movement appeared in 25% of attacks.[12] You should utilize threat modeling to identify weaknesses in the applications or systems, which can then be addressed with mitigating and compensating controls.[13] Organizations are now implementing various compensating controls and techniques to prevent lateral movement, including segmentation, microsegmentation, air gapping (removing network interfaces), and zero trust.[14] Many of these techniques can be used for the lab and test environments.

## Infrastructure Security Controls 06–07

Control IS-06: Maintain patches and updates, where appropriate, for all applications, systems, and environments.

Control IS-07: Identify threats to applications, systems, and environments. Implement mitigating and compensating controls to prevent threats.

# Preproduction and Production Environments

Preproduction (or staging) and production environments are usually managed by operations teams to maintain business continuity for internal or external users. In many modern development lifecycles, testing or preproduction environments may not even exist. As with all previously mentioned environments, you should implement least-privilege controls, log and monitor events, and pay careful attention to privileged-access actions. You should also prioritize any events and alerts generated from the production environment, looking specifically for malicious actors or events such as DDoS (distributed denial-of-service) attacks, which can overwhelm the environments with internet traffic.

When possible, connect these environments to a SOC, SIEM (security information and event management), or SOAR (security orchestration, automation, and response) system and process. Rapid detection of unauthorized events can potentially reduce damage and limit risk. Famous "remote code execution" exploits such as Log4j present immediate risk to vulnerable systems. In less than two weeks after the Log4j disclosure, Akamai Technologies Inc. observed millions of Log4j exploit attempts each hour.[15] Malicious actors are constantly scanning for vulnerable environments, which requires extreme diligence from operations teams to keep environments patched to prevent serious incidents such as exploitation, corruption, and data breaches.

> ## Infrastructure Security Control 08
>
> Control IS-08: Prioritize logging, monitoring, and patching of production environments. Integrate with SOC/SOAR/SIEM processes and systems.

# Software Distribution and Deployment Locations

Software distribution can happen in a number of ways, as shown in Figure 3-3: software packages placed in a specific distribution location; deployment through application stores and update services; or deployment of code or services to a cloud environment. Software packages generally are a collection of installation executables, application executables, configuration files, help files, templates, and more. These packages can be placed into many locations such as distribution servers (usually internal to a company), download centers (e.g., printer drivers located on a manufacturer website), or application stores (Apple App Store or Google Play). In the cloud world there are deployment packages or containerized services where small objects are moved to an environment. For more information on cloud infrastructure and deployment, see Chapter 6.

---

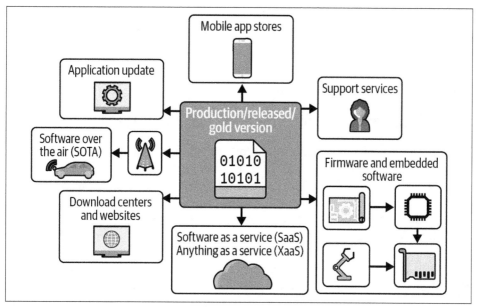

*Figure 3-3. Software distribution channels*

The software package may move along a path from the build environment to a staging environment to a production environment, or directly from development to production. The package may also move to a download repository or application store that contains applications for laptops, tablets, cell phones, IoT devices, or OT devices. The various software distribution locations present a risk because at any point along the distribution process, a malicious actor can replace or modify the software package or deployment, as was seen when malware was included in signed "live chat" software downloadable from a company's website in September 2022.[16] One method to secure software, as described in detail within Chapter 5, is signing software before distributing it to the various channels. This allows operating systems to automatically validate the authenticity of the software, assuming the signing credentials have not been stolen by a malicious actor.

To begin evaluating the potential risk points, you should map the software distribution processes to identify all the locations where a malicious actor or threat can manipulate the package or deployment. Pay careful attention to any locations or download centers where a collection of software packages may be stored for end-user access. Malicious actors may download and modify the software before creating fake websites. As mentioned earlier in the chapter, typosquatting of websites is a common practice to distribute fake software packages.[17] Downloading a software package from any site other than the direct publisher or manufacturer should be seen as risky.

# Manufacturing and Supply Chain Environments

For software and firmware that move through manufacturing and supply chain environments, as shown in Figure 3-4, there are additional risks and controls to consider. As mentioned in "Software Distribution and Deployment Locations" on page 48, the software or firmware must be signed and carefully monitored for malicious activity. Manufacturing and supply chain environments are another set of environments that may not normally be managed by IT departments. These environments usually have a number of unique systems—often running older Microsoft Windows versions—and OT devices and systems. For example, sensors and programmable logic controls (PLCs) are often positioned throughout a manufacturing line to operate different functions. More and more of these devices are connectable to a network and therefore should be secured using zero-trust technologies, segmenting networks, network access control, firewalls, wireless access restrictions, and additional compensating controls.

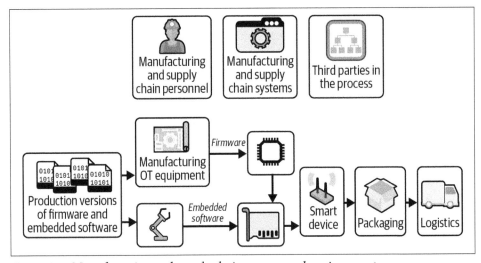

*Figure 3-4. Manufacturing and supply chain process and environments*

Manufacturing and supply chain environments have suffered over the past years from ransomware attacks such as WannaCry and NotPetya.[18] Similar to IT components and systems, the OT devices and systems must be included in an asset inventory, as well as follow proper security practices and manufacturer guidelines for securing the

---

devices. Monitoring for intrusions and logging is just as important in an OT environment, although usually it is managed with specific OT monitoring tools. As with other environments, patch management should be performed regularly during maintenance cycles.

---

### Infrastructure Security Control 10

Control IS-10: Maintain an asset inventory (including tools, applications, services, and APIs) for the manufacturing and supply chain environments. Secure the environments with proper security and compensating controls. Log and monitor all events for devices and systems that have access to software or firmware.

---

# Customer Staging for Acceptance Tests

In some software delivery workflows, there can be a staging area that holds the production-level product or systems along with specialized configurations for the customer. These environments may be cloud environments, physical systems, or a combination (hybrid). Sometimes the staging environments have specific devices, set-ups, and configurations requested for the customer environment. For example, the customer may be using one specific brand of firewalls, and the staging environments are built with those firewalls in mind.

The responsibility of the staging environments may sometimes be with the customer, the manufacturer, or with a third party such as a service provider or engineering firm. It is important to establish clear guidelines on the cybersecurity responsibility for those systems during the contracting process. There needs to be clear ownership of who will be responsible for the infrastructure of the environment to ensure that no malicious actors or threats enter that environment while it is being established, configured, and tested. If the environment is a physical product, there should also be physical security controls to prevent any intrusions. Sometimes these environments will not have established logging and monitoring yet, and thus the responsibility for any changes made to the system should also be included in the contract agreement. And with all systems, personnel must be using secure endpoints with least-privilege permissions to access the staging environments.

---

### Infrastructure Security Control 11

Control IS-11: Contract agreements must clearly state the cybersecurity responsibilities for the infrastructure, access, logging, and monitoring throughout the customer staging process. This includes any customer-specific requirements, personnel access procedures, and change logs.

---

## Service Systems and Tools

Infrastructure concerns exist even after customer delivery or deployment. Once the production environments have been established, there are potentially service applications, tools, and systems that have access to the product or environments; the deployment of these items may not have been tested or inspected during the deployment process. Examples of service tools include remote access tools, such as TeamViewer and Microsoft Remote Desktop as well as diagnostic tools such as WireShark and Nmap. There have been many cyberattacks using remote access tools such as two attacks in 2021 on wastewater treatment plants.[19] Service tools, especially open source tools, should be evaluated, documented, and deployed securely in production environments. Pay careful attention to any scripts such as PowerShell, which is frequently used for automation but can be leveraged by malicious actors, and confirm that any debug capabilities have been removed.[20]

Similar to the development tools, any systems or tools used during the service process should be assessed and monitored for threats. In situations where there is service personnel accessing customer environments or systems, the endpoints themselves should be complying with infrastructure controls. Endpoints can include items such as laptops, cell phones, tablets, or even special IoT diagnostic tools, which could have USB, WiFi, or Bluetooth connectivity.

---

### Infrastructure Security Control 12

Control IS-12: Maintain an asset inventory for all applications, systems, tools, and scripts used by the service organization. Monitor all service endpoints and tools for malicious threats.

---

## Summary

Infrastructure security is well recognized as important for enterprise applications and systems, but may not get the same attention and oversight in development, lab, or manufacturing environments. These environments and processes present security risks that can be reduced with access controls, monitoring, and logging, similar to what occurs for enterprise applications and systems. Adding the infrastructure controls from this chapter to an existing IT controls framework will provide an end-to-end set of controls for the software supply chain infrastructure and processes. In Chapter 4, I'll describe the first foundational element, a secure development lifecycle, to establish within an organization that is building or buying software.

# References

1  "The 18 CIS Critical Security Controls" (*https://www.cisecurity.org/controls/cis-controls-list*), Center for Internet Security®, accessed December 8, 2023.

2  John Rofrano, "Creating Reproducible Development Environments" (*https://medium.com/nerd-for-tech/creating-reproducible-development-environments-fac8d6471f35*), Medium, April 12, 2021.

3  Riya Sander, "What Is a Code Signing Certificate? How Does It Work?" (*https://www.computer.org/publications/tech-news/trends/what-is-a-code-signing-certificate*) IEEE Computer Society, August 31, 2021.

4  Sudhakar Ramakrishna, "An Investigative Update of the Cyberattack" (*https://orangematter.solarwinds.com/2021/05/07/an-investigative-update-of-the-cyberattack*), Orange Matter, May 7, 2021.

5  "SolarWinds Cyberattack Demands Significant Federal and Private-Sector Response (Infographic)" (*https://www.gao.gov/blog/solarwinds-cyberattack-demands-significant-federal-and-private-sector-response-infographic*), US Government Accountability Office, April 22, 2021.

6  Jeff Johnson, Fred Plan, Adrian Sanchez, Renato Fontana, Jake Nicastro, Dimiter Andonov, Marius Fodoreanu, and Daniel Scott, "3CX Software Supply Chain Compromise Initiated by a Prior Software Supply Chain Compromise" (*https://www.mandiant.com/resources/blog/3cx-software-supply-chain-compromise*), Mandiant (blog), October 23, 2023.

7  David Cassel, "The Junior Dev Who Deleted the Production Database" (*https://thenewstack.io/junior-dev-deleted-production-database*), The New Stack, June 10, 2017,.

8  CI/CD is a process for frequent integration (compiling, linking, or merging) and delivery (also known as deployment), usually through automation.

9  Dan Goodin, "Apple Scrambles after 40 Malicious 'XcodeGhost' Apps Haunt App Store" (*https://arstechnica.com/information-technology/2015/09/apple-scrambles-after-40-malicious-xcodeghost-apps-haunt-app-store*), Ars Technica, September 21, 2015.

10  Sergiu Gatlan, "Jenkins Discloses Dozens of Zero-Day Bugs in Multiple Plugins" (*https://www.bleepingcomputer.com/news/security/jenkins-discloses-dozens-of-zero-day-bugs-in-multiple-plugins*), Bleeping Computer, July 1, 2022.

11  "PROV-Overview" (*https://www.w3.org/TR/prov-overview*), World Wide Web Consortium, April 30, 2013.

12    VMware, *Global Incident Response Threat Report* (*https://www.vmware.com/content/dam/learn/en/amer/fy23/pdf/1553238_Global_Incident_Response_Threat_Report_Weathering_The_Storm.pdf*), 2022.

13    Mitigating controls may reduce the chances of a threat occurring, while compensating controls are alternative methods to threat reduction. For example, restricting user access can be a mitigation control, and using a multifactor authentication token can be a compensating control.

14    Zero trust is a security framework requiring all users and systems to be continuously authenticated and authorized. For more information, see Mary K. Pratt, "What Is Zero Trust? A Model for More Effective Security" (*https://www.csoonline.com/article/3247848/what-is-zero-trust-a-model-for-more-effective-security.html*), CSO, March 7, 2023.

15    "Threat Intelligence on Log4j CVE: Key Findings and Their Implications" (*https://www.akamai.com/blog/security/threat-intelligence-on-log4j-cve-key-findings-and-their-implications*), *Akamai* (blog), December 17, 2021.

16    "CrowdStrike Falcon Platform Identifies Supply Chain Attack via a Trojanized Comm100 Chat Installer" (*https://www.crowdstrike.com/blog/new-supply-chain-attack-leverages-comm100-chat-installer*), *CrowdStrike* (blog), September 30, 2022.

17    Adam Rowe, "Fake Zoom Websites Are Tricking Users into Downloading Malware" (*https://tech.co/news/fake-zoom-websites-downloading-malware*), Tech.Co, September 27, 2022.

18    Yoni Shohet, "Ransomware Attacks Hit Manufacturing—Are You Vulnerable?" (*https://www.industryweek.com/technology-and-iiot/article/22027363/ransomware-attacks-hit-manufacturing-are-you-vulnerable*) IndustryWeek, March 26, 2019.

19    Kevin Collier, "50,000 Security Disasters Waiting to Happen: The Problem of America's Water Supplies" (*https://www.nbcnews.com/tech/security/hacker-tried-poison-calif-water-supply-was-easy-entering-password-rcna1206*), *NBC News*, June 17, 2021.

20    Ionut Arghire, "Hackers Are Loving PowerShell, Study Finds" (*https://www.securityweek.com/hackers-are-loving-powershell-study-finds*), SecurityWeek, March 27, 2019.

# CHAPTER 4

# Secure Development Lifecycle

Secure software is software that has been designed and developed in a way that will continue to function normally even when subjected to malicious attacks. A secure development lifecycle (SDL, although your organization may use another name) consists of activities that strengthen an application or product's security posture during the software development lifecycle (SDLC). This can also be known as a secure software development lifecycle (S-SDLC) or a Secure Software Development Framework (SSDF).

There are three primary reasons to use an SDL as early and often as possible: to reduce vulnerabilities, reduce the impact of vulnerabilities, and address the original causes of vulnerabilities. As with any software defect, it's always cheaper and more effective to identify these issues early, and "early" goes all the way back to the initial creation and design of the software. An SDL can provide customers with assurance that a formal process has been followed and can also prevent organizations from repeating the same security mistakes with each release.

As we saw in previous chapters, software supply chain security requires secure development as one of the foundational elements and is now a required element in many cybersecurity legal agreements and certifications. Your organization may already have SDL processes within its existing SDLC or DevOps processes, even if they aren't called as such. This chapter will discuss the details of secure development lifecycles, augmenting SDLCs, and the more popular SDLs you can use in your organization. For a more detailed discussion of secure development, I recommend the book *Alice and Bob Learn Application Security* by Tanya Janca.[1]

The decision of which SDL to use is usually up to your organization and almost always requires the secure development lifecycle to be adapted to your processes. Once your organization has selected an SDL, document the decision and appropriate details in a corporate SDL policy.

> ## Secure Development Lifecycle Control 01
>
> Control SDL-01: Maintain a secure development lifecycle (SDL) framework and policy that requires employees, contractors, and third parties to follow SDL practices for applications and products.

# Key Elements of an SDL

An SDL is the foundation for a secure software supply chain. There are five key elements of an SDL that exist across the various frameworks: security requirements, secure design, secure development, security testing, and vulnerability management. Although you can reduce risk by implementing key elements—such as secure testing—without an SDL, you may still find yourself at a disadvantage since the development team cannot be certain that it has tested what truly needs testing. An SDL's prescriptive process and controls will enable you to implement a secure software supply chain with secure requirements, design, and development in a reproducible process.

## Security Requirements

Security requirements may be defined by laws, regulations, SDL frameworks, and standards, or identified by customers, marketing, internal guidelines, known vulnerabilities, and threat analysis. It is not unusual to have hundreds of security requirements of varying complexity as part of a product, application, or system. For example, marketing requirements for data security can be high-level, such as "personal data shall only be seen by the user," and then decomposed into dozens of more-detailed, lower-level security requirements, such as "data in transit must be encrypted" and "user access must be authenticated."

Sometimes there are specific regulations associated with the marketing or technical requirements. For example, there could be cryptography requirements at the marketing level, but regulations may require NIST FIPS 140 for cryptographic modules.[2] SDL frameworks can also introduce requirements such as the file integrity requirement in ISA/IEC 62443, which ensures users have a way to verify that software has not been altered. Before building applications, you should identify any standards that may apply or certifications you want to pursue, such as the CREST OVS (OWASP Verification Standard) for web and mobile application security standards.[3]

Product, application, system, and infrastructure security requirements coming from internal technical guidelines, known vulnerabilities, and threat analysis must be continuously updated to address new threats and attack paths. The typical approach for threat analysis comes in the form of threat modeling—a process by which potential threats, such as structural vulnerabilities or the absence of appropriate safeguards, can be identified and enumerated and countermeasures prioritized.

Another threat analysis approach is to use knowledge bases of curated adversary techniques from real-world observations, such as the MITRE ATT&CK® framework with attack techniques for enterprise systems, mobile applications, and industrial control systems (ICS).[4] MITRE techniques may include procedure examples, mitigations, detection information, and subtechniques.

The Cyber Kill Chain® framework, developed by Lockheed Martin, is another framework for the identification and prevention of cyber intrusions. The seven-phase attack framework shows the adversary's actions alongside the defender's actions to prevent the intrusion.[5]

Similar to the MITRE frameworks, the Open Software Supply Chain Attack Reference (OSC&R) specifically addresses the techniques used to attack software supply chains. In addition to using the information and controls within this book, I recommend you carefully review the OSC&R framework to identify requirements for your organization, products, and applications.[6]

For some software supply chain security risks, you can transform the security control into a security requirement. One such example would be the Infrastructure Security Control IS-08 for patching, as seen in Chapter 3. An application security requirement or user story specifically to "auto-update software" would resolve part of the IS-08 security control.

At some point, all of these security requirements should be documented in a requirements or user stories database—including the requirements that map to the SDL controls and governance process. Traceability between these requirements, the threat models, and secure test cases are important for validating the requirements prior to a software release and satisfying proof of controls for auditors. At least annually you should review the existing security requirements for enhancements or additions following any changes or improvements to the SDL process and controls as well as new requirements and threats that may have surfaced.

---

## Secure Development Lifecycle Control 02

Control SDL-02: Document and maintain security requirements for applications and products. Include security requirements that are required by processes, controls, applicable laws, and regulations.

---

# Secure Design

The concept of secure design (or secure-by-design) is not only about architecture and infrastructure but also about the security requirements implemented into the system. Within a product or application, secure design is when the team has gone through activities to evaluate the requirements and potential threats to limit risk. Risk to software supply chain security is greatly reduced when secure design activities such as threat modeling are performed. Even products that have been previously designed will benefit greatly from a complete threat model that analyzes entry points, code, services, protocols, APIs, and more.

Threat modeling must be a team sport, or as the *Threat Model Manifesto* states, there should not be a single hero threat modeler, but multiple people providing representations and views to illuminate different problems.[7] Threat models should be considered living artifacts that the team must reexamine when architecture, technology, or threats change. This demonstrates that threat models should be updated frequently since the threat landscape is shifting rapidly. Each time risks are identified through threat models, additional security requirements must be added to the product or application.

Additional techniques for securing the product, application, or system design include:

- Analyzing and selecting technologies, components, programming languages, and infrastructure with reduced risk compared to other choices
- Utilizing modular code for easier code updates or reuse
- Isolating critical components and security components from other components during execution
- Providing features for secure deployment, operation, and maintenance

Another type of secure design is "privacy by design" (sometimes called PbD). This includes data security, data protection, and data localization requirements for personal or business data. Considering PbD early in the design process can significantly reduce rearchitecting databases, structures, and common methods such as encryption to meet changing privacy requirements.

---

## Secure Development Lifecycle Control 03

Control SDL-03: Use secure-by-design and privacy-by-design concepts when designing applications and products. Conduct threat modeling on all code, services, systems, infrastructure, APIs, and protocols.

---

# Secure Development

Secure development, another key element in an SDL, involves the methods, techniques, and practices developers should follow and use during code development. This includes important areas such as proper error handling, fault handling, memory management, and secure coding standards. Secure coding standards should always prevent back doors, debug interfaces, error information, or intellectual property from being released. Secure coding rules must be specific for the technology and languages your organization uses, but if your organization does not have secure coding standards in place, refer to "Code Quality" on page 80 for a list of various standards.

There are many tools available that review code for secure coding risks. Code quality and software composition analysis (SCA) tools are designed to locate faults in free and open source software (FOSS or OSS) by examining code for known vulnerabilities. These tools can also identify license information for potential compliance risks. Some tools even look for hardcoded credentials or compliance to secure coding rules. For more information on open source or code analysis, refer to Chapter 5.

When selecting tools, check for compatibility with applications, operating systems, or platforms. Although OWASP (Open Worldwide Application Security Project) materials were originally designed for web applications, they have expanded to cover more than web technologies. OWASP is known in software development for its "OWASP Top 10" project, which outlines the 10 most critical security concerns for web application security and is revised approximately every three to four years.[8] The 2017 OWASP list had quite a number of frontend security risks, but the updated 2021 list also highlights risks due to poor SDL practices such as software integrity failures, insecure design, and vulnerable and outdated components.

---

### Secure Development Lifecycle Control 04

Control SDL-04: Follow secure coding rules, leverage tools, and mitigate known weaknesses to develop secure products and applications.

---

# Security Testing

Security testing is the fourth key element in an SDL. Like threat modeling, it's never too late to start a security testing practice. As shown in Figure 4-1, there are multiple ways to perform security testing, including static application security testing (SAST), dynamic application security testing (DAST), interactive application security testing (IAST), runtime application security protection (RASP), and penetration testing.[9] Fuzz testing, which is an automated software testing method that injects malformed, invalid, or unexpected inputs in order to reveal software defects and vulnerabilities, is an effective form of security testing. Additional types of testing include cloud container and deployment testing, as discussed in Chapter 6. The various testing methods should be used in combination with each other and will vary depending on the product, application, system, or infrastructure.

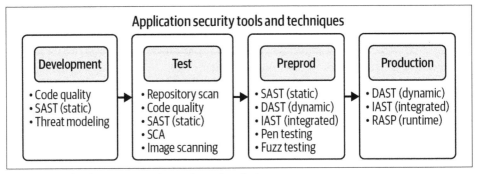

Figure 4-1. Application security tools and techniques

These tools are only effective at reducing security risk when mitigations (reducing the impact) or remediations (removing the threat) are performed on the findings. Also, these tools may locate hundreds or thousands of vulnerabilities, and most are ineffective in determining if the vulnerability can be exploited. Prioritization, tracking, and V&V (verification and validation) security testing should be used in conjunction with testing tools.

---

## Secure Development Lifecycle Control 05

Control SDL-05: Execute security testing using various tools and techniques on applications and products.

---

## Vulnerability Management

Although vulnerability management activities are contained within the primary SDL practices, this subprocess is critical for identifying, evaluating, and remediating security weaknesses. Throughout the development lifecycle, there are many activities that can identify vulnerabilities, such as during threat modeling, development, code analysis, scanning, and testing. This continuous process is vital for securing products and applications until they reach the end of their lifecycle. To demonstrate your organization's maturity, you can even choose to certify your vulnerability handling process to the ISO/IEC 30111:2019 standard.[10]

In a perfect world, all vulnerabilities would be fixed before releasing the product or application. Unfortunately, we do not live in a perfect world, and thus every release has vulnerabilities that may or may not be exploitable. In 2021, an exploitable vulnerability in Kaseya's remote monitoring tool gave malicious actors the opportunity to distribute malware to over 1,000 customers before Kaseya could take the software offline.[11]

When a vulnerability is found, it is usually rated with a scoring system, such as the Common Vulnerability Scoring System (CVSS) standard designed by the Forum of Incident Response and Security Teams (FIRST).[12] However, CVSS is not perfect, and therefore several other scoring and ranking systems now exist to help prioritize vulnerabilities.

The CVSS standard assigns severity scores to vulnerabilities on a scale of 0 to 10, with 10 being the most severe. The current version of CVSS is a calculated score, generally referenced in vulnerability catalogs, consisting of many metrics, including the attack complexity and what privileges are required. There are three other scoring and ranking systems in use: the Stakeholder-Specific Vulnerability Categorization (SSVC) model, the Exploit Prediction Scoring System (EPSS) model, and the Known Exploited Vulnerability (KEV) catalog.

The SSVC model, designed by Carnegie Mellon University's Software Engineering Institute and the US Cybersecurity & Infrastructure Agency (CISA), is a decision tree used to prioritize vulnerabilities based on five values, including exploitation status and technical impact.[13] In the same time period, EPSS was designed by FIRST to estimate the likelihood that a vulnerability will be exploited in the wild.[14] For ease of use, however, the searchable or machine-readable CISA KEV catalog is continuously updated with vulnerabilities that are currently being exploited.[15]

Ultimately when prioritizing vulnerabilities, I encourage you to begin with remediating KEVs first, and then the critical and high CVSS vulnerabilities. Remediation can take many forms, such as compensating controls, patching, updating, or replacing the source code. Ideally, all third-party libraries are kept up to date with the latest security patches applied in the source code, but there are situations where the only option is to implement compensating controls in order to prevent exploitation.

In the situation where a third party has reported a vulnerability, you should follow your organization's vulnerability handling process, and then disclose the mitigations or remediations taken according to your organization's disclosure policies, as discussed in "Vulnerability Disclosures" on page 139.

---

## Secure Development Lifecycle Control 06

Control SDL-06: Maintain a vulnerability management framework, vulnerability handling policy, and vulnerability disclosure policy for identifying, evaluating, remediating, and disclosing vulnerabilities to external parties.

---

# Augmenting an SDLC with SDL

Depending on your organization, you may already have a software development life-cycle (SDLC) with an SDL integrated into it. For those that do have an SDLC without security considerations, you should adjust existing SDLC processes, gates, reviews, templates, checklists, and training to integrate the key SDL elements. By doing so, the SDL will be less of a "checklist" and more of a natural task in the overall development process. Ultimately you want your SDL to be fully integrated and part of the natural day-to-day mindset of your teams, including management, as you develop your applications and products.

The following sections will describe the more popular SDL standards and frameworks. The market to which you sell your application or product can also dictate which SDL would be better received by your customers. If you have not already adopted an SDL, I recommend augmenting your SDLC with ISA/IEC 62443-4-1 (the most comprehensive) or NIST SSDF (rapidly gaining acceptance and free).

## ISA/IEC 62443-4-1 Secure Development Lifecycle

The International Society of Automation (ISA), the International Electrotechnical Commission (IEC), and the International Organization for Standardization (ISO) collaborated to create and release the "62443-4-1:2018 Secure product development lifecycle requirements" (hereafter referred to as "4-1 SDL"), which are available for purchase on the ISA and IEC web stores.[16] The 4-1 SDL standard specifies secure development process requirements for industrial automation and control systems products. These process requirements can be applied to new or existing software or firmware products.

The 4-1 SDL standard is the most robust SDL available for developing software and firmware. The technical committee that created the standard had taken many inputs from the available SDLs, security frameworks, security standards, and industry experience securing critical systems. The 4-1 SDL standard is one part of the overall ISA/IEC 62443 series, which provides standards for components, systems, integrations, deployments, and operations.[17] The 4-1 SDL standard is a baseline requirement for products and systems to receive additional ISA/IEC 62443 certifications, but as an SDL, it is broadly applicable for any product or application, not just for those in industrial systems.

The following list notes the eight practices within ISA/IEC 62443-4-1 SDL, as shown in Figure 4-2:

- Security management
- Specification of security requirements
- Secure by design

- Secure implementation (development)
- Security verification and validation testing
- Management of security-related issues (vulnerabilities)
- Security update documentation
- Security guidelines

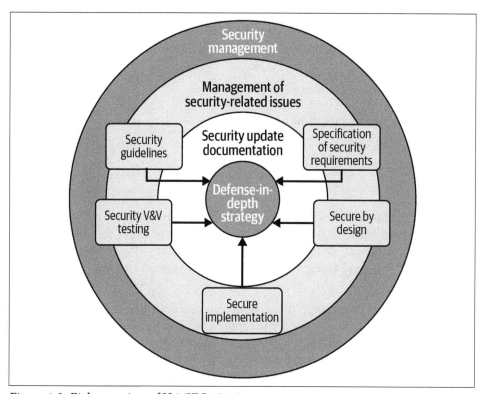

*Figure 4-2. Eight practices of ISA/IEC 62443-4-1*

The MDCG 2019-16 (Medical Device Coordination Group Document—Guidance on Cybersecurity for medical devices) document also uses these same eight practices.[18] Organizations that   develop products for industrial control systems (ICS), which are used in manufacturing, energy systems, water treatment, and more, often use 4-1 SDL as the foundation for their corporate SDLs and certify their global SDL frameworks through independent third-party certifiers. 4-1 SDL is a strong, solid framework for software and firmware, but needs some updates to reflect requirements for cloud-hosted applications and small Agile teams.

# NIST SSDF

The United States National Institute of Standards and Technology (NIST) produces many supply chain security documents and standards, one of which is NIST Special Publication 800–218. The NIST SP 800-218 document is better known as the "Secure Software Development Framework (SSDF) Version 1.1: Recommendations for Mitigating the Risk of Software Vulnerabilities," or shortened as SSDF.[19] The February 2022 document, current at the time of writing, includes an impressive cross-reference to the various secure software development frameworks. You can leverage this document for augmenting or establishing secure SDLC practices for your software suppliers.

The SSDF is organized into four main practice areas:

- PO: Prepare the Organization
- PS: Protect Software
- PW: Produce Well-Secured Software
- RV: Respond to Vulnerabilities

SSDF is a good foundation for an SDL, but it is not comprehensive enough to establish a secure software supply chain even when incorporating the NIST CSF (as described in Chapter 2). To evaluate and identify the risks in the entire software supply chain, you will need multiple frameworks or the core set of controls as identified throughout this book.

The SSDF does not provide specific guidance on implementing each SDL practice or control. However, there is an excellent supplemental spreadsheet provided with the SSDF document. The supplemental spreadsheet contains notional implementation examples, which can be useful to provide explanations and potential use cases. If you have already implemented other framework controls such as ISA/IEC 62443 or NIST SP 800–53, you will find the cross-reference available in the supplemental spreadsheet to be very helpful.

## Microsoft SDL

Microsoft first introduced its SDL (which Microsoft refers to as a Security Development Lifecycle) in 2008 and has been a solid supporter of SDL practices in all the standards and frameworks mentioned in this chapter.[20] Microsoft provides a free document titled "Simplified Implementation of the Microsoft SDL" for download on its website along with a Simplified SDL spreadsheet.[21] Prior to the release of NIST SSDF, the Microsoft SDL documentation was my recommended guidance to nonindustrial control system companies, especially small organizations or startups.

Although Figure 4-3 implies a waterfall process, Microsoft SDL is adaptable to Agile processes as well.

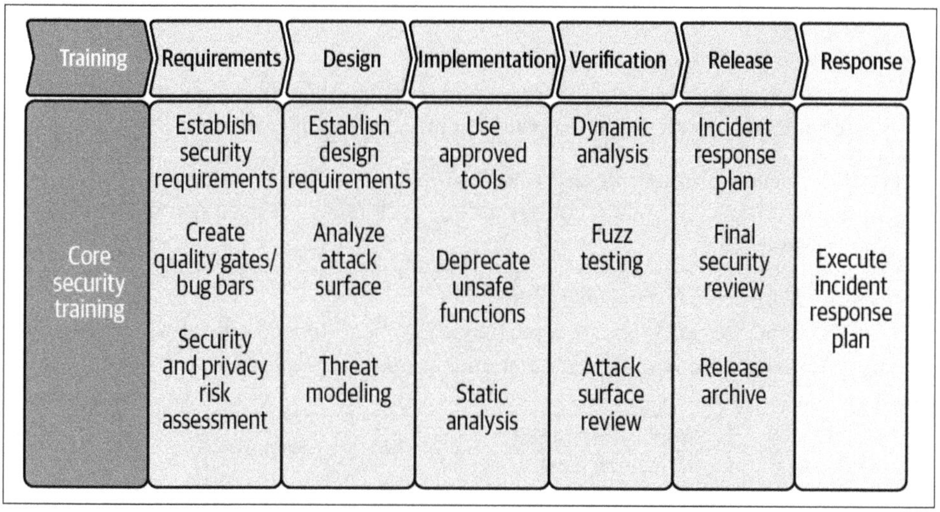

| Training | Requirements | Design | Implementation | Verification | Release | Response |
|---|---|---|---|---|---|---|
| Core security training | Establish security requirements | Establish design requirements | Use approved tools | Dynamic analysis | Incident response plan | Execute incident response plan |
| | Create quality gates/ bug bars | Analyze attack surface | Deprecate unsafe functions | Fuzz testing | Final security review | |
| | Security and privacy risk assessment | Threat modeling | Static analysis | Attack surface review | Release archive | |

*Figure 4-3. The Microsoft Security Development Lifecycle—simplified*

Microsoft has supplemented its SDL with other topics on its Security Engineering portal.[22] The most important enhancement is the Secure DevOps practices, as mentioned in Chapter 6, which can be considered as the basis for a Cloud SDL.[23]

## ISO/IEC 27034 Application Security

The International Organization of Standardization (ISO) and the International Electrotechnical Commission (IEC) collaborated to create and release ISO/IEC 27034 as part of the overall ISO 27k series. The ISO/IEC 27034-1:2011 standard "Information Technology—Security Techniques—Application Security" offers guidance for organizations acquiring, developing, or managing applications.[24] The ISO 27034 series also provides guidance to implement and demonstrate application security governance as well as application security management by helping to define, implement, and maintain a level of trust related to each application's lifecycle.

The 27034 standard works well for software applications in organizations that have adopted the ISO 27k standards and for those that are just starting to implement security for their applications. It is closely aligned to the ISO 27005 information security risk management standard. There are five main elements to the 27034 standard:

*Application Security Controls (ASCs)*
   Verifiable controls linked to the organization's security requirements, classified by level of trust, to prevent weaknesses in and around applications, as shown in Figure 4-4.

*Organization Normative Framework (ONF)*
    A repository of ASCs and processes used to normalize application security best practices across the organization.

*ONF Management Process*
    Manages an organization's priorities and defines ASCs in addition to other processes and security activities for the organization's applications.

*Application Security Management Process (ASMP)*
    Assesses risks, defines requirements, and tests ASCs using verification measurements.

*Application Normative Framework (ANF)*
    Collects and stores ASCs for a particular application as a subset to ONF, as well as process outcomes as security evidence for that application.

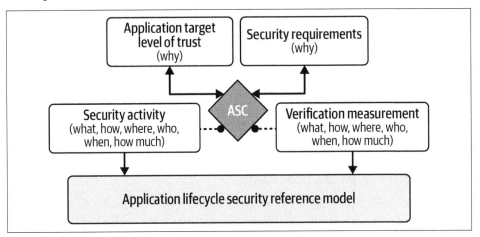

*Figure 4-4. ISO/IEC 27034 Application Security Control*

At first glance, many organizations consider the ISO 27034 standard to be complex, abstract, and of limited use to software manufacturers. However, while the mapping to specific situations may seem overwhelming to most businesses, the 27034 standard offers a step-by-step approach that allows companies to integrate application security into their existing processes according to their level of maturity, their priorities, and the resources they have available. This approach allows individuals, small organizations, and agile organizations to develop the ASCs for their applications in their context, and then continue to integrate the elements proposed by the 27034 standard as and when their security needs arise. For organizations already certified to many ISO 27k standards, the 27034 standard is worth considering.

# SAFECode

The Software Assurance Forum for Excellence in Code (SAFECode) is a nonprofit collaboration of companies that first documented SDL practices starting in 2008. Now in its third edition, "Fundamental Practices for Secure Software Development" provides a good foundation for secure development and testing.[25] The document references separate publications, including "Practices for Secure Development of Cloud Applications," which was released in 2013, and guidance for Agile practitioners in "Practical Security Stories and Security Tasks for Agile Development Environments" in 2012.[26,27]

All the SAFECode documents are well written and provide details on the core aspects of an SDL. The documents do not, however, provide prescriptive and enumerated requirements (e.g., Secure Design requirement number $n$). Without a set of controls, a development organization cannot demonstrate to a third party that SDL was followed for every release. I do believe the SAFECode publications can be used to augment a set of controls and provide materials for a solid training program. Although the cloud document is somewhat out of date and does not mention serverless computing, the Agile document contains many user stories, backlog tasks, and vulnerability weaknesses to support secure development and testing.

## SDL Considerations for IoT, OT, and Embedded Systems

An SDL is applicable for all products and applications, but there are additional considerations for devices such as IoT, OT (operational technology that can detect or cause a change in physical processes), and embedded systems (combination of computer hardware and software). As mentioned in "Device Protection Measures" on page 177, there are different ways to build in protection for devices through additional requirements, design considerations, development, and testing of the software, firmware, and hardware.

For IoT devices, there are new standards, baselines (minimum requirements), and labeling programs being released each year, and many are specific to the type of IoT device. Labeling programs require manufacturers to meet a certain cybersecurity standard before they can place a specific logo (trust mark) on the product. For example, the Singapore IoT Cybersecurity Labelling Scheme was released in 2021 and now includes many categories of consumer IoT devices such as routers, smart home hubs, and smart home devices.[28] Finland and Germany have also released cybersecurity labels, and the US IoT Cybersecurity Labeling for Consumers program is in design but was not officially released at the time this book was published.

In regard to OT products and embedded systems, the standards and baselines are very similar to IoT, but OT products generally have a correlation with safety either directly (e.g., controlling wastewater systems or manufacturing machinery) or indirectly (e.g., reading sensors located in a data center). There are a number of standards for IoT/OT, including some country- and industry-specific requirements. I have provided the following list, but you will need to monitor for new requirements since there are more releasing all the time:

- ISA/IEC 62443-4-2: technical security requirements for components[29]
- ETSI EN 303 645: cybersecurity for consumer IoT[30]
- ISO/IEC 27400:2022: IoT security and privacy guidelines[31]
- ISO/SAE 21434: automotive cybersecurity standard[32]
- UL 2900-1: network-connectable products[33]
- CTIA IoT Cybersecurity Certification: IoT baseline for the purpose of certification[34]
- UK Product Security and Telecommunications Infrastructure Act 2022: internet-connectable products[35]
- EU Cybersecurity Resilience Act (CRA): draft regulation includes IoT scope[36]
- US NIST IR 8259 Series: IoT recommendations and baselines[37]
- US California Law SB-327: first law specifically on IoT security[38]
- US Oregon Law HB 2395: consumer IoT law[39]

# Product and Application Security Metrics

A frequent question from those new to application security is "What metrics (a number) or measurements (relationship between numbers) do I use to assess an organization or product?" The answer, unfortunately, is not simple because it depends on where you are on your security journey and what is reasonable to capture.

My personal favorite for newer security programs is an SDL adoption measurement that uses compliance metrics from specific processes, such as penetration tests and security reviews. For example, there should be no easy vulnerabilities found in the penetration test, which has a complexity scoring system of easy, moderate, and difficult. You can combine any number of metrics and apply certain weights (e.g., three times the weight for a product that had an easy vulnerability) to define a measurement system that is unique to your organization.

For a list of many application security metrics and measurements, I recommend the "Capability Maturity Model and Security Metrics" chapter in *The Purple Book of Software Security*.[40] The Purple Book Community of software security experts, of which I am a founding member, has also designed the Scalable Software Security Maturity Model (S3M2) for organizations to assess their security maturity.[41] This software security model can be used by organizations of any size, even startups, and it is applicable to every industry and technology.

There are three other models available: ISACA/Carnegie Mellon University CMMI, Synopsys BSIMM, and OWASP SAMM. The Capability Maturity Model Integration (CMMI) uses well-known maturity levels to assess the capability of the process being measured. Available for purchase, CMMI is a good choice for organizations that have already adopted other capability maturity models and may not need a dedicated focus on software security.[42]

The Synopsys BSIMM (Building Security in Maturity Model) is available as an assessment service and thus is mainly used by larger companies. Although it is not a maturity assessment, it does provide assessment and comparison to peer companies and industry. Leveraging the results of the assessments conducted each year, Synopsys then produces a Trends & Insights report with key findings and recommendations.[43]

The OWASP SAMM (Software Assurance Maturity Model) project was specifically designed for application security and is available free to any organization.[44] It is a comprehensive application security maturity model, but it does not include other important areas of organization security posture such as network security and physical security. I suggest you review both the OWASP SAMM and the Purple Book S3M2 to find a maturity model that works well for your organization.

# Summary

Secure development lifecycles are the cornerstone of a secure software supply chain. With the attention being placed on secure development and secure testing practices, it will soon become common practice to have a corporate SDL policy for the development of internal, enterprise, or customer applications and products. Although there are various frameworks and approaches to SDLs, they all center around the main principles of security requirements, secure design, secure development, and security testing.

By incorporating these key principles into a corporate SDLC, the security posture of applications and products will improve and can respond when vulnerabilities are discovered. In Chapter 5, I'll discuss the various types of source code and how to secure the build and deployment processes.

# References

1 Tanya Janca, *Alice and Bob Learn Application Security* (Wiley, 2020).

2 "Security Requirements for Cryptographic Modules" (*https://csrc.nist.gov/publica tions/detail/fips/140/3/final*), NIST, March 19, 2019.

3 "CREST OVS Web Application Programme" (*https://www.crest-approved.org/ membership/crest-ovs-programme*), CREST, accessed December 10, 2023.

4 MITRE ATT&CK® (*https://attack.mitre.org*), accessed December 10, 2023.

5 Lockheed Martin Corporation, *Gaining the Advantage: Applying Cyber Kill Chain Methodology to Network Defense* (*https://www.lockheedmartin.com/content/dam/ lockheed-martin/rms/documents/cyber/Gaining_the_Advan tage_Cyber_Kill_Chain.pdf*), 2015.

6 "A New Open Framework for Releasing Secure Products" (*https://pbom.dev*), PBOM, accessed December 10, 2023.

7 "Threat Modeling Manifesto" (*https://www.threatmodelingmanifesto.org*), accessed October 26, 2023.

8 "OWASP Top 10" (*https://owasp.org/www-project-top-ten*), OWASP, accessed November 11, 2023.

9 Sherif Koussa, "What Do SAST, DAST, IAST and RASP Mean to Developers?" (*https://www.softwaresecured.com/what-do-sast-dast-iast-and-rasp-mean-to- developers*) Software Secured, accessed December 10, 2023.

10 "ISO/IEC 30111:2019 Vulnerability Handling Processes" (*https://www.iso.org/ standard/69725.html*), ISO, accessed December 10, 2023.

11 Charlie Osborne, "Updated Kaseya Ransomware Attack FAQ: What We Know Now" (*https://www.zdnet.com/article/updated-kaseya-ransomware-attack-faq-what- we-know-now*), ZDNET, July 23, 2021.

12 "Common Vulnerability Scoring System SIG" (*https://www.first.org/cvss*), Forum of Incident Response and Security Teams, accessed December 10, 2023.

13 "Stakeholder-Specific Vulnerability Categorization (SSVC)" (*https:// www.cisa.gov/stakeholder-specific-vulnerability-categorization-ssvc*), US Cybersecurity & Infrastructure Security Agency, accessed December 10, 2023.

14 "Exploit Prediction Scoring System (EPSS)" (*https://www.first.org/epss*), Forum of Incident Response and Security Teams, accessed December 10, 2023.

15 "Known Exploited Vulnerabilities Catalog" (*https://www.cisa.gov/known- exploited-vulnerabilities-catalog*), US Cybersecurity & Infrastructure Security Agency, accessed December 10, 2023.

16   See "ANSI/ISA-62443-4-1-2018, Security for Industrial Automation and Control Systems—Part 4-1: Secure Product Development Lifecycle Requirements (Formerly Part 4-1: Product Security Development Life-Cycle)" (*https://www.isa.org/products/ansi-isa-62443-4-1-2018-security-for-industrial-au*), International Society of Automation, accessed December 10, 2023; and "IEC 62443-4-1:2018" (*https://webstore.iec.ch/publication/33615*), International Electrotechnical Commission, January 15, 2018, IEC.

17   International Society of Automation-Global Cybersecurity Alliance, *Quick Start Guide: An Overview of ISA/IEC 62443 Standards* (*https://gca.isa.org/hubfs/ISAGCA%20Quick%20Start%20Guide%20FINAL.pdf*), June 2020.

18   Medical Device Coordination Group, *MDCG 2019-16—Guidance on Cybersecurity for Medical Devices* (*https://health.ec.europa.eu/system/files/2022-01/md_cybersecurity_en.pdf*), July 2020.

19   Murugiah Souppaya, Karen Scarfone, and Donna Dodson, "Secure Software Development Framework (SSDF) Version 1.1: Recommendations for Mitigating the Risk of Software Vulnerabilities" (*https://csrc.nist.gov/publications/detail/sp/800-218/final*), NIST, February 2022.

20   "Microsoft Security Development Lifecycle (SDL)" (*https://www.microsoft.com/en-us/securityengineering/sdl*), Microsoft, accessed December 29, 2022.

21   Microsoft Download Center (*https://www.microsoft.com/en-us/download/details.aspx?id=12379*), accessed December 29, 2022.

22   "Security Engineering Portal" (*https://www.microsoft.com/en-us/securityengineering*), Microsoft, accessed December 29, 2022.

23   "Security DevOps" (*https://www.microsoft.com/en-us/securityengineering/devsecops*), Microsoft, accessed December 29, 2022.

24   "ISO/IEC 27034-1:2011 Information Technology—Security Techniques—Application Security" (*https://www.iso.org/standard/44378.html*), ISO, accessed December 10, 2023.

25   SAFECode, *Fundamental Practices for Secure Software Development* (*https://safecode.org/wp-content/uploads/2018/03/SAFECode_Fundamental_Practices_for_Secure_Software_Development_March_2018.pdf*), third edition, March 2018.

26   SAFECode and Cloud Security Alliance, *Practices for Secure Development of Cloud Applications* (*https://safecode.org/wp-content/uploads/2018/01/SAFECode_CSA_Cloud_Final1213.pdf*), December 5, 2013.

27   SAFECode, *Practical Security Stories and Security Tasks for Agile Development Environments* (*http://safecode.org/wp-content/uploads/2018/01/SAFECode_Agile_Dev_Security0712.pdf*), July 17, 2012.

28    "Cybersecurity Labelling Scheme (CLS)" (*https://www.csa.gov.sg/our-programmes/certification-and-labelling-schemes/cybersecurity-labelling-scheme*), Cyber Security Agency of Singapore, accessed December 10, 2023.

29    "ANSI/ISA-62443-4-2-2018, Security for Industrial Automation and Control Systems, Part 4-2: Technical Security Requirements for IACS Components, 2nd Printing" (*https://www.isa.org/products/ansi-isa-62443-4-2-2018-security-for-industrial-au*), International Society of Automation, accessed December 10, 2023.

30    ETSI, *Cyber Security for Consumer Internet of Things: Baseline Requirements* (*https://www.etsi.org/deliver/etsi_en/303600_303699/303645/02.01.01_60/ en_303645v020101p.pdf*), March 31, 2021.

31    "ISO/IEC 27400:2022—Cybersecurity—IoT Security and Privacy—Guidelines" (*https://www.iso.org/standard/44373.html*), ISO, accessed December 10, 2023.

32    "ISO/SAE 21434:2021 Road Vehicles—Cybersecurity Engineering" (*https:// www.iso.org/standard/70918.html*), ISO, accessed December 10, 2023.

33    "UL 2900-1 Ed. 1-2017—Standard for Software Cybersecurity for Network-Connectable Products, Part 1: General Requirements" (*https://webstore.ansi.org/stand ards/ul/ul2900ed2017*), ANSI Webstore, accessed December 10, 2023.

34    "Internet of Things (IoT) Cybersecurity Certification" (*https://ctiacertifica tion.org/program/iot-cybersecurity-certification*), CTIA Certification, accessed December 10, 2023.

35    "Product Security and Telecommunications Infrastructure Act 2022" (*https:// www.legislation.gov.uk/ukpga/2022/46/contents/enacted*), legislation.gov.uk, accessed December 10, 2023.

36    "European Cyber Resilience Act (CRA)" (*https://www.european-cyber-resilience-act.com*), accessed December 10, 2023.

37    "NISTIR 8259 Series" (*https://www.nist.gov/itl/applied-cybersecurity/nist-cybersecurity-iot-program/nistir-8259-series*), NIST, accessed December 10, 2023.

38    "California SB-327 Information Privacy: Connected Devices" (*https://leginfo.legis lature.ca.gov/faces/billTextClient.xhtml?bill_id=201720180SB327*), California Legislature, September 28, 2018.

39    A-Engrossed House Bill 2395 (*https://olis.oregonlegislature.gov/liz/2019R1/Down loads/MeasureDocument/HB2395/A-Engrossed*), Oregon Legislature, accessed December 10, 2023.

40    Purple Book Community, "Capability Maturity Model and Security Metrics" (*https://www.thepurplebook.club/the-purple-book-chapters/capability-maturity-model-and-security-metrics*), in *The Purple Book of Software Security*, accessed December 10, 2023.

41  "Scalable Software Security Maturity Model (S3M2)" (*https://www.thepurple book.club/s3m2*), Purple Book Community, accessed December 10, 2023.

42  "CMMI Development" (*https://cmmiinstitute.com/cmmi/dev*), CMMI Institute, accessed December 10, 2023.

43  Synopsys, *BSIMM 13: Trends & Insights Report 2022* (*https://www.synopsys.com/ content/dam/bsimm/reports/bsimm13.pdf*), 2022.

44  "OWA Software Assurance Maturity Model" (*https://owaspsamm.org*), OWASP, accessed December 10, 2023.

# CHAPTER 5

# Source Code, Build, and Deployment Management

The true core of software supply chain security is the integrity of the product or application itself. From the moment one line of code is written until its delivery, there is risk of compromise. This compromise can come in the form of altered or injected code, malware, poor coding, weak build practices, and unverified deployments.

The development, build, and deployment processes are where the most well-known software supply chain attacks have occurred, at SolarWinds and Codecov, which are both described in more detail later in the chapter. Not only were their infrastructures compromised, but the attackers compromised their applications to gain access to many more customer organizations. The industry has reacted by focusing on improvements in the source code, build, and deployment processes.

This chapter will discuss the details of source code, how to improve code quality using secure coding standards and tools, the management processes, and integrity throughout the processes. The good news is that the controls in this chapter are not difficult to implement and will greatly increase the security posture of products or applications. Many of these controls build upon the infrastructure security controls in Chapter 3. The build and deployment processes in this chapter focus on more traditional products and applications. Therefore, refer to Chapter 6 for a discussion on cloud processes.

## Source Code Types

It's important to know the characteristics seen in different types of source code—such as open source, commercial, and proprietary, as well as operating systems and frameworks—because they hold different risks within the software supply chain. Risks also exist when using low-code or no-code platforms to build applications and generative AI platforms to write source code, as explained in this section. Your organization should always determine the data classification for source code, as discussed in Chapter 7. For example, open source code may be classified as public, but proprietary code may be classified as confidential.

## Open Source

Open source software (OSS) can be written by anyone and distributed under specific licenses that grant others the right to use, change, and share the code. In its *2022 Open Source Security and Risk Analysis Report*, Synopsys audited 2,400 code bases and determined that 78% were open source code.[1] The remaining 22% were a blend of proprietary and commercial code. With over three times the amount of code being open source, this highlights the importance of security practices for evaluating source code coming into the development process.

There are many risks to using open source, and those risks must be evaluated to determine whether or not open source should be used for a product or application. An open source project may have thousands of lines of code constructed from hundreds of authors. Many of the open source libraries are stored as code projects on public repositories such as GitHub, but you must remain cautious because not all code in GitHub, Stack Overflow, and other locations is safe to use.[2,3] The code may contain back doors, links to command-and-control servers, logic bombs, and intentional flaws. When searching for source code, only use legitimate, well-known public repositories and package managers. However, there is malicious code even in reputable repositories.

Instead of developing new code, using open source code can provide innovation and also reduce the time needed for development and testing. The advantage of using the more popular open source is that the code quality in those libraries is usually higher due to supervision, many code reviews, and extensive testing. The Apache Log4Shell project (where the Log4j critical vulnerability existed) is one of those libraries, but this vulnerability demonstrates that even well-tested code can eventually have vulnerabilities.

There are several techniques to reduce risks, including the use of software composition and code analysis tools. However, the tools can miss some security vulnerabilities. The most secure method for reducing risk is conducting line-by-line manual code reviews to inspect the code. Unfortunately, this is rarely done since open source can be thousands of lines long, and manual line-by-line reviews take time by even experienced reviewers.

There are many controls that an organization can implement to reduce OSS usage risk, and the best collection of controls and guidance can be found in the *Secure Supply Chain Consumption Framework (S2C2F) Simplified Requirements* document.[4]

Originally created as an internal Microsoft initiative, this framework is now freely available to any organization to build a strong open source software program, prevent the consumption of malicious code, and improve vulnerability remediation times, as shown in Figure 5-1.

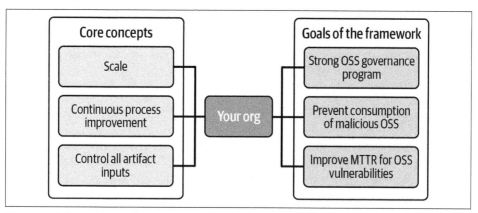

*Figure 5-1. Secure Supply Chain Consumption Framework concepts and goals*

To better understand the overall risk of OSS, you can use the free tool called OpenSSF Scorecard to check for vulnerabilities, dependencies, maintenance, tests, management, contributors, and build risks.[5] The tool generates a score and provides remediations to help strengthen the security posture. Another resource from OpenSSF is the "Concise Guide for Evaluating Open Source Software," which contains a comprehensive list of questions to consider when evaluating OSS.[6]

Additional approaches for reducing risk include examining who has contributed to the open source project and the frequency at which there are updates to the code. When open source has only one code maintainer—also known as single committers—there is a high probability that the person is doing this voluntarily. The maintainer may not have the capacity or capability to fix vulnerabilities, and sometimes the person will stop providing updates to the code. If the open source is abandoned, it essentially reaches "end of life" (EOL). This means your organization must take responsibility for fixing any publicly known vulnerabilities in the open source code within your software, or it should remove that open source from your software to reduce risk.

Open source has software licenses (e.g., BSD, GNU) associated with it, and these licenses provide details regarding how the open source may be used, modified, or shared.[7] One of the supply chain risks of open source is when a software license has additional conditions on the standard license text, such as restricting usage in certain government environments. Carefully review all the licenses for any potential license violations prior to using the OSS in your products and applications.

> ## Source Code, Build, and Deployment Controls 01–02
>
> Control SCBD-01: Use only open source that is well supported and available from legitimate sources. Continuously review all open source code, including updates or patches, for malicious threats and vulnerabilities. Continuously review the source code maintainers and contributors for ownership risk.
>
> Control SCBD-02: Review all open source and commercial licenses for agreement or potential license issues.

## Commercial

Commercial source code can be libraries, frameworks, binaries, or executables purchased for use within or by a product or application. Purchasing commercial code is similar to marriage—you want to understand your partner in hopes of having a long relationship because separating assets and obligations in a divorce can be very difficult. You can lower commercial code risk by performing proper code inspection, security tests, supplier management, and due diligence of the software publisher before and during the contract lifecycle.

Vulnerabilities exist in commercial source code, so in the contract it is important to document the service level agreements (SLAs) for vulnerability management and notifications. If you are only purchasing executables, and not the source code itself, you should minimize risk by requiring code to be placed with an escrow agent that can release the source code should the company close or default on its obligations. For more details on assessing suppliers and establishing contracts, see Chapter 9.

## Proprietary

Proprietary code is written by your organization or a third party contracted by your organization. Intellectual property rules and employer agreements do not normally grant or release code to the original employee or contractor. Usually proprietary code is owned by the organization unless a special agreement exists with employees or third parties.

## Operating Systems and Frameworks

Hardware platforms or chips may contain embedded operating systems (OSs), real-time operating systems (RTOSs), frameworks, libraries, or code. This code can be either open source (e.g., Apache Log4Shell), commercial (e.g., Microsoft .NET framework), or proprietary. To reduce risk, keep code patched or updated to resolve any design flaws or vulnerabilities. Some patches and security fixes can be "backported" to earlier versions without upgrading all the software libraries.[8] For example, patches backported from version 7.3 of a product can be incorporated into versions 7.0, 7.1, and 7.2, and those versions retain their original, earlier version number.

When incorporating operating systems into embedded software or firmware, during the build process you can use package managers to automatically manage dependencies and enable rapid updates, followed by thorough testing of the product. Platforms without embedded operating systems can usually leverage auto-update capabilities available in that version of the operating system. The Microsoft Windows and Mac operating systems have had update functionality for a long time, originally as a download and install process but now as a nearly seamless update. This capability has increased the security posture of the operating systems, but since only a limited number of software products and applications have auto-update functionality, it is important for organizations to understand and manage the patch cadence for all applications in every environment.

---

### Source Code, Build, and Deployment Control 03

Control SCBD-03: Update or patch software, firmware, and code to resolve any remediated vulnerabilities.

---

## Low-Code/No-Code

Many organizations have moved to low-code or no-code development platforms that provide the capability for anyone to create applications through a graphical user interface instead of coding in a programming language. Although the development environment and underlying application platform must be managed at an enterprise level, the applications created by users may also have a number of security vulnerabilities due to design errors. As seen in the "OWASP Low-Code/No-Code Top 10" list, there are still risks in the platform and applications such as account impersonation, authorization misuse, and data leakage.[9] SDL practices such as threat modeling and security testing are still required to reduce risk.

## Generative AI Source Code

Developers have been able to generate source code through IDEs (integrated development environments) and other tools for many years, but with the advent of modern generative AI systems, there are new security risks to consider when utilizing these tools. Coding assistants such as OpenAI's ChatGPT and GitHub's Copilot greatly increase developer efficiency, but introduce risks such as vulnerabilities, malicious code, poisoned training data, and quality and license risk.

Generative AI systems use training models to recognize data patterns and then use these patterns to generate new data. The content used to train the systems can come from public repositories, private repositories, or a combination of both. Since the source code training data likely has vulnerabilities, you should expect approximately 40% of the generated source code to also include vulnerabilities, according to research from Cornell University.[10]

In addition to vulnerabilities, generated AI code may also have end-of-life components, defects, design flaws, lack of documentation, and unnecessary code. Developers could find it difficult to understand the code logic and modify code when something goes wrong. Threat actors are taking advantage of the lack in transparency to specifically poison training data with vulnerabilities, malicious code, and biases that can lead to discriminatory practices in generated code. You can mitigate these risks by carefully reviewing the generated code to ensure it meets your standards of quality and testing the code carefully for threats and vulnerabilities.

If your organization allows or is considering the use of generated code, be cautious of ethics and policy concerns, as well as the licensing and use of the training data or generated code. Ethics, government policies, and organizational policies can all play a part in your decision to include generated code for internal applications or commercialized products. One ethical concern is the ambiguity over the authorship and copyright of AI-generated content. Your legal team should carefully review the license and, if applicable, the contract agreement before using the generative AI platform. To prevent the loss of intellectual property such as code or data, the legal team should also confirm if the training data and generated code is used in training models outside your organization.

---

### Source Code, Build, and Deployment Control 04

Control SCBD-04: Review all generative AI licenses for property rights concerns. Review all generated code for risks, threats, vulnerabilities, and lack of quality.

---

# Code Quality

As discussed in Chapter 4, secure development is one of the key principles in software supply chain security. An important aspect of secure development is ensuring code quality, which includes secure coding, the use of analysis tools, and code reviews.

## Secure Coding Standards

Secure coding standards are guidelines and rules for preventing security vulnerabilities. When used, these standards can help prevent attacks, detect problems or intruders, and stop malicious events or errors that could compromise software security. Standards for your organization will vary depending on the platforms and coding languages. Table 5-1 includes examples of secure coding standards that you can use to build a set of standards for your organization.

*Table 5-1. Secure coding standards*

| Title | Description |
|---|---|
| SEI CERT Coding Standards[a] | Language-specific coding rules for C, C++, Java, Perl, and the Android™ platform. |
| Common Weakness Enumeration (CWE)[b] | Security weaknesses in software and hardware. Includes languages C, C++, and Java. |
| OWASP Top 10[c] | Top web application security risks. Additional top 10 lists are available for desktop apps, mobile, APIs, serverless computing, low-code/no-code, large language model applications, Kubernetes, CI/CD build management, privacy, IoT, and more. |
| "OWASP Secure Coding Practices Checklist"[d] | Detailed checklist of best practices for secure coding. |
| Payment Card Industry Data Security Standard (PCI DSS)[e] | Secure coding guidelines for PCI DSS Requirement 6. |
| Secure Programming Cookbook for C and C++[f] | Recipes for cryptography, authentication, input validation, and more. |

a   "SEI CERT Coding Standards" (*https://wiki.sei.cmu.edu/confluence/display/seccode/SEI+CERT+Coding+Standards*), Carnegie Mellon University—Software Engineering Institute, November 18, 2020.
b   Common Weakness Enumeration (*https://cwe.mitre.org*), accessed November 12, 2023.
c   "OWASP Top 10" (*https://owasp.org/www-project-top-ten*), OWASP, accessed November 12, 2023.
d   "Secure Coding Practices Checklist" (*https://owasp.org/www-project-secure-coding-practices-quick-reference-guide/stable-en/02-checklist/05-checklist*), OWASP, accessed December 10, 2023.
e   Beth Osborne, "Secure Coding for PCI Compliance" (*https://resources.infosecinstitute.com/topic/secure-coding-for-pci-compliance*), Infosec, March 4, 2019.
f   John Viega and Matt Messier, *Secure Programming Cookbook for C and C++* (O'Reilly, 2003).

---

## Source Code, Build, and Deployment Control 05

Control SCBD-05: Maintain a set of secure coding standards specific to platforms and code languages. Educate developers on secure coding practices.

---

## Software Analysis Technologies

Examining source code for risks at the time of development can give developers direct feedback as they build products and applications. One technology used to improve secure coding is the set of plugins or features within integrated development environments (IDEs) where developers write code. Enhanced IDEs can provide immediate feedback to the developer before the code is even analyzed or tested. The IEEE Society has a list of free and commercial plugins categorized by IDE platform, code language, and source availability.[11] Be cautious, however, when using IDEs and plugins, because they can be compromised with malware, as happened in the "Octopus Scanner" attack on the Netbeans Java IDE.[12]

Software analysis tools, of which there are two main types, examine source code for security purposes. Static Application Security Testing (SAST) tools examine proprietary software for vulnerable code patterns, and Software Composition Analysis (SCA) tools examine open source components for known vulnerabilities.

SAST tools apply secure coding rules and need to support the programming languages used in your organization's products and applications. These testing tools leverage requirements, design, and specifications to test source code for known security vulnerabilities, but there can be many false positives (the tool claims there is an issue when there is not). SCA tools review code for known vulnerabilities, but there can be false negatives (missed issues) if the open source software library is not recognized by the tool. Both types of tools are extremely valuable in developing secure products and applications.

An additional analysis tool, known as a secrets scanning tool, is used to detect and identify sensitive information such as API keys, access tokens, credentials, and other confidential data within code repositories and other data sources. This valuable technology can help prevent breaches due to the loss of intellectual property, as described in Chapter 7.

---

### Source Code, Build, and Deployment Control 06

Control SCBD-06: Use features and plugins for enhancing integrated development environments (IDEs) and Static Application Security Testing (SAST) tools to identify secure coding rules and vulnerable coding patterns. Use Software Composition Analysis (SCA) tools to identify vulnerabilities in open source.

---

## Code Reviews

Reviewing open source, commercial, proprietary, operating system, framework, and generated source code is an important step in evaluating code for security risk and quality.[13] A manual line-by-line code review by experienced reviewers, as mentioned earlier in "Open Source" on page 76, can reduce risk. Reviews do not have to be formal but instead can be a lightweight process before the code is allowed into the build or deployment. Code reviews may only have one reviewer, though two or more peers are recommended especially when adding open source code. Reviewers can use this approach to mentor new developers or cross-train on another developer's code, which can quicken issue resolution when a flaw is discovered. Peer reviews can also help to mitigate insider threats, meaning that it would take collusion to insert malicious code.

# Source Code Integrity

In response to the SolarWinds attack, where malicious actors compromised code and build integrity, Google released its "Supply-Chain Levels for Software Artifacts" (SLSA) framework to make it more difficult or potentially prevent attacks on other software developers.[14] The SLSA framework ensures the integrity of artifacts interacting with source code management (SCM), continuous integration/continuous deployment (CI/CD), and distribution, while also providing details about the potential threat entry points, as shown in Figure 5-2.[15]

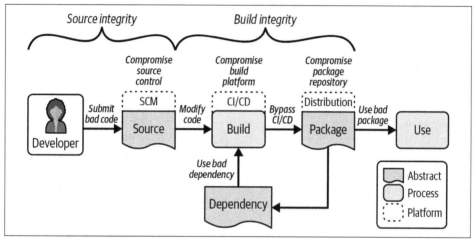

*Figure 5-2. Potential threats in the development lifecycle*

Although SLSA version 1.0 does not have the Source track at the time this book was published, SLSA version 0.1 is still available and has some source integrity requirements. The SLSA 1.0 Build track has requirements for provenance of the code package, signed provenance, and a hardened build platform.

In addition to the SLSA framework, the NIST SP 800-218 SSDF (Secure Software Development Framework) also contains source and build management requirements that can strengthen software supply chain security. Specifically the SSDF control PO. 3.2 provides examples for securing tools, repositories, and build pipelines. References to SSDF are included throughout the document called "Securing the Software Supply Chain: Recommended Practices Guide for Developers," published by the Enduring Security Framework (ESF).[16] Although the guide contains many of the risks, controls, and mitigations I mention in this book, the June 2022 ESF guide has some editorial challenges, making it difficult to implement due to repetitive topics that were likely the result of multiple authors contributing content.

There is another document, the "CIS Software Supply Chain Security Guide," that has a very comprehensive set of controls for source code, build pipelines, dependencies, artifacts, and deployment.[17] Each control has a description, rationale, audit recommendation, and remediation suggestion. The guide is ideal if you are looking for a more detailed set of controls that you can implement and then use to check compliance.

## Change Management

The process of change management within software development consists of securing access, tracking changes, reviewing changes, and controlling changes. You can perform change management using the various tools and systems already available in the development process. However, in many environments, the features or policies are not implemented or strong enough to stop malicious actors and threats. To identify the gaps within the change management process, you can perform threat modeling and penetration testing of the source and build environments.

The controls provided in Chapter 3 will strengthen the systems and environments, but the processes for code management also need careful review. For example, your organization should have policies that require code to be peer reviewed and scanned prior to inclusion in the build pipeline. You should also have the appropriate controls and policies in place that enable the propagation of code through the environments using least-privilege principles. As required by Control IS-02, every event should be logged to create audit documentation, such as the identification of individuals who have updated systems and environments.

---

### Source Code, Build, and Deployment Control 07

Control SCBD-07: Establish and maintain strict change management policies for code, systems, applications, and environments.

---

## Trusted Source Code

Trust is a complicated topic in the world of software development and geopolitics. Countries and customers want trustworthy suppliers providing products and applications. More narrowly, trusting the source code is one part of building customer trust, but gaining that trust can be quite difficult when all the information is not known. Historically, developers—which can be humans, systems, bots, or artificial intelligence—have not documented the origin for each line of source code. With thousands to millions of lines of code in an application, the true origin is unknown unless the information was captured as each line was written. Generally one has to accept that the source code's "country of origin," as required by some governments and customers, could be considered "any" or "all" countries. However, for definition within this book, you can consider the country of origin to be the location of the build pipeline or the primary maintainer.[18]

Source code origin is only one of the attributes of software provenance. Software provenance has many definitions, as explained in "Development Tools" on page 44, but as a baseline it is the verifiable information of where, when, and how the software artifact was produced. Open source, commercial, and proprietary code may capture provenance information, though this is not common yet in today's build pipelines. Due diligence in the form of code reviews, SCA tools, and vulnerability scans are the best way to reduce risk when uncertain about the provenance of source code.

Receiving or providing trusted source code also means that the source code, build process, and history have not been altered in any way.[19] In the case of SolarWinds, as shown in Figure 5-3, a malicious software library was injected into the build process and then SolarWinds signed the software as part of its Orion platform. This was a sophisticated software supply chain compromise that Google's SLSA framework could not have prevented unless implemented at the highest security level.

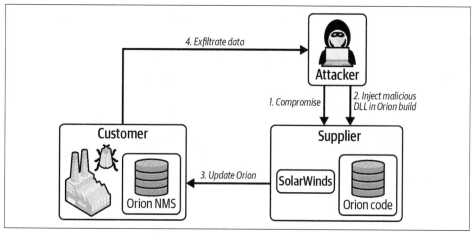

*Figure 5-3. SolarWinds Orion hack*

There are several ways to improve the trust for the source code your organization develops or consumes. Using frameworks such as SDL (secure development lifecycle), SLSA (Supply-Chain Levels for Software Artifacts), and S2C2F (Secure Supply Chain Consumption Framework), along with the practices mentioned in this chapter will strengthen trust as well as integrity. For open source code, the Open Source Security Foundation (OpenSSF) has a Best Practices Badge Program that allows open source projects to self-attest against the established criteria.[20] The badge program, combined with the OpenSSF Scorecard mentioned earlier in this chapter, can help to determine the level of trust for an open source project.

## Trusted Dependencies

Often during development there is a need to include or link to code, libraries, packages, or services from locations other than your organization's secure code repositories, tools, and systems. In cloud environments with dependencies, establish a hermetic (no network access) environment for the container during each build step to stop inclusions from remote resources. Dependencies on referenced items can lead to software supply chain attacks if malicious actors have compromised any of the referenced artifacts. Instead of linking to external artifacts, first quarantine the artifacts until you can fully inspect them, and then you can store the artifacts internally as if they were proprietary code. When the public version of the artifacts are updated, you should also quarantine the updates and follow best practices for assessing open source, as mentioned earlier in this chapter.

Beware of dependency confusion, especially in the popular programming languages of Node, Python, and Ruby, which use the tools npm, pip, and gems, respectively, as code package repositories. In Alex Birsan's blog post, he details how dependency confusion (a vulnerability where the code package is not from the intended location) can load external code packages rather than internal packages.[21] This vulnerability can lead to injected malware during the build process, as was the case when a security researcher uploaded a malicious version of the open source PyTorch machine-learning library to the PyPI code repository.[22] Because the malicious library had a higher version number, it had replaced the legitimate version for nearly a week in December 2022.

Malicious actors are now targeting open source developers through phishing campaigns, and uploading compromised packages to the PyPI code repository. For example, users downloaded 700,000 compromised packages for two popular Python applications in 2022.[23] If open source code or artifacts need updating, assume the artifact is compromised and perform the same due diligence as the first time by carrying out code reviews, tests, and scans. For more detailed information, Google has a "Dependency management" guide, which provides best practices for many different artifacts and platforms.[24]

> ### Source Code, Build, and Deployment Control 09
>
> Control SCBD-09: Internally host all code packages and library dependencies.

# Build Management

When establishing the process for building software packages, there are various actors, artifacts, and systems involved in the creation of software packages. In software supply chain security, the risks in build management reside mainly in authentication, the authorization of the build itself, the build scripts, and any automation. Refer to "Code Repositories and Build Platforms" in Chapter 3 for information and controls to secure the infrastructure before performing build management.

## Authentication and Authorization

Authentication, which verifies the identity of the user or service, and authorization, which determines the authenticated entity's access rights, are extremely important to secure build management processes, pipelines, and automation. If authentication and authorization are not controlled or monitored, malicious actors and threats can cause severe harm by manipulating the process or including malicious code. Essentially, you need to make sure that the correct people, tools, and services are allowed to do what they need to do for your software build, stop them from doing what they are not supposed to do, and ensure that the entity doing or accessing something is indeed the entity it claims to be.

Over time, the build process may have expanded to various people, tools, and services, and thus the authorization may not be correct. A thorough review of authorized access should be performed with some frequency. Not only should the accounts and keys be examined, but the permissions associated with those accounts should be set to least-privilege access with multifactor authentication enabled. Best practices suggest severely limiting the capability to check in artifacts, access the build process, and execute the build or deployment. For more information on how to reduce access and authorization risk, refer to Chapter 3 and follow control IS-03.

## Build Scripts and Automation

Whether it is through build scripts or some type of automation, there is risk that the build process itself may become compromised. Malicious actors can inject code into the scripts, configuration files, and any critical piece if not secured, monitored, and detected. This was the case for both the CCleaner and ASUS supply chain attacks, when malicious actors infiltrated the build systems to inject malware before the final applications were compiled.[25] Follow Control IS-04 in Chapter 4 to monitor accounts for unusual behaviors and code injections.

## Repeatability and Reproducibility

A build or CI/CD process cannot prove its integrity if it is not repeatable, reproducible, and has an attestation from the software publisher. Having a repeatable and reproducible process, usually through automation, allows for the validation of both the process and the activities. There are several ways to secure build integrity, but the strongest technique is to introduce "ephemeral" (short-living) build environments that exist only for the moments during the build activity. The containers or environments are then discarded after use to prevent malicious actors from accessing a static environment and manipulating the build process, as shown earlier in Figure 5-2.

The main way to check if the reproduced build is the same as the previous build is by comparing checksums, which are also known as cryptographic hashes or fingerprints. A checksum is an alphanumeric representation of the contents of a file created by applying a checksum algorithm to the file. There are three common hash algorithms used for files, in order from simple to complex: MD5, SHA1, and SHA256. MD5 and SHA1 have been broken by cryptography experts, but when verifying file integrity, you still may find some websites with documentation showing those hashes. During the build steps, the build process can generate the hashes of files and store them in a separate, highly secure repository. The build and deployment processes can conduct and compare integrity checks against the hashes in each step of the process using various tools, as noted on the Reproducible Builds website (*https://reproducible-builds.org*).[26]

---

### Source Code, Build, Deployment Control 10

Control SCBD-10: Use ephemeral (short-living) environments for build and CI/CD processes. Perform repeatable and reproducible integrity checks on the build and deployments.

---

## Code Signing

Code signing, a form of public key infrastructure (PKI), is a digital signature that verifies the file has not been altered after it was signed.[27] At a minimum, all code, drivers, product, and application files need to be signed with a certificate from a trusted Certificate Authority (CA). Every developer has the capability to sign code using the free service "sigstore" to automate digital signing, verification, and key management.[28] As shown in Figure 5-4, a hash is encrypted into a hash digest (the output of a hash function) with a private key, which the CA has generated. The private key is bound mathematically to a public key, which is made available to the user. The user can verify and validate the certificate through manual or automated means.

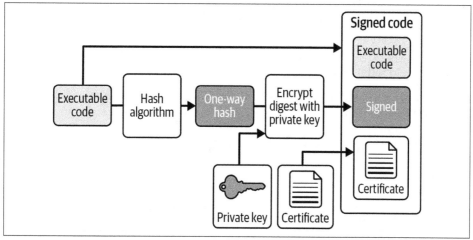

*Figure 5-4. Code-signing process*

There are examples where malicious actors have stolen code-signing keys, which was the case when Nvidia had private keys stolen during a data breach.[29] A stolen private key can be used by malicious actors to bypass operating system defenses—which prevent unsigned software from running—as experienced by unsuspecting users after the stolen Nvidia keys were used to sign malware. If the certificate exists for a file, you can find it on the Digital Signatures tab in the file's Properties within Windows 11, or on a keychain's Certificates category in the Keychain Access app within macOS.

## Source Code, Build, and Deployment Control 11

Control SCBD-11: Sign all code, drivers, scripts, and application files using a trusted Certificate Authority private key.

# Deployment Management

There are many approaches used to deploy and distribute software, as shown within Figure 3-3. Whether the deployment is directly to a cloud environment or posted onto a website, you should ensure that all access points in the deployment management process are secure. Each distribution channel should be penetration tested and monitored for malicious actors who could tamper with the contents of the package, thereby compromising the integrity and potentially replacing it with malicious code.

The deployment management process may be as simple as uploading a file to a website, as automated as deploying cloud infrastructure, or as complicated as moving software packages through the manufacturing process. Regardless of the process, each step should have secure access control in place. At any step, a malicious actor can attempt to compromise the software package, but the risk is lowered if authentication and authorization are carefully controlled. Follow Control IS-09 in Chapter 3 to secure distribution paths.

The most common method for validating the integrity is through signed certificates and hashes created during the code-signing process. Signature validation is usually performed automatically by an operating system (OS) or framework. Using the public key, the OS or framework decrypts the hash digest and compares it to the hash of the executable, as shown in Figure 5-5.

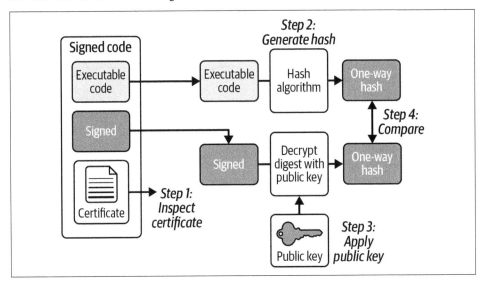

*Figure 5-5. Certificate validation*

To check the hash before installation, such as during the steps in a manufacturing process, you will need the hash digest for the software package. By decrypting the hash digest with the public key, you can compare that one-way hash with the hash of the executable code. This can be done either manually or through automation. If hashes cannot be verified at each step, perform ad hoc checks at different points or full verification when the package arrives in the final distribution location. In the case of the Codecov hack illustrated in Figure 5-6, it was a customer who noticed the hash of the Bash Uploader script did not match the hash listed on Codecov's GitHub (unfortunately the script had been compromised for two months).[30]

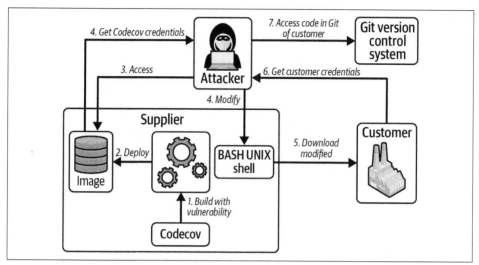

*Figure 5-6. Codecov hack*

---

### Source Code, Build, and Deployment Control 12

Control SCBD-12: Validate software package integrity through the deployment process by verifying certificates, signatures, and hashes.

---

## Summary

The risk of compromise throughout the product and application lifecycle can be reduced when we properly manage and control source code, builds, and deployment. Proprietary, commercial, open source, low-code/no-code, and generated code, as well as operating systems and frameworks, must be examined for code quality and integrity before the code can be trusted. With proper due diligence, such as code reviews, testing, and scanning, we can reduce some risk in the software development process.

After securing the source code, performing a thorough review of build and deployment processes will likely identify gaps and improvement actions. After the attacks on SolarWinds, Codecov, and others, the developer community released many articles and best practices, including Google's SLSA framework. Using the controls from this chapter and Google's SLSA framework, the likelihood of compromise will lower and the security posture of your product or application will elevate. In Chapter 6, I focus on cloud software, environments, and processes rather than the traditional software process.

# References

1   Synopsys, *2022 Open Source Security and Risk Analysis Report* (*https://www.synop sys.com/content/dam/synopsys/sig-assets/reports/rep-ossra-2022.pdf*), April 12, 2022.

2   GitHub Developer Platform (*https://github.com*), accessed December 10, 2023.

3   Stack Overflow (*https://stackoverflow.com*), accessed December 10, 2023.

4   Andrian Diglio and Jasmine Wong, *Secure Supply Chain Consumption Framework (S2C2F) Simplified Requirements* (*https://github.com/ossf/s2c2f/blob/main/specifica tion/Secure_Supply_Chain_Consumption_Framework_(S2C2F).pdf*),            GitHub, accessed December 10, 2023.

5   "OpenSSF Scorecard" (*https://securityscorecards.dev*), accessed December 10, 2023.

6   "Concise Guide for Evaluating Open Source Software" (*https://best.openssf.org/ Concise-Guide-for-Evaluating-Open-Source-Software*), OpenSSF Best Practices Work-ing Group, November 21, 2023.

7   "OSI Approved Licenses" (*https://opensource.org/licenses*), Open Source Initiative, accessed December 10, 2023.

8   "Security Backporting Practice" (*https://access.redhat.com/security/updates/back porting*), Red Hat Customer Portal, accessed November 11, 2023.

9   "OWASP Low-Code/No-Code Top 10" (*https://owasp.org/www-project-top-10-low-code-no-code-security-risks*), OWASP, accessed November 11, 2023.

10   Hammond Pearce, Baleegh Ahmad, Benjamin Tan, Brendan Dolan-Gavitt, and Ramesh Karri, "Asleep at the Keyboard? Assessing the Security of GitHub Copilot's Code Contributions" (*http://arxiv.org/abs/2108.09293*), arXiv, December 16, 2021.

11   Aniqua Z. Baset and Tamara Denning, "Poster: IDE Plugins for Secure Coding" (*https://www.ieee-security.org/TC/SP2017/poster-abstracts/IEEE-SP17_Posters_paper_34.pdf*), IEETC, accessed December 10, 2023.

12   Amnon Even-Zohar, "Beyond SolarWinds: The 'Octopus Scanner' Supply Chain Attack" (*https://cycode.com/blog/beyond-solarwinds-the-octopus-scanner-supply-chain-attack*), Cycode, January 12, 2021.

13   "How to Do a Code Review" (*https://google.github.io/eng-practices/review/ reviewer*), Eng-Practices, accessed November 12, 2023.

14   "Introducing SLSA, an End-to-End Framework for Supply Chain Integrity" (*https://security.googleblog.com/2021/06/introducing-slsa-end-to-end-framework.html*), *Google Security Blog*, June 16, 2021.

15   SLSA (*https://slsa.dev*), accessed December 10, 2023.

16    Enduring Security Framework, *Securing the Software Supply Chain: Recommended Practices Guide for Developers* (*https://media.defense.gov/2022/Sep/01/2003068942/-1/-1/0/ESF_SECURING_THE_SOFTWARE_SUPPLY_CHAIN_DEVELOPERS.PDF*), August 2022.

17    "CIS Software Supply Chain Security Guide" (*https://www.cisecurity.org/insights/white-papers/cis-software-supply-chain-security-guide*), Center for Internet Security, June 2022.

18    David Gallacher, "Country of Origin for Computer Software—US Customs Finally Sheds Some Light on the Issue" (*https://www.governmentcontractslawblog.com/2013/02/articles/baa-and-taa/country-of-origin-for-computer-software-u-s-customs-finally-sheds-some-light-on-the-issue*), *Government Contracts & Investigations Blog*, February 11, 2013.

19    Marcellus Buchheit, Mark Hermeling, Frederick Hirsch, Bob Martin, and Simon Rix, *Software Trustworthiness Best Practices* (*https://www.iiconsortium.org/pdf/Software_Trustworthiness_Best_Practices_Whitepaper_2020_03_23.pdf*), Industrial Internet Consortium, March 23, 2020.

20    "OpenSSF Best Practices Badge Program" (*https://www.bestpractices.dev/en*), OpenSFF, accessed November 12, 2023.

21    Alex Birsan, "Dependency Confusion: How I Hacked Into Apple, Microsoft and Dozens of Other Companies" (*https://medium.com/@alex.birsan/dependency-confusion-4a5d60fec610*), Medium, February 9, 2021.

22    Ofek Itach, "In-Depth Analysis of the PyTorch Dependency Confusion Administered Malware" (*https://blog.aquasec.com/pytorch-dependency-confusion-administered-malware*), *Aqua Blog*, January 4, 2023.

23    Amitai Ben Shushan Ehrlich, "PyPI Phishing Campaign | JuiceLedger Threat Actor Pivots From Fake Apps to Supply Chain Attacks" (*https://www.sentinelone.com/labs/pypi-phishing-campaign-juiceledger-threat-actor-pivots-from-fake-apps-to-supply-chain-attacks*), SentinelLABS, September 1, 2022.

24    "Dependency Management" (*https://cloud.google.com/software-supply-chain-security/docs/dependencies*), Google Cloud, December 4, 2023.

25    Michael Gorelik, "Inside the ASUS Supply Chain Attack" (*https://blog.morphisec.com/asus-supply-chain-attack*), *Cybersecurity Blog*, March 28, 2019.

26    Reproducible Builds (*https://reproducible-builds.org*), accessed December 10, 2023.

27    PKI is a common protection measure that combines encryption and authentication to prove trust in communications. Firmware code signing is described further in Chapter 10.

28 Sigstore (*https://www.sigstore.dev*), accessed December 10, 2023.

29 Gareth Corfield, "Leaked Stolen Nvidia Key Can Sign Windows Malware" (*https://www.theregister.com/2022/03/05/nvidia_stolen_certificate*), The Register, March 5, 2022.

30 Ax Sharma, "What You Need to Know about the Codecov Incident: A Supply Chain Attack Gone Undetected for 2 Months" (*https://blog.sonatype.com/what-you-need-to-know-about-the-codecov-incident-a-supply-chain-attack-gone-undetected-for-2-months*), *Sonatype* (blog), April 19, 2021.

CHAPTER 6

# Cloud and DevSecOps

Our world is more connected than ever, and we rely on cloud infrastructure for practically everything. When you turn on your phone's "airplane mode," you quickly realize how very little can be done without connecting to the internet, cloud services, and cloud infrastructure. With the world so dependent on the connectivity to our supply chain, we are incapacitated when there is a failure, or exposed when there is a breach, in the systems and applications we depend on every day. Because there are so many paths for attack, every connection, piece of software, and byte of data is at risk in any cloud infrastructure and is thus a risk within our supply chains.

Cloud security requires much more than setting up servers to prevent intrusion by malicious actors. The responsibility for software security in a cloud environment goes beyond infrastructure security (Chapter 3), the secure development lifecycle (Chapter 4), and deployment management (Chapter 5). Designing a cloud environment or a cloud application requires additional knowledge in many topics such as network security, configuration, tokenization, patch management, threat detection, and more. The attack surface for cloud is much larger than software or firmware because you must consider all the different layers of a cloud environment that may have many owners and a variety of skill sets necessary to secure everything.

There are many types of cloud models, and you may have every type within your organization. Table 6-1 describes some of the most common ones.

*Table 6-1. Common cloud models, capabilities, and connections*

| Type | Description |
|---|---|
| Software as a service (SaaS) | Cloud-based software delivery model to access software applications over the internet |
| Infrastructure as a service (IaaS) | On-demand service for compute, storage, networking, or virtualization |
| Platform as a service (PaaS) | Provider hosts integrated hardware and software |
| Container | Packages of software that contain all of the necessary elements to run in any environment |
| Virtualization | Virtualize an entire machine down to the hardware layers |
| Serverless | Method of providing backend services on an as-used basis, typically for developer environments |
| Infrastructure as code (IaC) | Managing and provisioning of infrastructure through code instead of through manual processes |
| Multicloud | Using services from more than one public cloud provider at the same time |
| IoT gateway | Physical device or virtual platform that connects sensors, IoT modules, and smart devices to the cloud |
| Edge device | Hardware that controls data flow at the boundary between two networks or for cloud connectivity |
| API gateway | Manage incoming calls for multiple services and route them to the appropriate endpoints |

For each of these models, the security responsibilities are distributed among consumers (your organization), providers, and what you both share (e.g., network security and middleware security). Often the shared responsibilities are poorly understood by cloud customers. In cases where both parties assume the other is taking care of security, it may mean no one is managing it. In many cases, the cloud provider is explicitly responsible only for infrastructure such as servers and networks, and it falls to the customer to manage resources including users, storage authorization, and application functions. So it is essential to clearly identify who is taking accountability and ownership for the security and risks of every cloud environment and application. Known as the *shared responsibility model*, these responsibilities may be defined in a contract, statement of work, or license agreement. The shared responsibility model should be documented alongside all the roles and responsibilities in the supply chain. To learn more about the shared responsibility model and cloud security in detail, I recommend Chris Dotson's book *Practical Cloud Security: A Guide for Secure Design and Deployment* (2nd ed.).[1] Dotson discusses cloud, data, and identity assessment management, as well as vulnerability, patch, and incident management.

In the first half of this chapter, I will review the different cloud security frameworks, controls, and assessments to provide a foundation for what is expected in cloud security and how cloud environments and the requirements they bring are different from classical infrastructure. Even if your organization does not design and deploy cloud environments or applications, the information I include in this chapter is relevant for anyone assessing a supplier's cloud product. I describe the cloud security standards, frameworks, and assessments such as SOC 2, ISO/IEC 27001, and US FedRAMP, as well as the work from the Cloud Security Alliance. However, you should not fully rely on assessments and reports because new threats against cloud environments and applications are being identified daily.

In the second half of this chapter, I describe how organizations can enhance their secure development lifecycle, infrastructure, and deployment processes with DevSecOps. I also discuss the importance of change management, how highly secure infrastructure should not be modified except through source control, and the importance of securing connections and APIs.

---

## Cloud Control 01

Control CLD-01: Document the roles and responsibilities of all parties who manage, administer, and operate cloud environments and applications.

---

# Cloud Frameworks, Controls, and Assessments

Before an organization starts to build a cloud product or service, it should apply the security controls from the ISO/IEC 27001 Information Security Management Systems standard to the organization's environments, systems, and processes.[2] Once the organization's internal systems and organization comply with this standard, the Cloud Security Alliance (CSA) is the best place to start for understanding cloud security controls and assessments.[3]

By understanding the CSA framework, with its Cloud Controls Matrix (CCM) and the Consensus Assessment Initiative Questionnaire (CAIQ), you will see what controls must be in place to secure cloud infrastructure and applications.[4] These controls establish the security requirements necessary for designing and operating cloud environments and applications, thus providing much of what is needed for cloud audits, reports, and certifications such as the ones I'll discuss in this section.

## ISO/IEC 27001 Information Security Management Systems

ISO/IEC 27001 is the leading information security standard followed by organizations. It was originally published in 2005, revised in 2013, and republished most recently in 2022. The standards are available for purchase from the ISO or IEC organizations, but the optional certifications to the standard are performed by accredited, third-party certification bodies. Certification costs vary depending on what standards are being audited and who is performing the certification.

As the foremost information security management system (ISMS), the 27001 standard details the requirements for establishing, implementing, maintaining, and improving cybersecurity with 114 controls divided into 14 domains:

---

- Information security policies
- Organization of information security
- Human resources security
- Asset management
- Access control
- Cryptography
- Physical and environmental security
- Operational security
- Communications security
- Systems acquisition, development, and maintenance
- Supplier relationships
- Information security incident management
- Information security aspects of business continuity management
- Compliance

Of the 14 domains, many are particularly relevant to cloud security, such as asset management, access control, physical and environmental security, operational security, and communications security. Some of the applicable cloud controls will be discussed later in this chapter.

---

### Cloud Control 02

Control CLD-02: Document security controls and requirements for cloud infrastructure and applications. Perform assessments to identify gaps and action plans.

---

## Cloud Security Alliance CCM and CAIQ

Unlike the ISO/IEC 27001 standard, which must be purchased, the Cloud Security Alliance's CCM (cloud controls matrix) and CAIQ (consensus assessment initiative questionnaire) are now combined into CCM version 4. The CSA is supported financially by cloud providers and corporations, but the CCM itself is freely available and widely adopted. With nearly 200 controls in CCM version 4, the spreadsheet identifies three main areas:

*Typical control applicability and ownership*
   Defines who owns the responsibility for this control, but usually it is the cloud service provider (CSP) or a shared responsibility between the CSP and customer.

---

*Architecture relevance for cloud stack components*
> Displays "TRUE" if the control is applicable for the physical, network, compute, storage, application, or data component stacks.

*Organizational relevance*
> Shows "FALSE" if the control is not applicable to the teams in cybersecurity, internal audit, architecture, software development, operations, legal/privacy, supply chain management, or human resources, along with governance, risk, and compliance.

The advantage of the CSA framework is that it provides the implementation guidance (or requirements) and the auditing guidelines for teams to prepare the organization, product, and services for assessments and audits. Organizations can capture all the documentation and answers to have it available for anyone who may send a CAIQ to an organization. Any gaps found during internal or external reviews should be tracked in action plans to ensure the actions are completed in a timely manner.

## Cloud Security Alliance STAR Program

The Security, Trust, Assurance, and Risk (STAR) Registry allows provider organizations to publish their compliance with the CSA CCM and other certifications.[5] This shows customers the security and compliance posture, including the regulations, standards, and frameworks the organization adheres to. The intention for this program is to reduce complexity and the need to fill out multiple customer questionnaires.

There are two levels of the STAR: self-assessment (Level One) and third-party audit (Level Two). Level One is a good foundation for organizations wanting to reduce the number of customer assessments they must complete. Level Two builds off of the requirements in ISO/IEC 27001 and SOC 2 by assessing an organization against additional cloud-specific criteria provided in the CSA CCM.

Organizations can submit their completed CAIQ to the portal for anyone to download. As a provider, be aware there are no access controls on the site for downloading assessments, so carefully consider what information you provide when answering the CAIQ and uploading it to the CSA portal. You can download other organization assessments to better understand how to answer your assessment, and also see how others are addressing the requirements. As a customer, when searching the registry, look for entries with both Level One assessments and Level Two certifications to find higher-quality assessments that have been audited by a third party.

# American Institute of CPAs SOC 2

The American Institute of Certified Public Accountants (AICPA) designed a suite of System and Organization Controls (SOC) for services and organizations.[6] A SOC 2 audit report has become the de facto standard for accrediting an organization's cloud services. A SOC 2 audit by a certified examiner reviews security, availability, processing integrity, confidentiality, and privacy. These reports can provide detailed information and assurance for the systems in question. Most customers are now requiring their cloud service providers (CSPs) to have passed SOC 2 audits before awarding contracts to the CSPs. As a provider, consider giving both a SOC 2 report and the CSA CCM assessment to customers in order to provide greater transparency into your cloud services.

SOC 2 requirements may, at first glance, look similar to the ISO/IEC 27001 Information Security Management Systems standard, but the main difference is in scope. ISO 27001 provides a framework for how organizations should manage their data and prove they have an information security management system in place, whereas SOC 2 focuses more narrowly on proving that the organization has implemented essential data security controls.

There are two versions of the SOC 2 report: Type 1 assesses the security processes at a point in time; and Type 2 assesses the effectiveness of the controls over an extended period of time. Thus, a Type 1 report may take weeks or a few months to receive, whereas a Type 2 report will usually take six months to one year.

# US FedRAMP

The United States Federal Risk and Authorization Management Program (FedRAMP) is a government-wide compliance program that provides a standardized approach to security assessment, authorization, and continuous monitoring for cloud products and services.[7] A cloud service provider (CSP) may go through either a government agency or a joint authorization board, using a third-party assessor, to obtain authorization for its cloud service offering.

FedRAMP differs from SOC 2 or CSA STAR because the FedRAMP controls are compliance measurements against a standard set of security controls, procedures, and policies based on the US NIST and Federal Information Security Management Act (FISMA) standards. NIST SP 800-53 Security and Privacy Controls for Information Systems and Organizations serves as the baseline for the security controls required by FedRAMP, and FedRAMP varies depending on the Impact Levels (Low, Moderate, or High) as defined in the CSP Authorization Playbook.[8]

As of late 2023, there are 125, 325, and 421 controls in the playbook for Low, Moderate, and High, respectively. Once an organization believes it has met the controls, the authorization process can take anywhere from six months to a year or more.

# Cloud Security Considerations and Requirements

The security requirements necessary to design, develop, configure, or deploy cloud infrastructure and applications can be interpreted from the cloud security frameworks discussed in the previous section. Over time, cloud environments have expanded beyond the standard architecture of web, application, and database servers hosted on premises in an organization's data center, room, or closet. Security controls can vary widely depending on the infrastructure or technology. As such, Table 6-2 lists a few security considerations for the most common cloud environment types. Be aware that considerations listed in one category type can also apply to other types, so consider all of them when assessing or designing cloud environments.

*Table 6-2. Security considerations for different cloud models, capabilities, and connections*

| Type | Security considerations |
| --- | --- |
| Software as a service (SaaS) | • Authenticate and authorize users.<br>• Encrypt sensitive data.<br>• Monitor data sharing.<br>• Keep a usage inventory. |
| Infrastructure as a service (IaaS) | • Use a cloud access security broker (CASB).<br>• Protect the cloud workload.<br>• Configure infrastructure securely. |
| Platform as a service (PaaS) | • Patch systems and software.<br>• Scan applications for vulnerabilities. |
| Container | • Secure the images.<br>• Manage secrets elsewhere.<br>• Restrict container privileges at runtime. |
| Virtualization | • Use firewall technologies.<br>• Log and monitor all activity.<br>• Limit applications to only those necessary for the purpose. |
| Serverless | • Build security around functions (not just applications).<br>• Secure and verify data in transit. |
| Infrastructure as code (IaC) | • Check for immutability of infrastructure (changes must be provisioned through a security pipeline).<br>• Scan for misconfigurations. |
| Multicloud | • Secure API layers.<br>• Maintain consistent identity access management. |
| IoT gateway | • Encrypt communications.<br>• Manage IoT certificates.<br>• Control security for baseband (e.g., radio) and ultrahigh frequencies (e.g., WiFi and Bluetooth). |

| Type | Security considerations |
|------|------------------------|
| Edge device | • Implement firewalls.<br>• Use intrusion detection/prevention systems.<br>• Prepare for malicious attacks. |
| API gateway | • Distributed denial-of-service (DDoS) preventions.<br>• Centralized authentication server.<br>• Limit API requests. |

Beyond applying security considerations, you should also think about implementing additional security features and requirements, as shown in Table 6-3. This isn't an exhaustive list, but it should serve to give you an idea of what requirements are available.

*Table 6-3. Some key cloud security requirements*

| Cloud security requirements | Description |
|------------------------------|-------------|
| Automated access prevention | The most popular, reCAPTCHA by Google, enables web hosts to distinguish between humans and automated access scripts for the purpose of blocking bots. |
| Boundary enforcements | Logical, compute, network, or storage separation to reduce the attack surface and restrict lateral movement.[a] |
| Cloud firewalls | Provides real-time monitoring, evaluates information traveling between source domains and data ports, and permits or blocks data, thereby thwarting potential threats. |
| Cloud workload protection | When monitoring workload behavior, it can detect an intrusion, send out an alert, and remove a threat from cloud workloads and containers where allowed. |
| Tokenization | Replaces sensitive data with nonsensitive data (known as a token) to ensure privacy compliance and reduce risk of data loss.[b] |
| Encryption | Transform plain-text data into indecipherable data (known as ciphertext) and return it to the original text using a digital key. |
| Data state encryption | Encryption techniques defined for data in transit, data at rest, and data in use. |
| Data localization | All data generated or collected within the country or jurisdiction remains on storage devices located within those borders. |
| Data sovereignty | Refers to the physical storage location of the data and the laws and regulations to which the data is subject at that location. |

a    "Cloud Security Guidance" (*https://www.ncsc.gov.uk/collection/cloud/understanding-cloud-services/technically-enforced-separation-in-the-cloud*), UK National Cyber Security Centre, accessed December 11, 2023.
b    "Guidance on Using Tokenization for Cloud-Based Services (ITSP.50.108)" (*https://www.cyber.gc.ca/en/guidance/guidance-using-tokenization-cloud-based-services-itsp50108*), Canadian Centre for Cyber Security, October 6, 2021.

Implementing these cloud security requirements does not guarantee the entire cloud environment or application is secure against malicious actors or attacks. In addition to the controls in the cloud security frameworks seen in Tables 6-2 and 6-3, an organization should also regularly perform extensive threat modeling using MITRE's ATT&CK® framework (as mentioned in Chapter 4), penetration testing, and patch management to mitigate known vulnerabilities.

# DevSecOps

Now that you understand the complexities of securing cloud infrastructure and applications, it's time to focus on what organizations must enhance in the infrastructure, secure development lifecycle, and deployment processes discussed in previous chapters. This can be done with DevSecOps (development, security, and operations) or DevOps, with the integration of security at every phase of the software development lifecycle. DevOps is simply a methodology that integrates and automates development with IT operations in order to shorten the lifecycle.

DevSecOps, as shown in Figure 6-1, makes application and infrastructure security a shared responsibility of development, security, and IT operations teams. It is an effective approach, usually with automation, for speeding up development cycles, integrating security tasks throughout the lifecycle, and improving reliability in cloud environments and applications. Integrating security into a DevSecOps pipeline can provide a unified culture between the developer, operations, and security teams with improved feedback loops and faster cycles for addressing security issues. This can lead to better collaboration, security, and repeatable, automated, and easy-to-audit configurations.

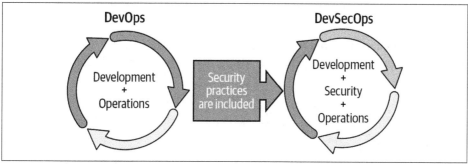

*Figure 6-1. DevOps and DevSecOps*

In Chapter 5, I discussed various approaches for bringing security into the development and CI/CD processes, and for additional guidance, I recommend reading NIST SP 800-204D, *Strategies for Integration of Software Supply Chain Security in DevSecOps CI/CD Pipelines.*[9] In the next section, however, I will focus on how operational security requirements and processes should be considered and included when operating cloud environments.

## Change Management for Cloud

When following strict change processes, every modification or suggestion to a configuration or file must be documented, reviewed, and approved. This creates the documentation needed for audits, stops unapproved changes to any component, and provides an audit log for monitoring and security purposes. Change management enables all forms of asset management tracking and provides a source of truth without the information getting out of date.

A core rule for anything in development, but especially when working with cloud infrastructure, is to treat every artifact, container, file, script, certificate, etc., as code. This means that almost everything (except for secrets and private keys) must be stored and managed in a project repository and all changes are managed using the same review and approval process as code. In cloud environments, change management is handled by dedicated repositories for source control, such as AWS Code Commit or Azure Repos. These services provide specific permissions for the DevSecOps pipeline.

Regularly review the permissions (see Control IS-04 in Chapter 3) and never have secrets such as passwords, private keys, API keys, or other sensitive information in the repositories (see Control IPD-05 in Chapter 7). For cloud environments, you can protect secrets using tools such as HashiCorp Vault, Azure Key Vault, or AWS Secrets Manager.

For the purpose of security, the following items should also be strictly tracked in a change management system for cloud environments and applications:

*User permissions*
Document and store the authorizations given to access specific resources such as infrastructure, secrets, private keys, data, code, administrative functions, etc.

*Digital certificates*
Keep a copy of all digital certificates (such as X.509 for public key infrastructure). You shouldn't have to go to the web server to get the most recent version.

*Firewall, network, and cloud configurations*
Store configurations to maintain a history of all changes and only use stored configurations when deploying configurations or new instances.

*Containers*
Maintain scanned and patched authoritative versions of containers (which are abstract units of software that have everything needed to run a workload or process).

*Scripts and files*
Keep all artifacts (e.g., Dockerfiles, PowerShell scripts) used in CI/CD pipelines, builds, deployments, operations, and hardening containers.[10,11]

Patching of the software, firmware, and systems occurs in every environment. However, updating cloud infrastructure should use patch baselines to have consistent change control over which patches are approved or rejected. A patch baseline could be a classification of patches, a set of rules, or a set of individual patches that can be installed or rejected. Predefined baselines are available through the cloud infrastructure's management platform, where you can use or modify existing baselines, as well as create new ones specific to your organization. Then the selected updates, such as critical patches, are automatically installed through a scheduler.

---

### Cloud Control 03

Control CLD-03: Control cloud infrastructure and artifacts in source repositories. Implement change management that only allows changes to be made within repositories.

---

## Secure Design and Development for Cloud Applications

Designing and developing secure cloud applications requires developers to fully understand cloud architecture and the attack surface of all layers within the cloud infrastructure and applications. For this reason, the best sources for understanding potential weaknesses are in the OWASP Top 10 lists and the MITRE ATT&CK® Framework, as mentioned in Chapter 4.

The following list of cloud computing vulnerabilities should be addressed in the design and development phase of both the application and the infrastructure:

- Abuse and nefarious use of cloud services
- Data exposure
- Denial of service
- Insufficient identity, credential, and access management
- Lack of encryption
- Shared technology issues (e.g., multitenant)
- Vulnerable interfaces and APIs

Despite the availability of tools and best practices, poor authentication and authorization are still issues today, as evidenced by the prevalence of phishing, botnet account attacks, and the hijacking of network traffic. You must design and develop cloud applications with strong capabilities to defend against these attacks.

Cloud applications should also be designed to include alerts and secure logging for the most important security events, such as multiple login attacks. In addition, you should design for centralized authentication integrations, client-side authentication checks must be duplicated on the server side, and tokens must be issued to users for authentication purposes.

# API Security

Securing APIs in cloud environments and applications requires API design, development, testing, and operational monitoring to be part of DevSecOps. Newer applications may be built with an API-first strategy, meaning that the APIs are the first items created before a user interface is put in place. It is critical to review and monitor all API access and integrations because at any time a malicious actor can be leveraging APIs to extract data or infiltrate systems.

In order to improve the security posture of APIs, the OWASP community maintains a set of API security risks as part of the OWASP API Security Top 10 project. Many items in the API Security Top 10 list involve broken authorization and authentication. For anyone developing and testing APIs, the list provides extremely valuable insights to lower the number of vulnerabilities within environments and software applications.

An API gateway—that is, a management tool that sits between an external client and a collection of backend services—can manage incoming calls for multiple services and route them to the appropriate endpoints. It consolidates security, authentication, access controls, and policy enforcements as well as decouples the API interfaces from backend services. API gateways can also integrate web application firewalls (WAF) to help prevent attacks and perform API validations to reduce the risk of injections and overflows.

There are several ways to set up an API Gateway, such as using the Azure API Management Services, the AWS API Gateway, or self-hosting software designed for API gateways. The benefits include denial-of-service (DoS) protections, centralized authentication, and no back door access, and it supports any authentication protocol (e.g., OAuth, AWS IAM, Active Directory). For security, it manages metering and rate-limiting (i.e., control the number of requests to APIs), concurrency limits (i.e., simultaneous connections), and policies (e.g., caching and batching multiple requests).

Large volumes of data can be retrieved using APIs, as experienced by T-Mobile customers when 37 million accounts were stolen in November 2022, according to a Bleeping Computer article.[12] It was not disclosed in the article how the T-Mobile infrastructure was compromised, but it might have occurred through an authentication weakness or a rogue API (which is an API not authorized by the organization). All API infrastructure, including gateways, must be thoroughly and frequently penetration tested for vulnerabilities, authentication weaknesses, and rogue APIs.

# Testing

Unlike waterfall or other linear development methodologies that require you to complete phases before moving on to the next phase, DevSecOps is meant for rapid and continuous deployments. Some organizations may push many builds for deployment every hour, day, or week. With these fast deployment cycles, you don't want testing and security to delay deployment or overwhelm your team with a never-ending set of builds to test. Instead, the goal is to trust your tests and scans enough that you can release without human intervention.

For cloud environments and applications, testing is more than verifying and validating application functionality. Testing should include: operating systems, applications (not just the one being built), containers, databases, configurations, scripts, automation files, certificates, and certificate chains.[13] You can automate functional and security tests, but all detected issues must be verified manually. Perform scans against container images and running containers to check for known vulnerabilities and configuration issues, as well as receive mitigations and hardening recommendations.

Once everything is fully tested—including penetration tested—the testing process can be automated and only "break the build" for serious issues.[14] For all other issues, you can address them by reporting defects or alerting the security team. In-depth testing should be performed periodically when significant code or configurations change, or when there are concerns about automated test results.

# Deploying Immutable Infrastructure and Applications

With all of the components, containers, software, connections, and infrastructure in cloud environments, it is easy to miss subtle changes made over time. When it comes time to re-create that environment for disaster recovery or testing purposes, the environment is then out of sync with what is documented. Situations such as configuration drifts—when new ports and accounts are opened over the lifetime of the infrastructure—happen even when the most stringent change management processes exist.

To prevent these subtle changes over time, DevSecOps teams fully replace containers and software with each deployment. Known as "immutable infrastructure," these systems are not changed in any way after being deployed but are instead completely replaced when something needs to be changed in the infrastructure or software. Immutable infrastructure is handled solely through source control where there are managed permissions and a full audit trail of changes.

Setting up an immutable infrastructure requires the operating system to be configured for not allowing changes, particularly configuration changes, to stay active in the system. In practice, operating systems introduce some changes while running, such as temporary files, but these changes can be discarded without negative impact whenever the system is replaced completely.

At the application layer, there are many models for deployment. Cloud orchestrator tools are the key to automating security updates for containers and containerized applications. These automatic security updates are referred to as "rolling updates" and they minimize downtime by scheduling new versions of containers when the old versions finish their workloads. If a container image has unauthorized changes or is defective, rolling updates can revert to older versions. Rolling updates also allow moving containers from one environment to another, such as moving from a test environment to a production environment.

Another deployment model, known as "blue green deployment," transfers user traffic from a previous version of the application to a newer version, both of which are running in production. Plus, if the application architecture is separated into microservices, you will only need to update a portion of the services, and therefore won't have to perform a complete replacement of the system at one time. Using blue green deployment and microservices will enhance rollback measures, disaster recovery, business continuity, and resilience by leveraging multiple production environments.

---

## Cloud Control 06

Control CLD-06: Scan for and prevent changes directly to production environments. Deploy cloud environments using the immutable infrastructure technique.

---

## Securing Connections

Establishing security for cloud environments and applications requires additional knowledge for securing encryption and network traffic. These are all areas that should be designed, tested, and monitored on a continuous basis as part of DevSecOps in order to ensure the security of your cloud environments or applications.

---

Encryption is important in all software applications and devices, but there are significantly higher risk and threats to defend against when systems and applications are exposed publicly. Environments, systems, and applications should use strong encryption and cryptographic protocols such as the latest version of TLS (Transport Layer Security) and protection for keys and secrets. HTTP Strict Transport Security (HSTS) is a policy mechanism to protect websites against man-in-the-middle attacks and should be set to only allow Hypertext Transfer Protocol Secure (HTTPS) connections.

To secure network traffic, enforce strong network isolation between containers by configuring the containerized infrastructure appropriately or by using container-aware tools. Network traffic between containers is often virtualized using software, making it difficult for traditional network monitoring and filtering software to capture the packets normally seen between environments. You can use specific tools, such as Wireshark, to gain valuable insights into the containers' network traffic for improving performance and identifying suspect network transactions.

---

### Cloud Control 07

Control CLD-07: Secure and monitor all connections to, and between, cloud environments, containers, and microservices.

---

## Operating and Monitoring

As part of DevSecOps, it is extremely important for development, security, and operations teams to cooperatively defend the infrastructure and applications in order to prevent potential attacks. Attack vectors continue to evolve, and thus the approaches to secure and defend the cloud environment must also mature and evolve.

In order to monitor the day-to-day health and security posture of cloud environments and applications, various dashboards should be accessible and send alerts to administrators, operations teams, and security operations centers (SOCs). These dashboards can display information on connections, backups, statuses, alerts, load balancing, performance, containers, policies, services, vulnerabilities, and logs.

Logging is a key component for effective monitoring. There are many logs in large cloud deployments, and each one might contain insights into attacks and security incidents. Logs should be connected to log aggregator tools and to Security Information and Event Management (SIEM) tools that specialize in finding unique security events. SIEMs are becoming more important with the advent of AI-generated attacks, but the SIEMs themselves can leverage AI to identify trends, patterns, and unusual activities.

A final technique that needs specific mention is the Information Security Continuous Monitoring (ISCM) tool. It monitors network security, personnel activity, configuration changes, system components, IT assets, log files, and more. The ISCM tool can generate alerts, block malicious code, provide recommendations, and scan for vulnerabilities.

As mentioned in the beginning of the chapter, I recommend reading *Practical Cloud Security: A Guide for Secure Design and Deployment* (2nd ed.), for details on securing cloud environments. Another good reference is *DoD Enterprise DevSecOps Reference Design*, which discusses all areas of DevSecOps and provides useful tables that list activities and tools.[15]

## Site Reliability Engineering

The final component I will mention that contributes to building security into your cloud environment and applications is site reliability engineering (SRE). SRE refers to a set of practices and principles that apply software engineering aspects to IT infrastructure and operations. In general, SRE includes managing system availability, performance, efficiency, monitoring, change management, and security engineering.

Good SRE practices lead to secure and efficient cloud environments that can quickly adapt to the changing threat landscape. The approach identifies weaknesses in the system by testing production environments and resolving problems before they become major incidents. To learn more about the nuances of SRE, I recommend the book *Site Reliability Engineering: How Google Runs Production Systems* for anyone serious about cloud performance and security.[16]

# Summary

In this chapter, I discussed the security framework, controls, and requirements organizations should follow when building cloud infrastructure and applications that are a critical part of the software supply chain within the supply chain. Before building cloud security, an organization usually starts by establishing an ISO/IEC 27001 Information Security Management System. From there, an organization can build strong foundations for cloud security using the Cloud Security Alliance's Cloud Controls Matrix and other requirements such as encryption and tokenization. Once an organization implements cloud security controls, the next step may involve assessments such as CAIQ, SOC 2, or FedRAMP.

When teams are ready to start designing, developing, and deploying cloud infrastructure and applications, following DevSecOps practices where the development, security, and operations teams collaborate is crucial for building secure cloud environments. This includes having rigorous change management practices such as keeping cloud components and artifacts in repositories so no changes can be performed directly on production environments. Also requiring immutable infrastructures that cannot be modified except through source control, and secure deployment models for applications, can increase the resilience of cloud systems.

Throughout the lifecycle of DevSecOps, the connections, environments, and configurations must be considered and maintained as technologies change or vulnerabilities are discovered. Cloud security doesn't stop when the environment is deployed—teams must continuously work together to maintain security, monitor the environments, and take action when situations arise. This teamwork involves development, security, operations, and, if available, site reliability engineers to keep cloud security posture high and lower risk throughout the lifecycle. In Chapter 7, I'll discuss the risks surrounding intellectual property and data, as well as the controls for protecting the people and technologies within the supply chain.

# References

1  Chris Dotson, *Practical Cloud Security: A Guide for Secure Design and Deployment* (O'Reilly, 2023).

2  "ISO/IEC 27001 Standard—Information Security Management Systems" (*https://www.iso.org/standard/27001*), ISO, accessed December 11, 2023.

3  Cloud Security Alliance (*https://cloudsecurityalliance.org*), accessed December 11, 2023.

4  "Cloud Controls Matrix (CCM)" (*https://cloudsecurityalliance.org/research/cloud-controls-matrix*), Cloud Security Alliance, accessed December 11, 2023.

5  "CSA STAR Registry" (*https://cloudsecurityalliance.org/star/registry*), Cloud Security Alliance, accessed December 11, 2023.

6  "2018 SOC 2® Description Criteria (with Revised Implementation Guidance—2022)" (*https://www.aicpa.org/resources/download/get-description-criteria-for-your-organizations-soc-2-r-report*), AICPA & CIMA, October 1, 2023.

7  "FedRAMP Authorization Process" (*https://www.fedramp.gov*), FedRAMP, accessed December 11, 2023.

8  "Cloud Service Providers" (*https://www.fedramp.gov/cloud-service-providers*), FedRAMP, accessed December 11, 2023.

9  Ramaswamy Chandramouli, Frederick Kautz, and Santiago Torres Arias, *Strategies for Integration of Software Supply Chain Security in DevSecOps CI/CD Pipelines* (*https://doi.org/10.6028/nist.sp.800-204d.ipd*), National Institute of Standards and Technology, August 2023.

10  A Dockerfile is a text document that contains all the commands to assemble an image on an operating system command line.

11    PowerShell is a cross-platform (e.g., Windows, Linux, macOS) task automation solution consisting of a command-line shell, a scripting language, and a configuration management framework.

12    Sergiu Gatlan, "T-Mobile Hacked to Steal Data of 37 Million Accounts in API Data Breach" (*https://www.bleepingcomputer.com/news/security/t-mobile-hacked-to-steal-data-of-37-million-accounts-in-api-data-breach*), Bleeping Computer, January 19, 2023.

13    A certificate chain (or Chain of Trust) is a list of certificates that starts from a server's certificate and ends with the root certificate.

14    This is when code is committed into a repository but doesn't compile or doesn't work (such as failing unit or regression tests).

15    Department of Defense, *DoD Enterprise DevSecOps Reference Design* (*https://dodcio.defense.gov/Portals/0/Documents/DoD%20Enterprise%20DevSecOps%20Reference%20Design%20v1.0_Public%20Release.pdf*), September 12, 2019.

16    Betsy Beyer, Chris Jones, Jennifer Petoff, and Niall Richard Murphy, *Site Reliability Engineering: How Google Runs Production Systems* (O'Reilly, 2016).

# CHAPTER 7

# Intellectual Property and Data

Manipulation or extraction of intellectual property (IP) and data is often the focus in software supply chain attacks. Intellectual property is any creation of human intellect in the form of documents, drawings, source code, designs, and more. Unintentional or intentional sharing of IP and data can ruin a company at any stage—from startup to maturity. There is no shortage of data breaches and leaks, as shown in the *Nira* blog article "51 Biggest Document Leaks & Data Breaches of All Time."[1] Additionally, malicious actors are always searching for publicly exposed data and intellectual property in cloud storage infrastructure and cloud-based technologies.

Everyone is familiar with malicious actors infiltrating networks to steal data, but the risk to the software supply chain is not only when they steal information, but also when they modify or inject false information into the IP or data. Once a malicious actor infiltrates a network, they generally perform reconnaissance, which could last days, weeks, or even months. During this time, they learn about the organization and determine how to cause the most significant damage or make the most money. The intention of the malicious actor is never clear, and we must do everything we can to protect our IP and data.

To reduce the risk of IP and data loss, begin by using the infrastructure controls, such as logging and monitoring, mentioned in Chapter 4. Within this chapter I discuss the importance of data classification, how people can impact IP and data loss, and the various threats associated with technologies.

# Data Classification

Before any discussion on IP or data loss can begin, you first must understand which data is and is not a risk to your organization if it is lost. A malicious actor downloading public documents from an internal repository would be of no risk to an organization, but downloading employee personal data would likely be a significant risk to the employees. As an organization, you should identify all types of data to determine their value and what risks exist from exposed data. An organization may have several levels of confidential and nonconfidential classifications.[2] At a minimum, your organization should have public, internal, and restricted levels. Data classification also ensures you comply with certain regulations and don't waste resources protecting nonsensitive data.

Create data classification processes and awareness campaigns for all employees and contractors. This should include a process for classifying data such as source code, architecture information, hardware designs, internal organization data, personal identifiable information (PII), and personal health information (PHI), and then implementing controls for securing the information. Your organization may even use the term "crown jewels" to represent data that is confidential, mandatory for business continuity, or a high-value target for malicious actors. It's critical to prioritize your security efforts and investment for crown jewels, such as PII, to reduce risk, impacts, and potential government fines or lawsuits if data is breached.

Every organization should have a data classification policy so its employees, contractors, and suppliers know exactly which data falls under which categories. The most important aspect of a data classification policy is providing the detailed definitions, criteria, and examples for your organization to follow. Without a policy, it is up to the discretion of each person to determine if something is public, internal, or restricted. This could lead to all types of data loss risk, such as someone releasing financials before the quarterly earnings call or a developer uploading proprietary code to a public troubleshooting site (i.e., Stack Overflow).[3] Once you know what you have to protect, the next step is to figure out what you need to protect it from. When it comes to IP data loss, you need to be vigilant against risks posed by people, processes, and technology.

---

### Intellectual Property and Data Control 01

Control IPD-01: Maintain a data classification policy with definitions, criteria, and examples.

---

# People

Whether you're in a small or large organization, there are people throughout who have knowledge of confidential information that the organization cannot afford to have released to the public. Leakage of restricted organizational processes, such as the software build process or configuration instructions, can result in significant intellectual property loss. It can be as innocent as incorrectly placing confidential process files in a public location or losing a USB drive, which can compromise an entire organization or customer.

In terms of software supply chain security, the people introducing risk are often the developers, architects, testers, build managers, product managers, and leaders who are building a product or application. The intellectual property may be written on whiteboards and in notebooks, documents, spreadsheets, presentations, and email; or it can be stored in many other places. Organizations are at risk when information is disclosed accidentally (human error) or intentionally (insider threat)—for example, through public social sites such as X (previously known as Twitter) before the product is made public, which happened to Microsoft, Apple, and other organizations.[4,5]

Accidental disclosure can occur when employees working with a supplier or customer mistakenly release information that should not have been sent to those parties. Many of these mistakes are unintentional and are simply people intending to be helpful. Social engineering or stolen access credentials, according to Verizon's *2023 Data Breach Investigations Report*, account for 74% of breaches involving the human element.[6] For example, malicious actors can use social engineering techniques to persuade technical teams to send IP about a product or project. IP loss also occurs when technical employees are phished through fraudulent job postings. During fake interviews, they may release information regarding technical details, administrative login information, suppliers or customers they are working with, or classified projects.[7] In Chapter 11, I will discuss approaches for better compliance, awareness, and training to reduce the risk of accidental disclosures.

Insider threats come from people within the organization, such as employees, former employees, or contractors, who have internal information concerning the organization's people, process, projects, data, and technology. IP theft is frequent enough in the technology space that the Digital Guardian blog was able to list nearly 50 espionage and IP thefts of secrets, data, technology, source code, customer information, and confidential documents.[8] Many of the cases resulted in significant legal costs, prison time, and businesses closing permanently, as was the case where someone was sentenced to 70 months in prison for stealing trade secrets of an anti-ice aircraft for a competitor.

It is important to maintain an ethics policy for employees and contractors, and the policy should be referenced in the data classification and security awareness programs.[9] You may also require your employees and contractors to sign nondisclosure agreements (NDAs) to prevent them from sharing confidential information, and this also provides your organization legal recourse if necessary. However, do not solely rely on an NDA to stop IP theft; as reported in *CPO Magazine*, an NDA was not enough to prevent someone from releasing 20 GB of confidential and restricted data about the Intel chipset platforms.[10]

---

### Intellectual Property and Data Controls 02–03

Control IPD-02: Maintain an ethics policy that references the data classification policy and the compliance responsibility for employees and contractors. Monitor for compliance with the policies and, when applicable, nondisclosure agreements.

Control IPD-03: Educate all employees and contractors about intellectual property and data loss risks with training on data classifications, ethics, and compliance.

---

# Technology

In addition to risk from people within the organization, IP and data loss can result from insecure or misconfigured technologies. Many of these technology risks have already been noted in Chapter 3, which describes developer tools and other technology controls meant to reduce the security risk.

All technologies in your organization are at risk if malicious actors take possession of business or development systems that contain restricted and confidential information. Even the business enterprise applications, such as the supply chain data within the enterprise resource planning (ERP) systems, present risks specifically to software and products. For example, the enterprise applications may contain supplier assessment results such as risks, deficiencies, and action plans. If a malicious actor gains access to the risk assessments performed on suppliers, they could use that information to locate the less secure suppliers and infiltrate one, thereby jeopardizing the software supply chain.

Although preventing attacks should be the primary focus of stopping data loss, you should implement detective controls such as monitoring and logging to find irregularities, suspicious behavior, and malicious actors. This would include any systems with restricted or confidential information, such as email platforms and collaboration tools (i.e., Slack, Microsoft Teams) that your organization uses as part of the software and product lifecycle. The following sections contain some additional examples of technology risks, which frequently lead to IP and data loss.

## Data Security

Protecting digital information from theft, corruption, or unauthorized access is one of the main requirements in securing the software supply chain. Many technologies and techniques exist for data security, including data encryption, data protection, and data loss prevention solutions that can identify, protect, and track sensitive data within a company.

Data encryption can come in many forms, but the best encryption to use will depend on the state of the data, as shown in Figure 7-1: data at rest, data in transit, and data in use. Data at rest is any stored data not being accessed and typically includes data in file servers, databases, USB keys, hard drives, etc. Data in transit is any data in motion as it travels through email, web servers, collaboration tools, and across communication protocols. Data in use includes data that is opened by applications for the consumption of users.

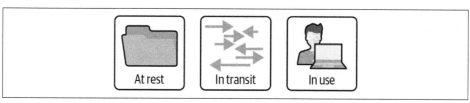

*Figure 7-1. The three states of data to encrypt*

Encryption techniques can come in many forms, as listed in Table 7-1. The data is considered secure as long as the decryption key is not located with the data and the encryption algorithm is currently unbroken. However, using multiple protections is best since quantum computing will eventually break modern cryptography.

*Table 7-1. Encryption techniques*

| Data type | Data security techniques |
|---|---|
| Data at rest | • Database encryption<br>• Data masking<br>• Full-disk encryption<br>• File-level encryption<br>• Device encryption<br>• Data loss prevention (DLP)<br>• Mobile device management (MDM)<br>• Digital rights management (DRM)<br>• Cloud access security brokers (CASB) |
| Data in transit | • Encrypted connections (HTTPS, SSL, TLS, FTPS, etc.)<br>• Email encryption<br>• Data loss prevention<br>• Managed file transfer (MFT)<br>• Cloud access security brokers |
| Data in use | • Identity access management (IAM)<br>• Role-based access tools (RBAC)<br>• Data masking<br>• Digital rights management |

Specifically designed for data security, the various data loss prevention solutions can identify violations of privacy regulations (e.g., GDPR, HIPAA, PCI-DSS) and an organization's internal data classification policies. However, DLP solutions are only effective when configured properly and given full visibility into the organization's applications and infrastructure.

A new concern for data security occurs when intellectual property and private data are used to train AI models. Data leaks can emerge if a user inserts confidential information into the AI prompt, as seen repeatedly when patient information and confidential business documents were uploaded to ChatGPT after it went public.[11] Even internal large language models (LLMs) can disclose confidential data if the information provided in the prompts is not classified properly. For example, if a payroll administrator uploaded a salary report into the LLM for it to create a summary, it's possible another user could prompt the LLM to find out who the highest-paid employees are in the organization. Your organization should evaluate the LLM licenses and set organizational policies on how to use AI tools to be compliant with the data classification policy and mitigate the data security risks.

## Loss of Code, Keys, and Secrets

One of the largest and most common issues in regard to IP and data loss in the software supply chain is when source code is accidentally released to public code repositories. Accidental code release is common enough that the GitHub code repository even provides instructions for removing sensitive data from a repository.[12] Code release is a concern for organizations of any size; there have been many situations where confidential source code from Toyota, Samsung, Intel, and Google have been placed in public locations.[13,14] The companies generally claim that the source code loss was not a significant risk since many different tools can reverse engineer the source code.

Unfortunately, when source code is accidentally released to the public, other secrets may become public at the same time, such as private keys and credentials, testing reports, project documents, threat models, and more. All information regarding data sources, file paths, accounts, connections strings, and configurations must be kept secure. For example, database information such as table names, column names, and security roles, as well as internal directory and file paths, can inform malware developers on approaches for infiltrating systems.

The loss of private keys and improper key management can lead to complete data loss or system compromise for an application or system. In the case of Toyota, the code was public for over five years with hardcoded data server access credentials. Samsung's source code contained 6,695 secrets, according to GitGuardian. One massive intellectual property loss was announced in October 2021, when over 120 security tools created by the Amazon-owned Twitch security team were leaked as part of a large data breach.[15] Several of the security IP leaks included Twitch's threat hunting playbooks and threat detection tools. This information can be valuable to a threat actor looking for gaps in Twitch's testing process.

Another loss of keys occurred in December 2022, when an engineer at a CI/CD software company, CircleCI, had malware on an engineering laptop.[16] This malware was able to execute a session cookie theft to steal the engineer's credentials for a production system. The malicious actor accessed and exfiltrated data including customer environment variables, tokens, and keys. A customer detected the theft within two weeks and alerted CircleCI, who reset all production credentials and employee accounts. There are many more real-life examples of lost or stolen code, key, and secrets. For specific guidance on preventing this loss, refer to the infrastructure and source code security controls in Chapters 3 and 6.

Key management tools such as HashiCorp Vault, Azure Key Vault, or AWS Secrets Manager can create, exchange, store, delete, and refresh keys, in addition to managing the access controls associated with those functions. Encryption keys should never be hardcoded into products and applications, or stored in web content directories and backups. At a minimum, an organization should have the following key management practices, as described in the OWASP "Key Management Cheat Sheet":[17]

- Key lifecycle management (generation, distribution, destruction)
- Key compromise, recovery, and zeroization
- Key storage
- Key agreement

Digital certificates authenticate the owner's identity and are another form of secrets that should be managed securely. The certificate uses cryptography and a public key to prove the authenticity of a server, device, or user. During the SolarWinds compromise, Mimecast had digital certificates stolen, and that allowed the threat actor to intercept traffic of organizations using Mimecast products on Microsoft 365 Exchange servers.[18] As mentioned in the previous section, you should deploy solutions that monitor for sensitive data and also configure existing platforms to log whenever someone accesses, moves, shares, modifies, or deletes data. If an action appears suspicious, the tools can raise alerts or send notifications to the security teams.

---

### Intellectual Property and Data Controls 07–08

Control IPD-07: Monitor for data loss of code, secrets, certificates, and keys using technologies and services.

Control IPD-08: Implement key management systems to secure secrets, tokens, keys, and other intellectual property.

---

## Design Flaws

Design flaws in the products or applications your organization creates can lead to data loss through many methods, including vulnerabilities in applications, improper access management or lack of access controls, and unencrypted data at rest or in transit. Threat modeling, security testing, and penetration testing can be used to detect design flaws before data loss occurs. Careful attention to design in the early stages of a project can potentially reduce rearchitecting the product or application to reduce design flaws.

The OWASP Top 10, as discussed in Chapter 4, and software composition analysis tools can also identify potential design flaws. Specifically, the OWASP "A04:2021—Insecure Design" weakness is the fourth-highest flaw in the web application secure development list.[19] Insecure design is the lack of adequate controls in the application or product to protect or resist against threat attacks. Design flaws can include ignoring secrets management, implementing weak identity management, designing poor access controls, rejecting uncontrolled external inputs, and accepting untrusted data.[20]

A strong list of potential design flaws is in the Common Weakness Enumeration (CWE) list maintained by MITRE.[21] This community-developed list describes one thousand weaknesses, which are referenced in the OWASP Top 10, the MITRE CWE Top 25, and in many security articles such as Endor Lab's Top 10 Open Source Software Risks.[22] The CWE warning notifications are reported by code analysis and threat modeling tools. These warnings, when remediated with secure design techniques, can prevent many design flaws.

---

### Intellectual Property and Data Control 09

Control IPD-09: Use secure by design, privacy by design, threat modeling, security testing, and penetration testing to prevent, detect, and remediate design flaws.

---

## Configuration Errors

Additional common data risks are when misconfigurations occur in technologies or systems such as databases, data storage services, integrations with third-party tools, and excessive permissions. Every month there are news articles where a researcher located a misconfigured cloud data repository (such as an Amazon S3 bucket). According to the research firm Gartner, "through 2025, 90% of the organizations that fail to control public cloud use will inappropriately share sensitive data."[23] Even high-technology companies, such as Microsoft, have misconfigured their systems, which then resulted in large data leaks. In 2022, SOCRadar disclosed Microsoft's 2.4 TB data leakage of five years of customer contracts and other data.[24] Then in 2023, Wiz Research detected a misconfigured token exposing 38 TB of Microsoft's private data when the Microsoft AI research team published a bucket of open source AI training data.[25] Although cloud repositories and systems are now usually set to "secure by default" on deployment, there still seems to be many cases where data is unintentionally left exposed with no logging to identify who has accessed or downloaded the data.

There are tools and services that scan for confidential information using techniques, such as file fingerprinting, or monitoring the dark web, where data may be available for sale.[26] The same risk management techniques, such as threat modeling and CWEs, mentioned earlier in "Design Flaws" on page 120, also apply to configuration errors. Specific attention should be given to unrestricted inbound and outbound ports, lack of monitoring and logging, protocol configurations, reviewing configurations on a repetitive basis, and access control.

---

### Intellectual Property and Data Control 10

Control IPD-10: Secure all infrastructure, system, and application configurations. Regularly review configurations and perform threat modeling to identify risks.

---

## Application Programming Interfaces (APIs)

Another data risk involves APIs, which provide access to data, applications, and services. APIs can retrieve enormous amounts of private data and need to be fully secured, as discussed in "API Security" on page 106. Unfortunately, there are many cases where APIs are compromised through poor authentication, which was the case for the data leaks at the Parler, Clubhouse, and LinkedIn organizations in 2021.[27]

Threats to products and applications will continue to grow as malicious actors leverage APIs to access products, applications, and systems. OWASP has a specific API Security Top 10 list, which should be used during design, threat modeling, development, and testing.[28] Security testing and penetration testing may sometimes not cover the full scope of risks, but automating tests on APIs is ideal to support regression tests. It is vital that APIs be tested fully to prevent data loss or manipulation, which can unfortunately lead to safety risks when products such as medical or vehicle systems are compromised. Fortunately, a team of researchers, led by Sam Curry, practiced responsible disclosure to vehicle manufacturers when they found a large number of API vulnerabilities that could have stopped and started engines, unlocked cars, changed vehicle ownership, and caused other serious issues.[29]

---

### Intellectual Property and Data Control 11

Control IPD-11: Design secure APIs and perform threat modeling, security testing, and penetration testing on APIs.

---

# Vulnerabilities

IP and data loss can often occur from vulnerabilities in products, systems, or infrastructure (e.g., Microsoft Active Directory, Linux operating system, or Cisco routers) not specifically associated with the data itself. Vulnerabilities can be leveraged in API attacks and by using misconfigurations or unremediated design flaws. Using vulnerabilities, the threat actors can enter systems, elevate their access, steal data, and then destroy system data through encryption or ransomware.

Patching systems is one of the best preventative measures to stop data loss due to vulnerabilities. One of the most recognized critical vulnerabilities, Log4Shell CVE-2021-45046, can lead to exfiltration of data from logging libraries.[30] Sometimes the application and system patches may not be available in time, which was the case for the ONUS fintech firm compromised through a Log4j vulnerability in its payment system.[31] Threat actors ransomed the data for $5M USD, and when ONUS refused to pay, its two million customers' data was put up for sale by the threat actors. When the threat actors were in the ONUS systems, they also leveraged a misconfigured Amazon S3 bucket to reach additional sensitive data.

---

### Intellectual Property and Data Control 12

Control IPD-12: Patch vulnerabilities in infrastructure, systems, and applications to prevent IP and data loss.

---

# Summary

In this chapter, I discussed the various risks and threats to software supply chain security with a focus on intellectual property and data loss. An organization can reduce many of these risks with data classification and ethics policies, education for employees and contractors on the policies, and compliance monitoring of the policies. Also, consider the threats insiders pose to organizations with the release of sensitive data and intellectual property.

Of course, technologies contribute to IP and data loss with accidental leakage to public locations, and through insecure design, misconfigurations, APIs, and vulnerabilities. Using the controls in this chapter, as well as in Chapters 3 and 4, will reduce the risk of IP and data loss. In Chapter 8, I describe how transparency of software, firmware, hardware, and processes can increase trust and awareness of the software supply chain.

# References

1   Ashleigh Bugg, "51 Biggest Document Leaks & Data Breaches of All Time" (*https://nira.com/data-breaches-and-leaks*), *Nira* (blog), November 17, 2021.

2   Sherif Koussa, "What Do SAST, DAST, IAST and RASP Mean to Developers?" (*https://www.softwaresecured.com/what-do-sast-dast-iast-and-rasp-mean-to-developers*) Software Secured, accessed December 11, 2023.

3   Ryan Donovan, "Copying Code from Stack Overflow? You Might Paste Security Vulnerabilities, Too" (*https://stackoverflow.blog/2019/11/26/copying-code-from-stack-overflow-you-might-be-spreading-security-vulnerabilities*), *Stack Overflow Blog*, November 26, 2019.

4   "Employee Accidentally Releases Microsoft Windows 11 Notepad. Read More" (*https://economictimes.indiatimes.com/news/new-updates/employee-accidentally-releases-microsoft-windows-11-notepad-read-more/articleshow/96520511.cms*), *Economic Times*, December 26, 2022.

5   Gordon Kelly, "Apple IOS 15.5 Code Leaks New Upgrades for iPads, iPhones" (*https://www.forbes.com/sites/gordonkelly/2022/04/19/apple-iphone-14-pro-max-ios-16-upgrade-new-features*), *Forbes*, April 19, 2022.

6   Verizon, *2023 Data Breach Investigations Report* (*https://www.verizon.com/business/resources/reports/dbir*), 2023.

7   Danny Palmer, "Security Warning for Software Developers: You Are Now Prime Targets for Phishing Attacks" (*https://www.zdnet.com/article/security-warning-for-software-developers-you-are-now-prime-targets-for-phishing-attacks*), ZDNET, August 13, 2019.

8   Chris Brook, "IP Theft: Definition and Examples" (*https://digitalguardian.com/blog/ip-theft-definition-and-examples*), *Digital Guardian* (blog), October 26, 2023.

9   "Ethics Policy" (*https://www.shrm.org/ResourcesAndTools/tools-and-samples/policies/Pages/employee-ethics.aspx*), SHRM, accessed January 3, 2023.

10   Alicia Hope, "Massive Data Breach Exposes Intel's Intellectual Property for Its Flagship CPUs and SpaceX Sensors" (*https://www.cpomagazine.com/cyber-security/massive-data-breach-exposes-intels-intellectual-property-for-its-flagship-cpus-and-spacex-sensors*), *CPO Magazine*, August 14, 2020.

11   Robert Lemos, "Employees Are Feeding Sensitive Biz Data to ChatGPT, Raising Security Fears" (*https://www.darkreading.com/risk/employees-feeding-sensitive-business-data-chatgpt-raising-security-fears*), Dark Reading, March 7, 2023.

12   "Removing Sensitive Data from a Repository" (*https://docs.github.com/en/authen tication/keeping-your-account-and-data-secure/removing-sensitive-data-from-a-repository*), GitHub, accessed December 11, 2023.

13   Dwayne McDaniel, "Toyota Suffered a Data Breach by Accidentally Exposing a Secret Key Publicly on GitHub" (*https://blog.gitguardian.com/toyota-accidently-exposed-a-secret-key-publicly-on-github-for-five-years*), *GitGuardian* (blog), October 11, 2022.

14   Mackenzie Jackson, "Samsung and Nvidia Are the Latest Companies to Involuntarily Go Open-Source Leaking Company Secrets" (*https://blog.gitguardian.com/samsung-and-nvidia-are-the-latest-companies-to-involuntarily-go-open-source-potentially-leaking-company-secrets*), GitGuardian (blog), March 9, 2022.

15   Mazin Ahmed, "Twitch Internal Security Tools: In-Depth Analysis of the Leaked Twitch Security Tools" (*https://mazinahmed.net/blog/indepth-analysis-twitch-security-tools*), *Mazin Ahmed* (blog), June 1, 2022.

16   Rob Zuber, "CircleCI Incident Report for January 4, 2023 Security Incident" (*https://circleci.com/blog/jan-4-2023-incident-report*), *CircleCI* (blog), January 13, 2023.

17   "Key Management Cheat Sheet" (*https://cheatsheetseries.owasp.org/cheatsheets/Key_Management_Cheat_Sheet.html*), OWASP Cheat Sheet Series, accessed December 11, 2023.

18   "Incident Report" (*https://www.mimecast.com/incident-report*), Mimecast, March 16, 2021.

19   "A04:2021—Insecure   Design"   (*https://owasp.org/Top10/A04_2021-Insecure_Design*), OWASP Top 10, accessed January 7, 2023.

20   Secrets management refers to the methods and tools for managing the credentials of passwords, keys, tokens, and APIs in products, applications, systems, services, accounts, and technologies.

21   Common Weakness Enumeration (*https://cwe.mitre.org*), accessed November 18, 2023.

22   Ron Harnik, "Introducing the Top 10 Open Source Software (OSS) Risks" (*https://www.endorlabs.com/blog/introducing-the-top-10-open-source-software-oss-risks*), *Endor Labs* (blog), March 1, 2023.

23   Kasey Panetta, "Is the Cloud Secure?" (*https://www.gartner.com/smarterwithgartner/is-the-cloud-secure*) Gartner, October 10, 2019.

24   "Sensitive Data of 65,000+ Entities in 111 Countries Leaked Due to a Single Misconfigured Data Bucket" (*https://socradar.io/sensitive-data-of-65000-entities-in-111-*

*countries-leaked-due-to-a-single-misconfigured-data-bucket*), SOCRadar, October 19, 2022.

25   Hillai Ben-Sasson and Ronny Greenberg, "38TB of Data Accidentally Exposed by Microsoft AI Researchers" (*https://www.wiz.io/blog/38-terabytes-of-private-data-accidentally-exposed-by-microsoft-ai-researchers*), *Wiz* (blog), September 18, 2023.

26   File (or data or document) fingerprinting is a technique to identify and track data across a network. Examples include locating source code in text files or specific financial data in spreadsheets.

27   Ran Ilany, "5 Real-World API Security Breaches from 2021" (*https://www.panoptica.app/blog/real-world-api-security*), *Panoptica* (blog), April 14, 2022.

28   "OWASP API Security Project" (*https://owasp.org/www-project-api-security*), OWASP, accessed January 8, 2023.

29   Sam Curry, "Web Hackers vs. The Auto Industry: Critical Vulnerabilities in Ferrari, BMW, Rolls Royce, Porsche, and More" (*https://samcurry.net/web-hackers-vs-the-auto-industry*), *Sam Curry*, January 3, 2023.

30   "CVE-2021-45046 Detail" (*https://nvd.nist.gov/vuln/detail/CVE-2021-45046*), NIST | National Vulnerability Database, accessed January 8, 2023.

31   Ax Sharma, "Fintech Firm Hit by Log4j Hack Refuses to Pay $5 Million Ransom" (*https://www.bleepingcomputer.com/news/security/fintech-firm-hit-by-log4j-hack-refuses-to-pay-5-million-ransom*), Bleeping Computer, December 29, 2021.

# CHAPTER 8

# Software Transparency

The practice of transparency—the deliberate disclosure of hidden software attributes including origins, composition, and build and test processes—has become important in today's technical world, where little is known about the software, firmware, or hardware that enables every aspect of our lives. Software transparency, and really any transparency in technology, means that the creator or manufacturer has disclosed information about what is inside the product or services and how it was made. This disclosure builds a connection between the parties and hopefully builds trust into the relationship.

Transparency measures are routine in many consumer products, such as the ingredients list on a box of packaged food. But there are significant differences between that example and software transparency. Generally, packaged food does not provide the source of the ingredients unless it is highlighted for marketing reasons. A stick of butter, for example, lists components (pasteurized cream and salt), potential risks (contains milk), and may include provenance of some components (cows from Ireland), but it does not describe the architecture (recipe), known risks (lactose intolerance), and other provenance (location where the salt was mined, what equipment was used, and the location where the butter was manufactured).

Now let's look at a more complicated example. Consider the transparency of a smartphone, as shown in Figure 8-1. Transparency would, at a minimum, include disclosing the following information for the smartphone:

*Hardware components*
    Which manufacturer created the Bluetooth hardware?

*Firmware*
    Who designed and developed the Bluetooth firmware?

*Embedded software*
What operating system is used?

*Application software*
Which preinstalled mobile applications are included?

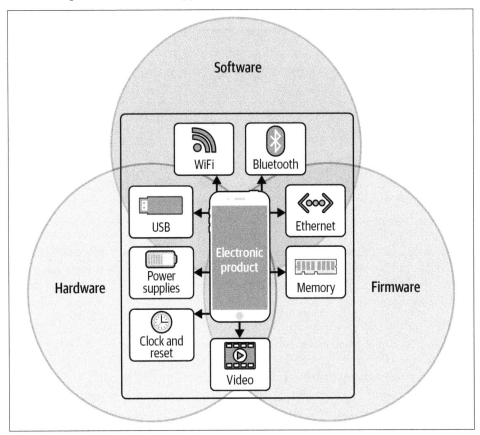

*Figure 8-1. Transparency of a device*

Transparency would also include information about who coded and administered the software, how the code was compiled and built, and where everything was designed, developed, produced, assembled, and delivered. Transparency gives you a view into how the product or service is made, and you can use this information to identify areas of risk throughout the product or service's supply chain. For example, a smartphone has many opportunities for compromise in the software supply chain during the software development or manufacturing processes, because there were thousands of participants and activities that went into building the device. Transparency will not give you the risks themselves, but it can indicate where there could be a risk. It does this by exposing the organizations who created the components, how they were created, and where the product or service was built.

---

## Software Bill of Materials (SBOM)

The definition of an SBOM, as written in US Executive Order (EO) 14028, is "a formal record containing the details and supply chain relationships of various components used in building software. Software developers and vendors often create products by assembling existing open source and commercial software components. The SBOM enumerates these components in a product."[1]

---

Some people might associate software transparency as being the same as an SBOM, but that is only part of it. Software transparency is about having visibility into the components or libraries, architectures, design elements, security features, testing results, potential threats and risks, known vulnerabilities, and provenance. Many decisions—such as whether to trust software—rely on transparency to provide the basis for trustworthiness. It also may be requested by laws or regulations, such as the US Food and Drug Administration's Section 524(b).[2] This chapter discusses these aspects as well as how to provide evidence of transparency through various mechanisms such as SBOMs, vulnerability disclosures, software attestations, provenance, and artifacts. For an even deeper discussion on software transparency, I recommend the book *Software Transparency: Supply Chain Security in an Era of a Software-Driven Society* by Chris Hughes and Tony Turner.[3]

# Software Transparency Use Cases

Before discussing how to provide evidence of software transparency (which includes SBOMs), you must first understand what transparency aims to capture and why having this information is so valuable. There are many potential ways that software transparency can benefit organizations, and these benefits or use cases can be split into three different roles:

*Producer*
Creates software transparency information for themselves and potentially others

*Chooser*
Uses software transparency information to understand the software before making a purchase decision

*Operator*
Makes decisions about software risk based on software transparency information

Depending on your organization's mission, you may be in just one role, two of the roles, or all three roles. For example, an organization may produce SBOMs for its products, it may choose a supplier based on the content within an SBOM, or it may reference an SBOM during the operation of a product. It is important to understand why your organization needs transparency and how that information will be used. When you know that, you can then determine what technologies and processes in your organization need transparency.

First, for producers of software, after gathering the software transparency information, you can use it for the following purposes:

- Monitoring components for vulnerabilities and end of life (EOL)
- Learning what is included within the software or component, which can promote code reuse and reduce work
- Understanding dependencies within larger projects
- Reducing code bloat by standardizing on component versions or removal of unnecessary code
- Knowing and complying with license obligations, as well as software prohibited by regulators or your organization

As a producer, your organization must define how the customers will obtain the software transparency information. This information can be provided with the product itself, through a third-party service, a customer portal, or another mechanism. You may choose to provide the software components, vulnerability information, and provenance details. Many of the decisions you make will depend on your customers and how they expect to retrieve and ingest the information.

Second, for choosers of software, after receiving the software transparency information prior to supplier selection, you can use it for the following purposes:

- Identifying potential vulnerable and end-of-life components
- Targeting analysis for security concerns and risks
- Verifying the sourcing and claims
- Understanding the software's integrations
- Knowing and complying with license obligations, as well as software prohibited by regulators or your organization

As a chooser, your organization may have certain guidelines prescribed by the procurement or security teams when selecting software. If you are operating critical infrastructure, for example, your organization may have regulations to comply with, such as minimum encryption requirements or compliance laws. Your procurement teams may use the absence of transparency as a negotiating point, perhaps to request discounts or other considerations, due to the additional unknown risk they may be accepting.

Third, for software operators, after receiving the software transparency information for operations, you can use it for the following purposes:

- Evaluating whether the software is using a specific component
- Identifying potential vulnerable and end-of-life components
- Making more informed risk-based decisions
- Defining mitigations or compensating controls
- Minimizing attack surfaces by disabling features or modifying configurations
- Knowing and complying with license obligations, as well as software prohibited by regulators or your organization
- Understanding the use cases in which software can be relied upon and when it cannot

As an operator, your organization may use the software transparency information in operations, but at the time of publication there were still a limited number of tools that could ingest, or consume, the information for operational decision making. In November 2023, the Enduring Security Framework released the document *Securing the Software Supply Chain: Recommended Practices for Software Bill of Materials Consumption* to guide organizations on the consumption and use of SBOMs.[4] Asset management databases, as well as security operations tools, are adding capabilities to take in the software transparency information for risk monitoring or determining actions. However, the ability to make automated decisions based on the information requires a level of detail not found in most software transparency information, specifically the Vulnerability Exploitability eXchange (VEX) details for an SBOM.

---

## Vulnerability Exploitability eXchange

According to the VEX working group, as part of a public-private partnership under the US Cybersecurity & Infrastructure Security Agency (CISA), a VEX is "a form of a security advisory that indicates whether a product or products are affected by a known vulnerability or vulnerabilities." A VEX allows a supplier or other party to assert the status of specific vulnerabilities in a product.[5]

---

The combination of SBOM and VEX together establishes a powerful approach to vulnerability management for software operators.[6] Organizations are starting to generate VEX records for their products, but the volume of VEX records and the time required by development teams to validate the statuses is very high if all potential vulnerabilities are assessed. However, by focusing on known exploitable vulnerabilities, such as the CISA KEV (Known Exploited Vulnerabilities) catalog, a team can focus on the highest-priority vulnerabilities.

For example, if you have a network router and want to know if it was susceptible to a new zero-day vulnerability, you would need to have the correct version of the SBOM and the manufacturer's (or trustworthy service's) VEX information confirming if the vulnerability was or was not affecting the router. Figure 8-2 shows the process flow on how, at some point in the future, the SBOM and VEX information can be used to make decisions or take action. In this example, the flow checks if a product deployed in an organization is affected by a known exploitable vulnerability—in this case, CVE 2034-98765—within an open source library. If the VEX information is not available, the organization should assume the product is impacted until confirmed by the vendor.

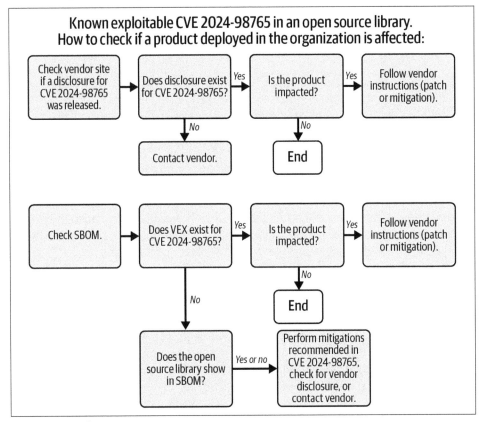

*Figure 8-2. Software transparency in operations*

There are many more use cases that your organization may have for software transparency information. By understanding the benefits, you can determine the value and potentially the return on investment (ROI) to your organization based on the various software transparency use cases.

# Software Bill of Materials (SBOM)

As mentioned previously, software transparency isn't only an SBOM, but an SBOM is an important part of software transparency. The National Telecommunications and Information Administration (NTIA), part of the US Department of Commerce, established in 2018 a series of software component transparency working groups that were reconstructed in 2022 within the Cybersecurity and Infrastructure Security Agency (CISA), part of the US Department of Homeland Security.[7] These working groups are partnerships between the government and private sector experts, such as myself, and our primary work products are the definitions and recommended practices for the use of SBOMs. For information on the working groups and documents, refer to the CISA SBOM website.[8]

To understand SBOMs, you must first recognize that a product or service can be a combination of many components. Figure 8-3 shows an SBOM graph example for a medical infusion pump product with four software components and three software subcomponents. This SBOM graph shows a very simple SBOM, but an SBOM could have dozens or hundreds of components; when the subcomponents are included, there could be a thousand or more components and subcomponents within a single SBOM.

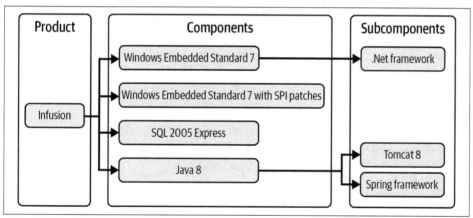

*Figure 8-3. Example SBOM graph*

The SBOM itself is usually a machine-readable file that lists various elements such as the software component names and versions used in the software or firmware. The highest-quality SBOMs are generated during the build process when all the components are known, though the tool may not know all the subcomponents. There are many different ways to generate an SBOM, as described in the following list:

- From source code repositories in prebuild using a tool, plugin, or version control system
- During the software build process using a specialized tool or plugin
- By orchestrating an SBOM during the prebuild, build, and postbuild activities
- With a postbuild binary analysis tool inspecting the binaries
- Using specialized tools while the software is running

Prebuild SBOM tools are specific to a programming language or ecosystem, such as C++, .NET, Node.js, NPM, Maven, Rust, Python, or Go. SBOMs should be generated for every build, and specifically the SBOMs of production software need to be retained for customers. For a list of build integration SBOM tools, I recommend the CycloneDX Tool Center and SPDX Tools page, which are both updated frequently with a large list of commercial and open source software tools.[9]

When the SBOM is generated postbuild using analysis or inspection tools, the tools generally cannot recognize commercial and proprietary components because the fingerprints for those components are not widely known. For example, a proprietary calculation library I'll call `cassie_calcs` would not be recognized by commercial or OSS tools, yet it could be used in a dozen different products within my fictitious organization. If at some time there was a critical vulnerability in `cassie_calcs`, it would be important to my customers to know which products contained that proprietary library. The only way they would know is if I provide SBOMs that noted the library. This transparency is also needed for any libraries I purchased from commercial suppliers.

For SBOMs to provide value to choosers of software or software operators, they must be shared beyond the development teams. There are so many possibilities to share or exchange SBOMs, as described in the following list:

- Direct sharing between a software publisher and customer through an SBOM-sharing mechanism (e.g., API, document repository, or email)
- Storing the SBOM or reference directly within the software or firmware or through a manufacturer usage description (MUD) schema[10]

- Publishing it on a publicly or privately accessible portal
- Publishing it to a third party such as an Information Sharing and Analysis Center (ISAC) or a risk management service

However, a number of organizations consider SBOMs to be intellectual property and thus may only provide SBOMs through restricted mechanisms and potentially under a nondisclosure agreement (NDA).

---

### Software Transparency Control 01

Control ST-01: Generate a software bill of materials (SBOM) for every production release of software.

---

## SBOM Formats

There are three main SBOM formats, as shown in Table 8-1: CycloneDX, Software Package Data Exchange (SPDX®), and a third format that does not have the popularity of the first two, Software Identification (SWID).[11] CycloneDX and SPDX are similar in nature and updated frequently to stay in sync with the quickly evolving SBOM use cases. The three SBOM formats are machine-readable JavaScript Object Notation (JSON) files, but since SBOM ingestion tools are not commonplace, there are still human-readable SBOMS in Adobe Portable Document Format (PDF), Microsoft Excel Binary File Format (XLS), or comma-separated values (CSV) format.

*Table 8-1. SBOM file formats*

| Format | Origins | Description |
| --- | --- | --- |
| CycloneDX[a] | OWASP community | Focuses on automation, adoption, and enhancement of SBOMs within build pipelines. Frequently updated. |
| SPDX[b] | Linux Foundation and ISO/IEC 5962:2021 | ISO/IEC 5962:2021 - Information technology SPDX® Specification V2.2.1 focuses on ingestion in development workflows and corporate compliance. Frequently updated. |
| SWID[c] | ISO/IEC 19770-2:2015 | Designed for software inventory and entitlement management. Rarely updated. |

a   CycloneDX (*https://cyclonedx.org*), accessed June 25, 2023.
b   "ISO/IEC 5962:2021" (*https://www.iso.org/standard/81870.html*), ISO Webstore, accessed January 19, 2024.
c   "ISO/IEC 19770-2:2015" (*https://webstore.ansi.org/standards/iso/isoiec197702015*), ANSI Webstore, accessed December 12, 2023.

Although not a statistical survey, when I query organizations as to which standard they have adopted, it appears to be divided equally between CycloneDX and SPDX. However, since the SBOM formats are digital, it is easier for tool vendors to maintain compatibility with both formats. It is too early to determine if one of them will become a leading format or if they will both remain equally distributed.

The example SBOM graph, shown previously in Figure 8-3, can be viewed online within the SwiftBOM tool.[12] SwiftBOM, a simple SBOM generator created for the SBOM healthcare proof-of-concept working group, includes samples of CycloneDX, SPDX, and SWID. The SwiftBOM samples show some of the various elements that I describe in "SBOM Elements" on page 136.

## SBOM Elements

The NTIA Framing Working Group released a set of elements (or attributes) to include in SBOMs, as shown in Table 8-2.[13] Although the SPDX and CycloneDX include these elements and more, the US government instructed NTIA to release a minimum set of elements necessary for any SBOMs that are to be provided to US government agencies.[14] For a current list of elements supported in the SPDX or CycloneDX formats—which far surpass the NTIA minimum elements or the framing document elements—refer to that format's specific documentation.

*Table 8-2. SBOM attributes[a]*

| Attributes | Description | NTIA minimum element |
|---|---|---|
| Author of SBOM data | Name of the entity that creates the SBOM data for this component. This does not have to be the software component publisher. | Yes |
| Timestamp | Record of the date and time of the SBOM data assembly. Although not specified, an international date and time format (YYYY-MM-DDThh:mm:ss) is recommended to avoid confusion between MM-DD and DD-MM and has T as the delimiter (i.e., 2025-11-24T14:55:39 for November 24, 2025, at 2:55:39 p.m. UTC). | Yes |
| Lifecycle phase | Stage (source, build, or postbuild) where the SBOM was captured. | No |
| Supplier name | Name of an entity that creates, defines, and identifies components. Usually this is the software publisher, manufacturer, vendor, developer, integrator, maintainer, or provider. | Yes |
| Component name | Designation assigned to a unit of software defined by the original supplier. Examples of components include a software product, a device, a library, or a single file. | Yes |
| Version of the component | Identifier used by the supplier to specify a change in software from a previously identified version. This can be any format since it is unique to the supplier, but semantic versioning (major.minor.patch) is recommended. | Yes |

| Attributes | Description | NTIA minimum element |
|---|---|---|
| Component hash | Unique identifier for a software component, the compiled binary form of that component, or a collection of components. Due to the uncertain nature of the hash being represented, and because some SBOM generation tools may not have direct access to the underlying component, this attribute is not required in the NTIA minimum elements. | No |
| License information | License information for open source and commercial libraries is an important element for compliance. Although not required in NTIA's minimum element, it is commonly included in SBOMs. | No |
| Other unique identifiers | Other attributes used to identify a component or serve as a lookup key for relevant databases. Examples of commonly used unique identifiers are Common Platform Enumeration (CPE), SWID tags, and Package Uniform Resource Locators (PURL).[b] | Yes |
| Dependency relationship | Characterizes the relationship that an upstream component $n-1$ is included in software $n$. A transitive dependency is when component $n-2$, which is a component of $n-1$, is associated with software $n$—essentially, dependencies of dependencies. At a minimum, all top-level dependencies ($n-1s$) must contain enough detail to identify transitive dependencies. For example, the Android operating system is a modified version of the Linux kernel. | Yes |
| Other dependency relationships | Some SBOM standards capture additional dependency relationships, such as derivation. Derivation is when a component has had modifications from the original version of a component. This may occur when code is removed from, or added to, the original component. Other dependencies could be dynamic dependencies or third-party services, which load components when called by the application. | No |

a    The attribute names are the ones defined in the NTIA minimum elements, which differ slightly from the names in the framing document.

b    See "National Vulnerability Database—Official Common Platform Enumeration (CPE) Dictionary" (*https://nvd.nist.gov/products/cpe*), NIST, accessed June 25, 2023; and "package-url/purl-spec" (*https://github.com/package-url/purl-spec*), GitHub, accessed June 25, 2023.

## SBOM Limitations

SBOMs aren't a perfect solution, nor do they solve all problems, and so I will describe some limitations that exist when using SBOMs to provide software transparency. At some point the tools, technologies, and standards may be able to resolve or reduce the limitations noted in the following list:

*Software naming/product naming*
> A single software product is known by different names in different ecosystems, and there is no single name that will work everywhere or single source of truth for that software. For example, if a company acquires another company, the software may be rebranded with a new name.

*Accurate SBOMs*

Depending on how and when the SBOM was created, the SBOM may be missing library references, especially proprietary or commercial libraries. This can occur if a software composition analysis (SCA) tool has reverse engineered the software binary. SCA tools also may incorrectly identify software libraries if there were portions of a library used, but the existing code is maintained by the software publisher. For example, if a portion of code was copied and pasted from an open source library, the SCA tool may recognize it even if the organization is fully maintaining any defects in the source code.

*Backporting patches*

Backporting is when a software update or patch is taken from a recent software version and applied to an earlier version of the same software. This can be used to address security flaws in older versions of the software that are still supported by the publisher. Backporting is useful for IoT and OT firmware products where hardware is specifically developed to support certain software libraries or functions. For example, earlier versions of the OpenSSL open source library could be maintained for backward compatibility and interoperability with other products. A manufacturer may then choose to backport the latest OpenSSL security patch into a previous version of OpenSSL within the firmware.

*SBOMs for operations*

Although there are a large number of SBOM generation tools, at the time of writing, there are limited technologies to ingest an SBOM and use it for operational functions. There are SBOM readers, such as the open source Dependency Track tool, which displays software dependencies to identify potential vulnerabilities. SBOM ingestion capabilities will also be beneficial to configuration management databases (CMDBs); security information and event management (SIEM) tools; security orchestration, automation, and response (SOAR) tools; security operation centers (SOCs); and vulnerability management tools and processes. Vulnerability management use cases are limited, however, unless VEX information is included to confirm or deny the impact from a vulnerability.

*SBOMs matching IT asset inventory*

Each SBOM is unique to a software version. Over the course of a product lifecycle, there may be dozens or hundreds of software versions and SBOMs. Unless the IT asset inventory has a record of the installed software, embedded software, or firmware, it is not possible to match the correct SBOM with the IT asset. For example, an IP-connected video surveillance camera may be running version 5 of its firmware, but the current version and new SBOM is for version 9. In that time, software libraries and vulnerabilities may have been patched. A false sense of security can happen if the SBOM for version 5 is not available.

## Additional Bill of Materials (BOMs)

Besides SBOMs, there are additional bills of materials (BOMs) that can provide transparency to software choosers and operators. The BOMs in the following list help organizations further illuminate supply chains:

*Software as a service BOM (SaaSBOM)*
A SaaSBOM is a logical representation of the system, services, dependency on other services, directional flow of data, data classifications, endpoint URLs, and, optionally, the software components for each service.

*Operational BOM (OBOM)*
An operational bill of materials decouples the dynamic information, such as runtime environments, configurations, and additional dependencies from the SBOM.

*Hardware BOM (HBOM)*
Providing transparency for a connectible, IoT, Industrial IoT, or OT device would include a hardware bill of materials that allows purchasers and operators to evaluate and mitigate risks in the supply chain. An HBOM identifies the finished product information, component parts, and production details, which should include the names and locations of suppliers, manufacturers, and assembly.[15]

*Artificial intelligence BOM (AI-BOM) and machine learning BOM (ML-BOM)*
The AI-BOMs and ML-BOMs provide transparency into the machine learning models and datasets, as well as software components and algorithms.

*Cryptography BOM (CBOM)*
The CBOM provides an object model to describe cryptography assets and their dependencies.[16]

# Vulnerability Disclosures

A significant part of software transparency is the disclosure of vulnerabilities. Vulnerabilities may exist in open source, commercial components, or an organization's proprietary code, but sometimes the disclosure is not voluntary. In other words, the disclosure might be announced by a third party such as a government agency or research firm. However, if the third party coordinates with the software publisher or manufacturer before announcing the vulnerability, this is known as "responsible disclosure." For more information on creating vulnerability disclosures, refer to the UK's "Vulnerability Disclosure Toolkit" published by the UK National Cyber Security Centre (NCSC).[17] The toolkit, based on the international standard "ISO/IEC 29147:2018 Vulnerability Disclosure," includes an example vulnerability disclosure policy.[18]

When an organization discloses vulnerabilities, it is usually in the form of a CVE (Common Vulnerabilities and Exposures) record, or through various methods such as release notes, security bulletins, the common security advisory framework (CSAF), vulnerability disclosure reports (VDRs), or vulnerability exploitability exchange (VEX) records. These multiple approaches and formats for disclosing vulnerabilities are described as follows:

*CVE record*

A list of vulnerability entries in a database, such as the US National Vulnerability Database (NVD), each containing a unique identification number, a description, and at least one publicly known reference.

*Release notes*

Usually a software publisher or manufacturer distributes a document, known as release notes, with each version. The release notes contain a list of changes and may reference security patches or fixes contained in the release. Some organizations include low and medium security fixes in the release notes only rather than generating a CVE record and potentially a security disclosure.

*Security bulletins or notices*

An organization may choose to release a human-readable document (known as a security bulletin, disclosure, advisory, or notice). This document typically contains a list of CVEs, affected products, and mitigations, which can include links to patches or updates.

*CSAF document*

A documented standard to disclose vulnerabilities in a machine-readable format, allowing suppliers to automate their vulnerability disclosures.[19] The CSAF file generally includes the publisher, tracking information, and a list of products and vulnerabilities. CSAF version 2.0 added support for VEX.

*Vulnerability Disclosure Report (VDR)*

An attestation of all vulnerabilities affecting a product or its dependencies, along with an analysis of the impact. It should include plans to address the vulnerabilities and be signed with a trusted, verifiable, private key. For a detailed explanation of VDR, refer to Richard Brooks's article "What Is a NIST SBOM Vulnerability Disclosure Report (VDR)."[20]

*VEX record*

A security advisory to state all the vulnerabilities not affecting a product, product family, or organization. It also can state which vulnerabilities do affect a product, if there is an investigation in progress, or what plans exist to address the vulnerability. The VEX should be signed with a trusted, verifiable, private key. For a detailed explanation showing the key differences between a VDR and VEX, refer to Steve Springett's article "Vulnerability and Exploitability Transparency—VDR & VEX."[21]

---

### Software Transparency Control 02

Control ST-02: Establish a vulnerability disclosure process and publish vulnerability information based on the organization's disclosure criteria.

---

# Additional Transparency Approaches

In addition to SBOMs and vulnerability disclosures, there are other approaches to demonstrating software transparency. These frameworks, methods, and artifacts are all working toward a similar goal of providing the end customer with information they feel is needed to assess risk in their organizations. Since software transparency is a relatively recent requirement from customers, transparency approaches are still evolving and thus may have changed after this book was published.

## US CISA Secure Software Development Attestation Common Form

In accordance with US Executive Order 14028, the US Cybersecurity & Infrastructure Security Agency (CISA) released the Secure Software Development Attestation Common Form for any organization that intends to sell software (including firmware or cloud products) to the US government.[22] This form requires organizations to self-attest—that is, to make a formal and legal statement—that the product, products, or company were consistent with the following practices:

- The software is developed and built in secure environments.

- The software producer has made a good-faith effort to maintain trusted source code supply chains.

- The software producer maintains provenance for internal and third-party code incorporated into the software.

- The software producer employs automated tools or comparable processes that check for security vulnerabilities.

Once this draft form is finalized, the US government and many other organizations, even if they are not government agencies, will adopt this form and language to assess suppliers on secure development practices. This will also be standard practice if the product is part of another product, system, or service being sold to the US government.

## Supply Chain Integrity, Transparency, and Trust (SCITT)

Formed through the Internet Engineering Task Force (IETF), the Supply Chain Integrity, Transparency, and Trust (SCITT) Working Group has created an initial design that allows implementers to build integrity and accountability into the software supply chain.[23] By creating a scalable, flexible, and decentralized architecture, software publishers and manufacturers can produce evidence that allows users to validate the integrity through a trusted mechanism. There are three core tenets for this trust guarantee to work:

- Statements made about supply chain artifacts must be identifiable, authentic, and nonrepudiable using a distributed public key infrastructure.

- Statements must be registered on a secure append-only log, so their provenance and history can be independently and consistently audited.

- Software publishers and manufacturers can efficiently prove to any other party the registration of their signed statements.

In 2023 the SCITT Working Group received approval from IETF to develop the architecture and standardize the technical flows for providing information about a software supply chain. I recommend reviewing the latest documents and architecture in the IETF SCITT project since the architecture was still in design at the time this book was published.

## Digital Bill of Materials and Sharing Mechanisms

Originally designed by Unisys Corp, and now available as a Linux Foundation open source project, the Digital Bill of Materials (DBoM) project enables API-based attestation sharing (e.g., deliverables such as SBOMs, HBOMS, and documentation) among supply chain partners and customers.[24]

The DBoM solution is composed of open source software components that allow sharing of attestations through a set of supported repositories such as databases, private and permissioned distributed ledgers, or public blockchains.[25] With DBoM, an organization can set up private or specific broadcast channels between two or more partners to share information between one or more DBoM nodes, as shown in Figure 8-4.

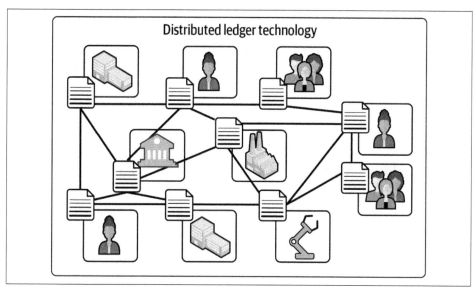

*Figure 8-4. Artifacts are shareable between many partners*

By establishing a DBoM node, an organization can provide specific channels for the communication of artifacts and access to the repositories. These private or broadcast channels will have certain access policies determined by the owner of the channel. As seen in Figure 8-5, any type of artifact can be distributed through the channels, but the most common for supply chain purposes are SBOMs, HBOMs, and vulnerability information.

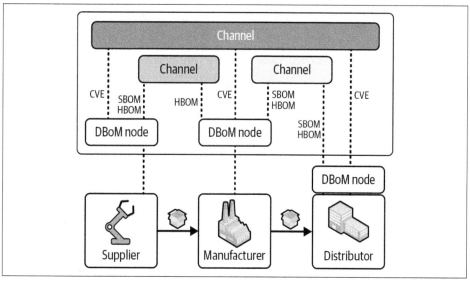

*Figure 8-5. DBoM nodes and channels for sharing artifacts*

DBoM and other sharing (or exchanging) mechanisms are frequently discussed in the SBOM community. There is no dominant mechanism at the time of publishing this book, but several vendors have models for sharing SBOMs through private or SaaS clouds. Other vendors and ISACs are focusing on niche repositories to store SBOMs for specific industries. Some people would prefer a global SBOM storage database, but until the naming problem mentioned earlier is resolved and organizations accept that SBOMs are accessible by anyone, it is highly unlikely a global repository will exist.

## Graph of Understanding Artifact Composition (GUAC)

Graph of Understanding Artifact Composition (GUAC) is a free tool developed by Google that can aggregate different sources of software security metadata into a graph database.[26] GUAC is more than an SBOM graph: querying this database can enable risk and policy management as well as trustworthy intelligence about project dependencies, and it can identify critical libraries. The tool has four major areas of functionality, as shown in the following list and represented in Figure 8-6:

*Collect*
    Connect to a variety of open, public, internal, or proprietary sources of software security metadata.

*Ingest*
    Import data on artifacts, projects, resources, vulnerabilities, repositories, and even developers.

*Collate*
    Assemble the data into a coherent graph of relationships.

*Query*
    Query for metadata attached to, or related to, entities within the graph.

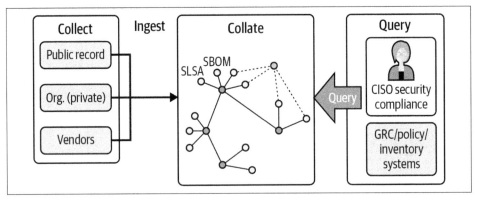

*Figure 8-6. GUAC graph*

Querying for a given artifact may return any number of items, including provenance, vulnerabilities, SBOMs, lifecycle events, and build chain data from the SLSA framework (as described in "Source Code Integrity" on page 83).

## In-Toto Attestation

Although the SLSA framework, discussed in Chapter 5, is specifically designed to provide a checklist of controls to improve integrity and prevent tampering, the provenance framework referenced by SLSA is the in-toto attestation framework. Using in-toto attestation, an end user can verify the integrity, authenticity, and auditability of a software product by providing transparency about the steps performed, who performed the steps, and in which order the steps were performed.[27]

The in-toto framework first requires the project owner to create a layout of the mandatory steps for build and deployment. Then the build tasks are performed and metadata concerning the tasks are recorded. Finally, the end user or policy engine checks that the metadata matches the intended layout with a bit-by-bit comparison to the final product reported by the last step in the supply chain. This allows the user to verify if a step in the build or deployment process was not performed to specification or was performed by someone else.

---

### Software Transparency Controls 03–04

Control ST-03: Produce required transparency artifacts such as software attestations.

Control ST-04: Identify and utilize sharing mechanisms for software transparency artifacts.

---

## Software Provenance

As mentioned in Chapter 5 and according to NIST, software provenance is defined as verifiable information of where, when, and how the software artifact was produced and sometimes by whom. According to the North American Electric Reliability Corporation (NERC), knowing the heritage of components allows users to better identify and defend against threats.[28] Transparency information, such as provenance, may be requested by organizations that want to purchase products and services. Any organization, whether purchasing or selling products, may be required to prove the provenance of software, firmware, or hardware for regulatory reasons, or as a potential risk vector stemming from adversarial countries. For example, the US has identified some vendors that cannot be part of products, and their technologies cannot be used to create or support products.

Some software provenance information can be included in an SBOM, SCITT artifact, or other transparency artifact. Organizations may require different provenance elements, depending on the products or services required. The following list contains some examples of provenance information requested by organizations:

- Development and testing tools and platforms
- Source code repository locations and access logs
- Logs of development and testing activities
- Build management tools, CI/CD tools, and access logs
- Production platforms and access logs
- Locations of developers, testers, and anyone with access to the source code and platforms
- Data models used for generative AI

There is a challenge with depending on provenance for software transparency information. Considering there are trillions of lines of code globally, the percentage of code that has some or all provenance information captured is extremely small. In situations where some information is available, it is likely to be a small percentage of the entire product or service.

Even with only a small percentage of information available, requests for provenance instigate conversations about software origin and its relationship to trustworthiness. In recent years, malicious actors have been increasingly targeting open source projects and components in public repositories and systems. The provenance of these systems may not exist or it may be false. Organizations need to carefully inspect any open source, as identified in control SCBD-02 and SCBD-06 from Chapter 5, for any hidden security risks.

Generative AI presents an additional challenge, as seen in the court case against GitHub, Microsoft, and OpenAI (which had not been settled at the time of this book's publication).[29] In this legal case, a number of developers have alleged that source code generated by AI did not identify the original source code and thus violated the open source licenses for that code. As organizations begin to use generative AI to create source code, they should capture all provenance details for future use cases, such as transparency, regulatory, or legal artifacts.

---

### Software Transparency Control 05

Control ST-05: Capture provenance information for software, firmware, and hardware.

---

# Practices and Technology

Another aspect of software transparency is all the practices (processes, procedures, policies, organization) and technology that contributed to the product, offers, and services. Often in contracts and assessments, customers will require organizations to provide details, and thus transparency, on these topics. Table 8-3 lists and describes some of these common practices and technologies.

*Table 8-3. Other information requested for software transparency*

| Practices | Description | Examples of practices and technology |
|---|---|---|
| Organizational setup | Security personnel structure and responsibilities | • Information security management policy<br>• Product security policy |
| Requirements | Requirements that contributed to the product or service | • ISA/IEC 62443-4-2 Technical Security Requirements for IACS Components<br>• ISA/IEC 62443-3-3 System Security Requirements and Security Levels<br>• ETSI EN 303 645 Cyber Security for Consumer Internet of Things: Baseline Requirements |
| Change management | Who or what has authority to make changes to the product or service | • Product owner<br>• Patch management tool |
| Design | Requirements and techniques that contributed to the product or service | • Secure-by-design requirements<br>• Privacy-by-design requirements |
| Development | Secure software development lifecycle framework used for development | • NIST SP 800-218 SSDF<br>• ISA/IEC 62443-4-1 Secure Development Lifecycle |
| Threat modeling | Details about the tools used and the model itself | • Microsoft Threat Modeler<br>• Threat modeling summary report |
| Security testing | When, where, and what types of tests were performed | • Fuzz testing<br>• Penetration testing report<br>• Security testing summary report |
| Build and release management | Process and tools used for compiling or deploying the product or service | • Build management tools<br>• Cloud deployment tools |
| Operations | Who performs and what tools are used | • Managed service provider<br>• Cloud monitoring tools |
| Vulnerability management | Framework used and what vulnerabilities exist in the product or service | • ISO/IEC 30111 Vulnerability Handling Processes<br>• List of publicly disclosed vulnerabilities |
| Supplier management | Process for selecting and assessing software and hardware suppliers | • Supplier management policy<br>• MITRE System of Trust |

These examples are just some of the artifacts that may be requested by organizations. Many of the artifacts can be prepared ahead of time and provided in a transparency package with the product or service during the procurement or delivery process.

> ## Software Transparency Control 06
>
> Control ST-06: Prepare and provide transparency packages for requested software, firmware, and hardware.

# Summary

The time for transparency has come. Organizations need to prepare artifacts such as SBOMs, policies, test reports, and attestations for review and assessment during the procurement cycle, and also provide ongoing information throughout the lifecycle of the product or service. It may never be possible to have all the details and history of the software supply chain, but transparency helps build trust in the organization and the software. There are many more ways to build trust in the software supply chain, and those are by understanding and assessing your suppliers, as I discuss in Chapter 9.

# References

1   "Improving the Nation's Cybersecurity" (*https://www.federalregister.gov/d/ 2021-10460*), Federal Register, May 17, 2021.

2   Consolidated Appropriations Act (*https://www.congress.gov/117/bills/hr2617/ BILLS-117hr2617enr.pdf*), 2023, HR 2617, 117th Cong. 2nd sess.

3   Chris Hughes and Tony Turner, *Software Transparency: Supply Chain Security in an Era of a Software-Driven Society* (Wiley, 2023).

4   Enduring Security Framework, *Securing the Software Supply Chain: Recommended Practices for SBOM Consumption* (*https://media.defense.gov/2023/Nov/ 09/2003338086/-1/-1/0/SECURING%20THE%20SOFTWARE%20SUPPLY%20CHAIN %20RECOMMENDED%20PRACTICES%20FOR%20SOFTWARE%20BILL%20OF %20MATERIALS%20CONSUMPTION.PDF*), November 2023.

5   "Vulnerability Exploitability eXchange (VEX)—Use Cases" (*https://www.cisa.gov/ sites/default/files/2023-01/VEX_Use_Cases_Aprill2022.pdf*), US Cybersecurity & Infrastructure Security Agency, April 2022.

6   "Minimum Requirements for Vulnerability Exploitability eXchange (VEX)" (*https://www.cisa.gov/resources-tools/resources/minimum-requirements-vulnerability- exploitability-exchange-vex*), US Cybersecurity & Infrastructure Security Agency, April 21, 2023.

7   "NTIA Software Component Transparency" (*https://ntia.gov/other-publication/ ntia-software-component-transparency*), NTIA, April 28, 2021.

8  "Software Bill of Materials (SBOM)" (*https://www.cisa.gov/sbom*), US Cybersecurity & Infrastructure Security Agency, accessed December 12, 2023.

9  "Tool Center" (*https://cyclonedx.org/tool-center*), CycloneDX, accessed December 12, 2023, and "Tools" (*https://spdx.dev/use/tools*), SPDX, accessed January 19, 2024.

10  Eliot Lear and Scott Rose, "RFC 9472: A YANG Data Model for Reporting Software Bills of Materials (SBOMs) and Vulnerability Information" (*https://www.rfc-editor.org/rfc/rfc9472.html*), RFC Editor, October 2023.

11  NTIA Multistakeholder Process on Software Component Transparency: Standards and Formats Working Group, *Survey of Existing SBOM Formats and Standards* (*https://ntia.gov/sites/default/files/publications/sbom_formats_survey-version-2021_0.pdf*), 2021.

12  "SwiftBOM (5.2.7)—SBOM Generator for PoC and Demos" (*https://democert.org/sbom*), Democert.org, accessed December 12, 2023.

13  NTIA Multistakeholder Process on Software Component Transparency: Framing Working Group, *Framing Software Component Transparency: Establishing a Common Software Bill of Materials (SBOM)* (*https://www.ntia.gov/files/ntia/publications/ntia_sbom_framing_2nd_edition_20211021.pdf*), October 21, 2021.

14  US Department of Commerce, *The Minimum Elements for a Software Bill of Materials (SBOM)* (*https://www.ntia.doc.gov/files/ntia/publications/sbom_minimum_elements_report.pdf*), July 12, 2021.

15  US Cybersecurity & Infrastructure Security Agency, *A Hardware Bill of Materials (HBOM) Framework for Supply Chain Risk Management* (*https://www.cisa.gov/sites/default/files/2023-09/A%20Hardware%20Bill%20of%20Materials%20Framework%20for%20Supply%20Chain%20Risk%20Management%20%28508%29.pdf*), September 2023.

16  Basil Hess and Nicklas Koertge, "OWASP CycloneDX: The Missing Standard For Describing Cryptography in Software" (*https://owasp.org/blog/2023/10/03/CycloneDX-Cryptography-CBOM*), OWASP, October 3, 2023.

17  "Vulnerability Disclosure Toolkit" (*https://www.ncsc.gov.uk/information/vulnerability-disclosure-toolkit*), UK National Cyber Security Centre, September 14, 2020.

18  "ISO/IEC 29147:2018 Vulnerability Disclosure" (*https://www.iso.org/standard/72311.html*), ISO, accessed December 12, 2023.

19  "Common Security Advisory Framework (CSAF)" (*https://oasis-open.github.io/csaf-documentation*), Oasis CSAF TC, accessed December 12, 2023.

20   Richard Brooks, "What Is a NIST SBOM Vulnerability Disclosure Report (VDR)" (*https://energycentral.com/c/pip/what-nist-sbom-vulnerability-disclosure-report-vdr*), Energy Central, August 24, 2022.

21   Steve Springett, "Vulnerability and Exploitability Transparency—VDR & VEX" (*https://owasp.org/blog/2023/02/07/vdr-vex-comparison*), OWASP, February 7, 2023.

22   "Secure Software Development Attestation Form" (*https://www.cisa.gov/secure-software-attestation-form*), Cybersecurity and Infrastructure Security Agency, accessed December 12, 2023.

23   "Supply Chain Integrity, Transparency, and Trust (SCITT)" (*https://data tracker.ietf.org/wg/scitt/documents*), IETF Data Tracker, December 12, 2023.

24   DBoM Technical Project (*https://dbom.io*), accessed December 12, 2023.

25   A distributed ledger is a database that is shared and synchronized across multiple sites, is accessible by multiple participants, and allows transactions to have public witnesses. Participants can own an identical copy of it, and any changes or additions made to the ledger are reflected and copied to all participants.

26   "Announcing GUAC, a Great Pairing with SLSA (and SBOM)!" (*https://security.googleblog.com/2022/10/announcing-guac-great-pairing-with-slsa.html*), *Google Security Blog*, October 20, 2022.

27   in-toto.io, accessed December 12, 2023.

28   NERC, *Security Guideline: Supply Chain Provenance* (*https://www.nerc.com/comm/RSTC_Reliability_Guidelines/Security_Guideline-Supply%20Chain%20Provenance.pdf*), March 22, 2023.

29   GitHub Copilot Litigation (*https://githubcopilotlitigation.com*), Joseph Saveri Law Firm, November 3, 2022.

# Suppliers

Suppliers can introduce risks to you through the people, practices, code, and technologies that they use to build their product or service. A single code library provided by a supplier, for example, can introduce critical vulnerabilities into your organization, products, or services. Your organization likely has a process for selecting suppliers, which usually includes an evaluation of the supplier's financial health, the quality of the product it produces, and its ability to deliver the volumes you need. When reviewing criteria for a potential supplier, cybersecurity should also be a weighted factor in your overall evaluation. These supplier evaluations now assess the risk of cybersecurity issues, data breaches, and regulatory compliance, or are used to meet insurance requirements. The evaluations are important, but they may not address the key risks for the supplier's scope of products or services. For example, the cybersecurity posture of a supplier's websites and attack surfaces does not necessarily mean that the supplier uses a secure software development lifecycle process or monitors its development environments.

Throughout this chapter, I use the term "supplier" to represent the direct supplier or vendor who provides goods or services to your organization, which would make it a "third-party" supplier. Each third-party supplier may have multiple suppliers itself, making them your fourth-party suppliers. This continues upstream to the fifth party all the way to the nth party. According to legal definitions, the first party is *your company* and the second party is the end user or customer, where applicable. These relationships are shown in Figure 9-1.

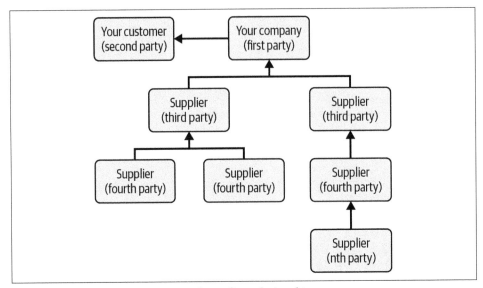

*Figure 9-1. Customer, company, and supplier relationships*

Third-party suppliers should have the same controls, assessments, and agreements with their fourth-party suppliers, who should do the same, and so on up the supply chain. Any upstream supplier or technology that creates, modifies, or has access to source code represents an inherent risk in the software supply chain. The goal is to manage and minimize the risks of third parties and beyond, even though you have limited or no control over their processes, performance, and controls.

There are three main processes involved in software supplier risk management: cyber assessments, cyber agreements, and supplier management. These processes can be performed in parallel to your organization's supplier management processes, independent from existing supplier management processes, and independent from each other. For a current supplier with a cyber agreement in place, as an example, you can implement the supplier management activities and wait until right before contract renewal to conduct a supplier assessment.

This chapter will discuss the details and controls for the three main processes of cyber assessments, cyber agreements, and supplier management. The controls in this chapter provide a specific focus on cybersecurity risk in the supplier software supply chain. You can integrate and expand the software supply chain controls from this chapter into your supplier evaluation process.

# Cyber Assessments

There are many cyber risk management companies that provide tools and services for supplier management and assessment. The tools monitor an organization's digital footprint, including DNS, insecure protocols, and so on, and the services provide real-time monitoring, dashboards, and alerts when there are certain situations such as a data breach. Primarily these services are only for the external-facing posture, which may indicate a supplier's level of IT hygiene but does not fully represent a supplier's overall cybersecurity posture. In addition to, or in lieu of, these monitoring tools, organizations may choose to perform cyber assessments to evaluate the security posture for specific products or services. The cyber assessment results should provide value into any of your decisions about suppliers, and if the cyber risks are above your risk threshold, the supplier process should allow you to reject the supplier or escalate the risk. A poor cyber performer is a liability and a cost to your organization—you are either paying to enhance the security in advance of using the performer's product or services, or you take the cost burden once a cyber event has occurred.

Typically cyber assessments exist in the form of questionnaires developed by cyber risk management companies, trade associations, regulatory groups, individual companies, or governments, such as the ones mentioned in the following list:

*CISA ICT SCRM Task Force—Small Business template[1]*
Designed for small businesses to assess information and communication technology (ICT) hardware, software, and services.

*CISA NRMC—Vendor Supply Chain Risk Management (SCRM) Template*
Standardized template of questions for enhanced visibility and transparency.[2]

*Enduring Security Framework—Supplier Artifacts and Checklist[3]*
Located in Appendix D in the publication "Securing the Software Supply Chain: Recommended Practices for Suppliers," this document provides examples of information to assess or questions to ask.

*North American Transmission Forum (NATF) Supply Chain Security Assessment Model[4]*
One of the first publicly available supplier assessment models, the NATF's Supply Chain Security assessment model is directed toward suppliers in the energy industry.

*Idaho National Laboratory—Cyber Security Evaluation Tool (CSET)[5]*
A desktop software tool for evaluating an organization's security posture. It provides a process to evaluate industrial control system (ICS) and information technology (IT) network security practices.

Suppliers are very familiar with receiving cyber questionnaires. In these questionnaires, you should ask the supplier to provide evidence to support the things it's claiming in the assessment. The level of transparency for evaluating cybersecurity posture can be difficult to prove since suppliers consider many of the details confidential and require a nondisclosure agreement (NDA) to provide answers and evidence (e.g., their policies, internal processes, bills of materials, audit results, and testing reports). Rather than providing evidence, suppliers may propose to show evidence only during review meetings. Before requesting evidence, you should carefully consider whether your organization will benefit from reviewing the evidence and whether you have the resources or capability to review and evaluate the evidence. Later in this section, I will discuss areas to focus on (e.g., IT security, product/application security, secure development lifecycle) for questions and evidence used to evaluate a supplier's risk to the software supply chain.

## Assessment Responses

One question that I am asked continuously is how to get suppliers to respond to questionnaires and assessments. Unfortunately, there are very few ways to enforce compliance with your supplier assessment process. Unless the supplier is already obligated by a contract, law, or regulation to provide answers, it may choose to ignore or indefinitely delay the assessment. Open source software maintainers will probably not be in the position to answer assessments, and some extremely large organizations may only provide responses to strategic accounts, or they may refer you to a portal that contains the information they feel is relevant to share. If an organization has a policy where it does not respond to questionnaires, it may note that somewhere on its website or open source project.

It is not unusual for assessment requests from smaller organizations to be ignored. However, the following is a list of suggestions that may increase the response rate from supplier organizations:

- Request escalation within the supplier's sales organization.
- Ensure the assessment is being routed to the cybersecurity team or CISO rather than staying with the supplier's sales organization.
- Contact a cybersecurity team member or the CISO on a social networking site, such as LinkedIn.
- Work with peer organizations and, by using a common template, send a joint request to the supplier.
- Include your legal team in the request, or ask the team to make the request.

If you still do not have answers after using these various methods, you will need to perform some research on your own, as described in "Research" on page 155, or use a third-party service to collect intelligence on the organization. Once you have collected and evaluated any available information, your organization will need to agree on how much risk it is willing to accept if this supplier is used.

## Research

The supplier selection process is generally led by purchasing, procurement, and financial teams to qualify a supplier's enterprise and financial risk. Carefully review the existing supplier selection process in your organization and identify any gaps in the due diligence with regards to security posture. In some cases, you may find the supplier has populated its website with cybersecurity information such as the processes it follows and the certifications it has received. A good example of this is Cisco's Trust Portal, which contains audit reports such as SOC2 and FedRAMP, as well as security testing information and questionnaire responses.[6]

To continue your due diligence, perform internet searches to identify any media attention that the company may have received for data breaches, software vulnerabilities, or cyberattacks such as ransomware. This due diligence would include reviewing the known vulnerabilities databases (US-based NIST NVD or China-based CNVD) and the US-based CISA Known Exploited Vulnerabilities (KEV) Catalog for any common vulnerabilities and exposures (CVEs) in the supplier's product.[7] CVEs are not a true indicator of the company's product quality but instead provide a view into the supplier's transparency and known exposures for future risk mitigations.

---

### Supplier Controls 01–02

Control SP-01: Incorporate cybersecurity into the supplier selection and evaluation processes.

Control SP-02: Research the supplier's cybersecurity posture for risk and transparency.

---

## IT Security Including Environmental Security

When performing an assessment for software supply chain security, there will always be elements of IT security to keep in mind. The assessments must include the environment controls mentioned in Chapter 3 and verification of the controls for developer systems, lab environments, build management systems, test environments, production environments, and, when applicable, manufacturing environments. Even cloud-first organizations and a cloud-based development infrastructure must maintain IT controls for proper access management, role-based access control, logging and monitoring, backups, disaster recovery, and business continuity.[8] Multifactor authentication, VPNs, and other IT controls are critical for retaining the confidentiality, authenticity, and integrity of the supplier's products and applications. Depending on the risk of the product, application, or data, you should ask for the penetration test results on the IT infrastructure used in the software development lifecycle. Most organizations perform IT and application penetration testing, but they do not scope a penetration test on the development environment infrastructure.

---

## Supplier Control 03

Control SP-03: Request evidence of a supplier's IT security controls specifically in defense of software development systems, environments, and infrastructure.

---

# Product/Application Security Organization

When receiving assessments, suppliers usually answer the cybersecurity organization questions from an IT security perspective. Sometimes the assessments may be completed by someone in the sales organization using preapproved cybersecurity answers, but the answers may not address software supply chain risks for the product or service. If you are making the investment to perform a supplier assessment, be sure to ask in the questionnaire about the organization, identity, and role of the responder to factor it into the evaluation.

Assessments for software supply chain security should always ask the supplier about its product or application's security organization (i.e., product security office or security engineering), which may be part of the CISO office or development organization. The assessment should ask if there is an application security leader, such as a head of application security or chief product security officer (CPSO), accountable for the secure development processes, controls, and compliance.

For evidence, request organizational charts showing application security leaders, security architects, and security testers. If the supplier does not have a product or application security organization, the supplier should demonstrate resources within the IT security or development teams who are accountable for secure development practices, security testing capabilities, and formal cybersecurity review checkpoints that examine product and application cyber risk.

I recommend that during and after the assessment process, you create and maintain a relationship directly with the cybersecurity leaders in the supplier's organization. By establishing a relationship, you can discuss security posture improvements as peers, and also have direct contacts in place should any concerns or incidents arise in the supplier's organization.

## Product Security Processes and Secure Development Lifecycle

When collecting assessment evidence, a supplier's product and application security processes should be documented in policies, procedures, reports, and dashboards. This should include secure development, secure coding rules, secure testing requirements, security features and requirements, penetration testing requirements, and release management criteria, as well as vulnerability and patch management policies and SLAs (service-level agreements). As covered in Chapter 4, the SDL process can be a specific framework such as ISA/IEC 62443-4-1, NIST SSDF, ISO/IEC 27034, or Microsoft SDL. Whichever process is followed, the company should have a documented policy stating the baseline and the cyber criteria required for release. There may be specific procedures and controls regarding which tools to use, what criteria is allowable for decision making, and who approves the release based on cyber risk. The software security process should also have some criteria for measurement and monitoring of an application or product's security posture.

It is common for suppliers, especially smaller companies or startups, to have a blend of secure development practices rather than follow a specific process framework. Be cautious when the response to a request for secure development evidence is an SOC 2 report and ISO 27001 certification since those processes and reports do not assess secure development practices. An SOC 2 report demonstrates the security and reporting controls for privacy, confidentiality, security, processing integrity, and availability. An ISO 27001 certification covers security policies, asset management, physical and environmental security, access control, incident management, and regulatory compliance. That evidence is valuable for other cybersecurity risks and may be required for cybersecurity compliance or regulation requirements, but it is not applicable to assess the security posture of secure development practices.

# Training

In security questionnaires, there is usually a question that asks if cybersecurity awareness training, which usually covers phishing and social engineering risks, is required for all employees. In a software supply chain security assessment, there should also be specific questions in regard to how the supplier trains its various teams such as IT, development, cloud operations, etc. As described in Chapter 11, these trainings should specifically address the secure development lifecycle process and also role-based training for topics such as secure coding and security testing. Smaller companies and startups should be held to the same training requirements as larger companies since there is no difference in risk to the product or service you are purchasing. However, one question that is rarely asked is "Have the application security teams completed the training before starting the project?" because there is little value for the team to have secure development training after they've developed the entire product or application.

---

## Supplier Control 06

Control SP-06: Request evidence of a supplier's training program for cybersecurity awareness, secure development lifecycle processes, secure coding, and security testing, along with the policy for mandatory training prior to development.

---

## Secure Development and Security Testing

During the development process, the supplier should utilize threat modeling, secure coding techniques such as peer reviews, and secure coding analysis (SCA) tools to evaluate code written by or included from open source and commercial vendors. During assessments, you should request evidence of threat modeling and secure coding practices that have been performed by the development team. Also request information as to which SCA tools are used and evidence that the tools have been utilized during the build process.

Assessment evidence should include the practices, tools, and reports that prove security testing was performed during builds and before the deployment or release. Security testing practices should include validation of security feature requirements, similar to how functional testing is done for other requirements. For example, there should be test cases performed on data protection requirements and OWASP Top 10 risks such as Broken Access Control. In addition to testing against security features, requirements, and risks, the supplier should provide evidence for other types of testing. As mentioned in Chapter 4, SAST and DAST tools provide effective use of secure testing but should not be the only security testing performed on a product or application.

**Supplier Control 07**

Control SP-07: Request evidence or a demonstration of a supplier's secure development practices that include threat modeling, secure coding practices, static code analysis, and security testing.

## Build Management, DevSecOps, and Release Management

As we saw in the SolarWinds hack of 2020, when a threat actor inserted malicious code into the software build process, build management practices are extremely important for software supply chain security. As previously described in Chapter 5, using a build integrity framework such as Google SLSA can provide specific controls and proper build management practices. During assessments, you should request evidence for which build tools were used, who is allowed to perform builds and where, how to confirm that code commits are valid before integration into a build or DevSecOps process flow, and the release management and approval practices associated with all levels of change from small to significant architecture adjustments.

DevSecOps and release management evidence should include code management and change management practices, software bills of materials (SBOMs), configuration changes, and changes made to the build and release processes. Evidence should also support that logs for tools and SIEM/SOAR systems have a log retention policy, that the logs are connected to off-site log repositories, and that the SIEM/SOAR system logs are inspected for unusual behavior and incidents.

**Supplier Control 08**

Control SP-08: Request evidence or a demonstration of a supplier's build management, DevSecOps, and release management practices, including tools, reports, processes, access controls, approvals, and logs for tools and event management systems.

## Scanning, Vulnerability Management, Patching, and SLAs

Third-party supplier assessments should always include questions and require evidence regarding scanning, vulnerability management, and patching. Frequent scanning of the source code, systems, environments, and networks must be conducted. Evidence of those policies, practices, reports, and scanning logs should be provided to you. Within the evidence, there should be a vulnerability disclosure policy and a vulnerability management procedure that describes how the supplier receives vulnerability reports, how it manages vulnerabilities in a timely fashion, and how it discloses vulnerabilities to customers and authorities.

Systems, environments, and applications must be patched to remediate any known vulnerabilities. There should be an SLA and a policy in regard to patching critical and high-risk vulnerabilities. Evidence of any internal SLAs or requirements should be provided by the supplier.

---

## Supplier Control 09

Control SP-09: Request evidence of a supplier's scanning, vulnerability management, and patching processes, including policies, procedures, reports, logs, and patching service-level agreements.

---

# Cloud Applications and Environments

For all cloud applications and environments used in the software supply chain, suppliers should provide evidence of management and hygiene, as discussed in Chapter 6. Evidence should include information about the appropriate people, processes, and technologies associated with the cloud environment, not just the infrastructure itself. For example, with regards to people and processes, suppliers must frequently review administrator privileges and practices along with private key management procedures. For technologies, suppliers should monitor their cloud providers and perform frequent checks to ensure that the environment remains correctly configured and secure by default.

Frequently, cloud suppliers introduce new tools or configuration options, which can change the security posture of cloud applications and services. Annual testing of cloud applications, configurations, and infrastructure must be performed by experienced penetration testers. Ask for evidence in the form of an AICPA SOC 2 Type 2 report or an ISO 27001 certification, which is not adequate for secure development processes, as mentioned previously, but is very applicable for cloud infrastructure. As described in Chapter 6, an SOC 2 Type 2 report is especially useful because it monitors the controls to safeguard customer data over a period of time for service commitments, requirements, and assurance.[9]

---

## Supplier Control 10

Control SP-10: Request evidence of a supplier's management practices and reports for cloud infrastructure, access controls, keys, configurations, testing, responsibilities, and service-level agreements.

---

# Development Services

If the supplier is going to provide you with any software or firmware development services, in addition to the secure development practices mentioned earlier in this chapter, there should be assessment questions related to code quality. The assessment will reveal if any adjustments may be required to the services or cyber agreements. For example, you should clearly define the responsibilities for ongoing development, testing, defect corrections, and vulnerability remediation.

Depending on where the software is used or sold, it may also be relevant to ask the location of the developers and if background checks have been performed on personnel, assuming that background checks are even allowed in that country. Evidence should include access control policies, mandatory multifactor authentication, SBOMs, and additional secure development practices, as mentioned in the previous sections.

---

## Supplier Control 11

Control SP-11: Request evidence of a supplier's development services, including code quality reports, test reports, and vulnerabilities. When applicable, request developer information such as locations and evidence of background checks.

---

# Manufacturing

Some suppliers may be providing third-party services such as flashing firmware or assembling products. Manufacturing suppliers that have direct access to the product should also be evaluated for risk of software or firmware compromise during the transportation, manufacturing, or distribution processes. For example, if you provide final firmware to a third-party supplier, that supplier should validate that the product has not been compromised.

The manufacturing process should also include final integrity checks prior to customer delivery. Validation and testing of this process should be performed at minimum annually, and the evidence of those tests should be made available as part of the assessment process. For further information regarding manufacturing security, refer to Chapter 10.

---

## Supplier Control 12

Control SP-12: Request evidence of a supplier's access controls and integrity checks for any personnel or process that has access to software or firmware.

---

# Cyber Agreements, Contracts, and Addendums

Although assessments help you to gain an understanding of a supplier's security posture, *cyber agreements* hold the supplier accountable and responsible for its ongoing security posture. Your cyber agreement should focus on the topics that were important to you in the assessment process. If you do not have a cyber agreement template, ask your legal team to work with you in adapting one for your organization, or you can reference an industry-specific template such as the one from the Edison Electric Institute.[10] When creating a cyber agreement, you will need to determine the minimum requirements and risks that you are willing to accept. Ideally you will have one cyber agreement for all supplier types, regardless of whether the supplier provides internal business applications or components to use in your commercial products.

Supplier agreements should include cyber conditions either in the main contract or in addendums. A master services agreement (MSA) or cyber agreement should include the following general cybersecurity items:

- IT security and management
- Data protection
- Requirements for data residency, defined as the physical or geographical location of data
- SLAs, including requirements for business continuity and resiliency
- Definitions of breach and incidents
- Incident management and notification
- Right to audit and assessment, usually annually or triggered in the case of data breaches, critical incidents, or critical vulnerabilities
- Safety and license obligations, including language for violations
- Cybersecurity insurance for breaches and other cyber incidents
- Indemnity, defined as compensation for loss or damage, or an exemption from liability

Specifically for software supply chain security, your agreements should also require the supplier to have the following elements:

- Secure development lifecycle
- Threat models
- Code analysis
- Security tests
- Penetration tests

- Software bills of materials (SBOMs)
- Vulnerability and patch management, including SLAs
- Vulnerability disclosure and notification
- Role-specific cybersecurity and application training

You can establish in the agreement what secure development lifecycle frameworks should be followed, such as ISA/IEC 62443-4-1, NIST SSDF, ISO/IEC 27034, or Microsoft SDL. You may also require the third party to have annual independent and third-party assessments such as SOC 2 and penetration tests for the full scope of the product. If you noted any deficiencies during the supplier assessment process, these should be added to the cyber agreement. For example, if no security tests were performed, then a condition could be made that a third-party company should conduct a penetration test and provide the results along with the remediations performed by the supplier.

A critical component within a cyber agreement includes the management of vulnerabilities and patches, along with the SLAs for that management. Usually, an MSA has some comments regarding software updates for new features or software defects, but vulnerability management, as well as the warranty and liability concerns in regard to vulnerability remediation, are often not addressed. For any on-premises software, IoT device, or operational technology (OT) device, the manufacturer should be providing updates and enhancements to the software for known vulnerabilities. In the situation where you are purchasing products through a value-added reseller (VAR), you may not have the ability in the reseller contracts to require vulnerability or patch notifications from the original manufacturer. In those cases, you should follow your organization's patch management policy to monitor the manufacturer for critical and high-risk vulnerabilities in the platforms, devices, and software.

Cyber agreements generally include an SLA for notification and remediation of critical and high-risk vulnerabilities. For fixes that are not available within the agreed timeline, contract language should state that notifications must be provided within the same SLA timelines. The industry standard is 30 days for critical vulnerabilities and 90 days for high-risk vulnerabilities, but medium and low vulnerabilities are not usually mentioned in the cyber agreement since they are rarely exploitable and thus are usually fixed in a future software update. Remediations in cloud and mobile applications can happen quickly, but for IoT and OT devices, there will be extensive testing required to ensure that hardware compatibility, backward compatibility, interoperability, and safety have been taken into consideration. In some cases, due to hardware dependencies or end-of-life components, patching may not be feasible and the device manufacturer can only recommend mitigations and compensating controls. SLAs should also account for longer timelines when vulnerabilities exist in the supplier's third-party components. For example, if a fourth-party library of chip firmware has a vulnerability, the supplier must wait until the fourth party makes the correction and releases it to the supplier.

Usually patch management may not be described in detail within a cyber agreement, but when over-the-air (OTA) updates or auto-updates are required, there should be specific language regarding downtime during the patching process. The language should specify that updates must be tested to prevent unexpected downtime while the software is being actively used, since downtime could result in safety issues or loss of business revenue.

The topic I see most often missed in an agreement is the software termination process and the cyber responsibilities of the supplier upon termination. If you continue to use a product or service after the agreement has expired or been terminated, security vulnerabilities may still place your organization at risk. Or if you've purchased commercial code libraries and the agreement does not allow for use after termination, the code may need to be removed from your product or application, leaving limited options for replacements.

In the agreement, you need to define what will happen if either party could not or would not continue the relationship. In some cases, a termination clause may include the cost for continuing support or updates. A termination clause may also require the supplier to keep code in escrow in the event of the supplier closing its business. Termination clauses should consider all areas of business continuity, business resilience, and lifecycle management.

If the event that a supplier cannot agree to the conditions stated in the agreement, then it is possible that its cybersecurity practices are not mature and you will need to invest in compensating controls up to and including the selection of another vendor.

---

### Supplier Control 13

Control SP-13: Incorporate cyber agreements into the supplier contracting process that include cyber risk and minimum security standards according to the purchasing organization's policies.

---

# Ongoing Supplier Management

A supplier's security posture may change over time. One would hope that the security posture continuously improves, but there are situations where the security posture may decline due to reasons such as supplier organizational realignment. To maintain competitiveness and innovation, supplier management should include the evaluation of other suppliers. However, there should be change management controls in place to prevent switching suppliers only for cost savings.

I recommend having critical supplier reviews at least quarterly and monitoring the vulnerability databases for any new disclosures that may not have been reported to you directly by your suppliers. As mentioned earlier, a supplier cyber risk management service can review the external-facing security posture and provide some alerting if something is of noticeable concern. The following sections describe the ongoing software supply chain management topics, which should include monitoring, supplier reviews, and the right to audit.

---

### Supplier Control 14

Control SP-14: Incorporate cyber topics and monitoring into the existing supplier management process. Monitoring and reviews should include vulnerabilities, data breaches, and supply chain issues and may require an audit or reassessment.

---

## Monitoring

Monitoring suppliers for health and vulnerabilities is common in the industry, but in regard to software supply chain security, the monitoring needs to be more specific. This should include monitoring of CVEs in the NVD or CNVD and monitoring for any potential breaches or other software supply chain issues. You can also leverage the SBOMs, which you requested in the agreement, for monitoring software components that could potentially create risk to your organization.

Suppliers may have cybersecurity pages or portals that you can monitor and register to be notified of updates to software, products, and vulnerabilities. One such way to monitor is through the common security advisor framework (CSAF) machine-readable files, which list a product's vulnerabilities. Ideally, these CSAF files would be used by your risk management platforms and asset management tools for alerts.

Either on the dark web or even on social sites such as YouTube, there may be instructions or videos on how to illegally access software and crack license keys. Some cyber risk management services include monitoring of the dark web for discussions or data in regard to suppliers or their products. This can include data such as customer details, personal identifiable information (PII), credit card data, intellectual property, and access to suppliers' environments.

## Supplier Reviews

Whether on a quarterly, biannual, or annual basis, a review of your critical suppliers should be an important part of your third-party management program. Some critical suppliers may be large organizations that choose not to participate in quarterly updates with smaller organizations. In this case, monitoring activities, as mentioned in the previous section, are more important than normal.

As part of your regular supplier review, be sure to cover the topics that were included in your cyber agreement. These would include vulnerability management, patch management, and SLAs. Use these meetings to discuss vulnerabilities and how the supplier managed certain events (i.e., Log4j or the latest critical vulnerability).

If you use a cyber risk monitoring service, you should discuss any changes you observed in the supplier's digital footprint. Take the opportunity to ask if there have been any changes to its cybersecurity processes or organization. You can also use this review time to inform the supplier of potential requests (either your own or your customers') if you have them. For example, if you need a software bill of materials or "country of origin" information, these meetings provide a direct opportunity for you to collect information on the supplier's software supply chain security.

## Right to Audit and Assess

Although many suppliers request to remove the "right to audit" or assessments from their contracts, this is an extremely important part of the supplier management process for software security. At a minimum, you should work with the supplier to allow audits for incidents containing your data. The audit costs should be paid for by your organization and usually are stipulated to have a mutually agreed-upon third party to perform the services. However, a supplier will often proactively hire a third-party auditor for any breach that has received media attention.

When there is a publicly known incident, data breach, or critical vulnerability, a supplier may document information on its website for its customers and submit reports to government authorities if required by law. This could be through security notifications, security bulletins, blog articles, or filings with government agencies or regulators. For example, after the incident on the Orion platform, SolarWinds wrote blog articles and emails on mitigations, platform updates, and how it updated its build management practices. This level of disclosure is higher than what is normally provided by companies after an incident or breach.

# Summary

This chapter discussed the details and controls for cyber assessments, cyber agreements, and supplier management. To start with, cyber assessments provide you with supplier responses and evidence to understand the supplier's security posture and potential cyber risks. Next, cyber agreements provide a common understanding on key topics including vulnerability, patch, and incident management. Lastly, the supplier security process requires management and monitoring to ensure the supplier's software supply chain is secure. In Chapter 10, I will discuss the software security risks seen within the manufacturing supply chain, which includes the significant dependencies on suppliers.

# References

1    "Operationalizing Vendor SCRM Template for SMBs Spreadsheet" (*https://www.cisa.gov/resources-tools/resources/operationalizing-vendor-scrm-template-smbs*), CISA, October 26, 2021.

2    US Cybersecurity & Infrastructure Security Agency (CISA) | National Risk Management Center, *Vendor Supply Chain Risk Management (SCRM) Template* (*https://www.cisa.gov/sites/default/files/publications/ICTSCRMTF_Vendor-SCRM-Template_508.pdf*), April 2021.

3    Enduring Security Framework, *Securing the Software Supply Chain: Recommended Practices Guide for Suppliers* (*https://media.defense.gov/2022/Oct/31/2003105368/-1/-1/0/SECURING_THE_SOFTWARE_SUPPLY_CHAIN_SUPPLIERS.PDF*), September 2022.

4    "NATF: Promote Excellence in the Reliable Operation of the Electric Transmission System" (*https://www.natf.net/industry-initiatives/supply-chain-industry-coordination*), North American Transmission Forum, accessed December 12, 2023.

5    "Downloading and Installing CSET" (*https://www.cisa.gov/downloading-and-installing-cset*), US Cybersecurity & Infrastructure Security Agency, accessed December 16, 2023.

6    "Trust Portal" (*https://trustportal.cisco.com/c/r/ctp/home.html*), Cisco, accessed December 12, 2023.

7    See "National Vulnerability Database" (*https://nvd.nist.gov*), NIST, accessed December 12, 2023; China National Vulnerability Database (*https://www.cnvd.org.cn*), accessed December 12, 2023; and "Known Exploited Vulnerabilities Catalog" (*https://www.cisa.gov/known-exploited-vulnerabilities-catalog*), CISA, accessed December 12, 2023.

8    An approach where organizations prioritize cloud applications, platforms, environments, and infrastructure over physical, on-premises, or hybrid models.

9    "A Guide to Understanding SOC 2 Reports" (*https://ermprotect.com/blog/how-soc-2-reports-safeguard-data-and-elevate-customer-confidence*), ERMProtect, accessed December 12, 2023.

10    Edison Electric Institute, *Model Procurement Contract Language Addressing Cybersecurity Supply Chain Risk* (*https://www.eei.org/-/media/Project/EEI/Documents/Issues-and-Policy/Model--Procurement-Contract.pdf*), October 2022.

# CHAPTER 10

# Manufacturing and Device Security

According to the World Economic Forum, the manufacturing sector has become one of the most targeted sectors for cyberattacks.[1] Usually, we attribute software supply chain security risk to something within the software development lifecycle, but the risk may exist in a compromised chip, component, or product through connectable IT, IoT, Industrial IoT (IIoT), or operational technology (OT) installed in your infrastructure. But even if you don't have a manufacturing program in your organization, risks can be introduced by your suppliers' manufacturing processes. This chapter will help you understand the overall risks in supply chain security for the products your organization purchases or produces.

When you consider all the physical and digital components, along with the processes used to build a device, there are hundreds, and potentially thousands, of opportunities for compromise. Each physical device, such as a laptop, usually has firmware, embedded software, and hardware components (e.g., motherboard, laptop screen). A printed circuit board assembly (PCBA), such as the one pictured in Figure 10-1, may have a dozen integrated circuit (IC) components, or chips, that support operation of the device, and many of them contain embedded code libraries at the time of purchase.[2]

The logic on these ICs can include cybersecurity flaws or intentional compromises from upstream suppliers, and they can result in breaches that are very difficult to detect and prevent. The following sections discuss the risks within the manufacturing process for ICs and devices, as well as ways to safeguard manufactured products.

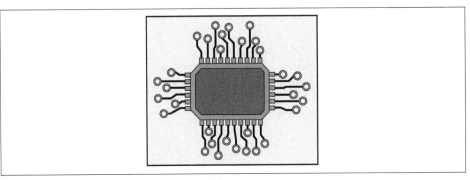

*Figure 10-1. Printed circuit board assembly*

# Suppliers and Manufacturing Security

As you have learned throughout Chapter 9, risks can originate from any supplier. A single error or intentional compromise in a device can lead to disastrous consequences, resulting in safety issues, data breaches, or product recalls. To limit the risk of a supply chain compromise, every product should undergo a thorough supply chain assessment and verification process of the activities described in the following list:

- Designing, developing, and testing the hardware and software components
- Operating manufacturing tools and processes
- Receiving supplier goods
- Examining integrated circuits, chips, and modules
- Installing firmware (also known as flashing) on components or devices
- Testing the assembly of printed circuit boards and the device
- Warehousing, shipping, and transporting the manufactured product

The supplier is not alone in the creation of the product. As shown in Figure 10-2, suppliers may also have participated in product design and creation as an original design manufacturer (ODM); they may private label an existing product; they may act in the role of electronic manufacturing service (EMS); or they may perform contract manufacturing (CM), where they design, test, manufacture, and repair products.

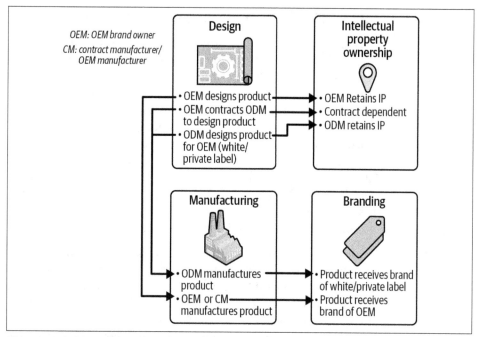

*Figure 10-2. Manufacturing relationships*

When you are evaluating manufacturers, you should consider what cybersecurity knowledge, experience, and certifications they have in their organizational and manufacturing processes and locations. The manufacturer should have a strong IT cybersecurity and data protection posture by following standards such as the ISO 2700x information security, cybersecurity, and privacy protection standards, along with ISA/IEC 62443 industrial automation and control system standards. If the manufacturer conforms to the NIST Cybersecurity Framework, it should also implement the adjunct publication, NIST IR 8183, *Cybersecurity Framework Manufacturing Profile*, within its organization.[3]

## Manufacturing and Device Security Control 01

Control MDS-01: Validate that manufactured devices were designed, developed, manufactured, tested, and shipped using information security, cybersecurity, and data security best practices.

# Equipment, Systems, and Network Security Configurations

By following information security and data protection standards, the manufacturer should have secured its digital and physical infrastructure using policies, processes, procedures, and technologies such as defense-in-depth to keep malicious actors from infiltrating its environments. As described in Control IS-10 from Chapter 3, the manufacturing and supply chain environments must be inventoried and monitored for threats. Manufacturing environments have a number of unique devices and systems, as shown in Figure 10-3, that also need to be managed similar to typical IT assets. The assets in manufacturing often include manufacturing execution systems (MES), human machine interfaces (HMIs), programmable logic controllers (PLCs), and OT, IT, and IIoT products. The assets should be deployed using secure configurations, integrations, and best practices, paying special attention to securing the communication protocols, which may not be encrypted in legacy devices.

IT security is just as important in manufacturing environments as it is in corporate environments. The network strategy should include segmentation and technology controls to secure and, where applicable, separate the corporate systems from the manufacturing systems. Manufacturing environments should also implement additional controls and zero-trust strategies on systems and equipment, such as disabling USB storage, adding tamper detection on equipment, and incorporating patches and updates into the manufacturing maintenance schedules. However, the threat landscape for firmware attacks is quickly increasing, and thus constant attention should be given to internet-facing devices and systems.[4]

To further secure the manufacturing environment, wireless capabilities should be set to allow equipment such as autonomous robots, barcode scanners, and radio frequency identification (RFID) readers to operate, but the controls should prevent cell phones or nonapproved devices from accessing the network. Along with general IT management technologies, the manufacturer should also leverage tools specifically designed to secure and monitor OT, IoT, and IIoT devices within the plant.

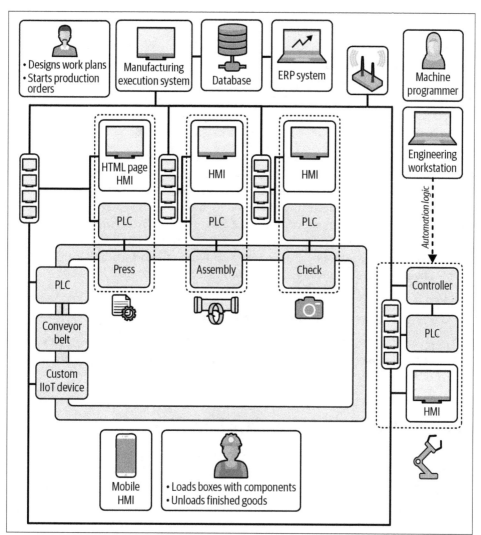

*Figure 10-3. Manufacturing line example*

## Physical Security

Manufacturing involves many people, systems, and processes, as shown previously in Figure 10-3. Physical security controls ensure that only approved personnel have access to manufacturing sites, production floors, warehouses, distribution centers, and any other physical locations where supporting processes are performed. Unapproved persons pose a significant threat to supply chain security if they have physical access to the equipment, systems, and networks within a location.

Manufacturers should have detailed policies and procedures for physical security that must contain the instructions employees, contractors, and visitors are required to follow. This should include, for example, a policy that does not allow visitors to be unaccompanied in the manufacturing plant or in any company location. To stop or prevent potential supply chain compromise and enhance the defense-in-depth strategy, everyone must be trained in the physical security procedures for that location. Penetration testing of the physical controls should be performed at locations where supply chain security can greatly impact a product or service.

---

### Manufacturing and Device Security Control 02

Control MDS-02: Institute clear policies and procedures for access to secured facilities. Train all personnel on the physical controls and procedures. Maintain and test physical security controls for the organization and locations.

---

# Code, Software, and Firmware Integrity

A single device, whose manufacturing cycle is presented in Figure 10-4, will often be produced by many organizations, people, and processes interacting with the code, software, firmware, and components. With so many opportunities for compromise to the software supply chain, it's necessary for all parties to have control points and tests to verify code, software, or firmware integrity throughout the entire product lifecycle, and to also include counterfeit checks for each of the physical components.

According to the research paper "Stealthy Dopant-Level Hardware Trojans: Extended Version," it is possible to manipulate components during the fabrication process where the modifications would not be detected using the standard visual or integrity checks.[5] Such a compromise requires extensive skill and access, so I wouldn't consider manipulation during chip fabrication to be a major threat, but the best safeguard is to perform integrity checks along the process. There are various ways to check for integrity throughout the process, such as comparing checksums, as mentioned in "Repeatability and Reproducibility" on page 88. The following sections provide additional guidance on validating integrity along the manufacturing process.

---

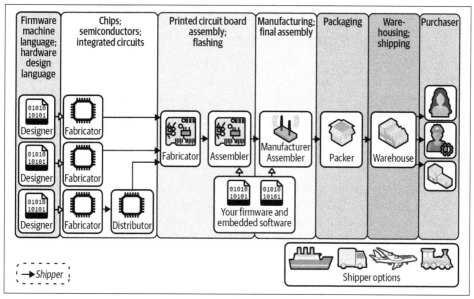

| Firmware machine language; hardware design language | Chips; semiconductors; integrated circuits | Printed circuit board assembly; flashing | Manufacturing; final assembly | Packaging | Ware-housing; shipping | Purchaser |

Designer | Fabricator

Designer | Fabricator

Designer | Fabricator | Distributor

Fabricator | Assembler

Manufacturer Assembler

Packer

Warehouse

Your firmware and embedded software

Shipper

Shipper options

*Figure 10-4. Many opportunities for compromise*

## Tests for Integrity

A detailed hardware bill of materials (HBOM) should list all components but also include suppliers, fabricators, manufacturers, and assemblers who have provided materials and components and performed activities toward the creation of the physical product. For each company identified in the HBOM, it should have performed quality and integrity checks during each transition between companies and through each step of the process. As an example, the logistics actions represented by the arrows in Figure 10-4 introduce risk when information or components are shipped digitally or physically.

Using the information provided in a software bill of materials (SBOM), suppliers and customers should always cryptographically authenticate any code received from another party, including internal code transfers between departments and work-groups. Similar to quality checks, integrity testing procedures should evaluate components or devices from each developer, fabricator, distributor, assembler, and manufacturer. Additional tests, which are created specifically by the engineers who design the manufacturing lines, should confirm the integrity of the components or products through each step of manufacturing and assembly.

> ## Manufacturing and Device Security Control 03
>
> Control MDS-03: Using the information available in the hardware bill of materials (HBOM) and software bill of materials (SBOM), authenticate the components and conduct integrity checks throughout the manufacturing process on any chips, integrated circuits, components, firmware, and embedded software.

## Counterfeits

Counterfeit chips are not a new problem, but with the chip shortages in 2020–2022, there is an increase in fake parts and disreputable sellers. Fake chips can come in several forms: previously failed chips, recycled chips, counterfeit chips, and cloned chips. Counterfeit chips can lead to failed quality tests, product recalls, and safety concerns. Worst of all, they may also include vulnerable or malicious code that can result in compromise of a product.

In order to reduce the likelihood of receiving counterfeit parts, an organization should ensure in advance that the suppliers and manufacturers are reputable, trustworthy, and preferably following a standard such as ISO 20243-1:2023, "Open Trusted Technology Provider Standard (O-TTPS)," as described in Chapter 2. Sometimes a supplier may be a broker or reseller, thereby sourcing components or products from other parties. This situation is highly susceptible to counterfeit or malicious components, so manufacturers should insist on anticounterfeit measures in the components and packaging. These measures may be in the form of microscopic or chemical markings, electrical or optical watermarks, or unique embedded cryptographic identities.

Components and products should always be sent within tamper-resistant packaging. The supplier should provide, through a separate communications channel, what the tamper-resistant packaging should look like and how to perform authentication and integrity checks. To truly reduce counterfeits, however, the receiver must perform the verification checks upon the receipt of goods to ensure the materials are authentic. When materials are received, they must be carefully inspected to identify compromised components. This includes inspecting packaging, verifying serial numbers, sampling components, and performing quality and integrity tests.

> ## Manufacturing and Device Security Control 04
>
> Control MDS-04: Verify that chips, components, and products are authentic before using them in the manufacturing process.

# Chain of Custody

*Chain of custody*, defined as the record of the people and organizations that possessed an item, is an important concept for establishing the integrity of products and their underlying components. Figure 10-4 demonstrates that many parties exist along the supply chain, but there may not be a mechanism for tracking the provenance and chain of custody, referred to as *traceability*, for each component from its origin to the final product. As mentioned previously in Chapter 8, the country of origin, original creator, or provenance may not be clearly evident, but the moment a component or part appears in the supply chain, traceability can begin.

Traceability can exist in documents, in systems, and in the form of barcodes, QR codes, RFID tags, and NFC (near-field communication) on products, packaging, cases, and pallets. These tracking mechanisms, along with tamper-evident packaging, seals, markings, or other methods, reduce the risk of tampering along the supply chain. The chain of custody documentation, along with a description of the tamper-evident mechanisms used for the product, can provide a level of assurance and attestation, which may be required by the customer.

---

### Manufacturing and Device Security Control 05

Control MDS-05: Trace the physical and digital parts, components, and products through the supply chain to capture the chain of custody for the product.

---

# Device Protection Measures

During the design, development, and manufacturing processes, organizations can strengthen device security by implementing firmware and hardware-based security protections such as digital signatures, secure hardware and software modules, and device authentication. These protections, as described in the following sections, also improve the security posture of the final product.

---

### Manufacturing and Device Security Control 06

Control MDS-06: Implement hardware, firmware, and embedded software protection measures within the device.

---

# Firmware Public Key Infrastructure (PKI)

The foundation for device protection starts with digitally signing firmware and embedded software using a firmware public key infrastructure (PKI) and is similar to the software code signing described in Chapter 5. Without code signing, a malicious actor can replace the embedded software or firmware images without any indication that a change has occurred. In 2020, Eclypsium released research showing unsigned firmware was on devices such as network adapters, graphics cards, USB devices, and more.[6] The company demonstrated that firmware in modern computers could easily be replaced with a malicious version.

A number of IoT devices have unsigned firmware due to the architecture requirements necessary for verifying signatures at boot time, or due to a lack of infrastructure for firmware signing. Organizations should implement firmware signing practices for the devices they produce and require all purchased products to have signed firmware.

# Hardware Root of Trust

Cryptographic hash comparison and digital code signature validation techniques, as mentioned in Chapter 5, can verify integrity, but for IoT and OT devices, a *hardware root of trust* is another method that should be leveraged by manufacturers. A hardware root of trust, of which one type is a hardware trusted platform module (TPM), contains the keys used for cryptographic functions and enables a secure boot process.

A TPM conforms to a secure cryptoprocessor international standard, ISO/IEC 11889, and is also the name for a microcontroller chip following that standard.[7] Both software- and hardware-based authentication are subject to supply chain vulnerabilities, but a hardware root of trust presents special challenges for manufacturers. Like any hardware, a hardware root of trust must contain testing interfaces to verify integrity during manufacturing. However, due to the high levels of security required, the interfaces and test processes must be explicitly designed for the device.

# Secure Boot

For many years, each original equipment manufacturer (OEM) had its own basic input and output system firmware, usually referred to as a BIOS, to perform hardware initialization during the booting process. Now on most modern computers, the Unified Extensible Firmware Interface (UEFI) standard has replaced the OEMs' BIOS interface between operating systems and firmware. As shown in Figure 10-5, secure boot is a UEFI security feature that adds a layer of protection to the preboot process by maintaining a cryptographically signed list of authorized binaries to run, or forbidden binaries to not run, at boot time. If properly designed, this ensures that the forbidden firmware will not even load.

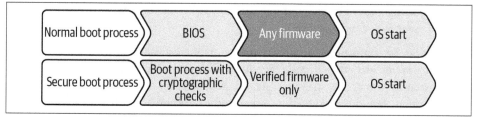

*Figure 10-5. Normal boot versus secure boot sequence*

Secure boot requires UEFI-supported hardware on the device to support the enhanced boot sequence and cryptographic checks necessary to verify the firmware. However, due to its widespread adoption, UEFI has become a popular attack surface because once a threat actor has compromised it with malicious code, they can launch any code before the operating system or any security software starts.[8]

## Secure Element

A secure element is a chip or component designed to prevent unauthorized access, run a limited set of applications, and store cryptographic and confidential data. Product design teams use secure elements, in the form of SIM cards, smart cards, microSD, or chips, within cell phones, tablets, hardware cryptowallets, wearables, and other IoT devices. The secure element acts as a vault to protect the applications and data from malware attacks against the device's operating system and other components.

## Device Authentication

IT, IoT, and OT devices can include security features that prove the authenticity of the device through incoming requests from an external system or another device. This ensures that only authorized devices can connect to specific networks, services, or sites. Device authentication is a basic requirement for zero-trust architecture and should always be enforced in addition to strong user authentication.

## Summary

Software supply chain security extends past the moment software development is complete. As shown throughout this chapter, compromise during the manufacturing process can occur in the locations, equipment, systems, and even the final products. Cybersecurity controls and security measures must be in place for not only the IT environments, but also for the manufacturing systems and networks. This must include physical security measures at the manufacturing plants, distribution centers, and suppliers.

From the moment software or firmware leaves development, the authentication and integrity checks should exist within each step to prove that the code has not been compromised. With so many participants and threat opportunities in fabrication, manufacturing, and logistics, maintaining traceability data is required to confirm the chain of custody for the product.

Products can be compromised by malicious actors if the proper device security is not in place, beginning with digital code signing for all embedded software and firmware. Device security protection measures such as secure boot, secure elements, and device authentication should be designed into the product and incorporated within the manufacturing process. In Chapter 11, I will discuss how people in manufacturing and all phases of the product lifecycle have an enormous impact on the software supply chain.

## References

1   Mansur Abilkasimov, Dawn Cappelli, Filipe Beato, and Giulia Moschetta, "Why Cybersecurity Risks Matter—and How to Raise Security" (*https://www.weforum.org/agenda/2023/03/why-cybersecurity-in-manufacturing-matters-to-us-all*), World Economic Forum, March 27, 2023.

2   A printed circuit board (PCB) is without any components or chips; a PCBA contains all the components and chips required for the board to function.

3   Keith Stouffer, Timothy Zimmerman, Cheeyee Tang, Joshua Lubell, Jeffrey Cichonski, and John McCarthy, *Cybersecurity Framework Manufacturing Profile* (*https://doi.org/10.6028/nist.ir.8183*), NIST, September 2017.

4   Bill Toulas, "SonicWall Devices Infected by Malware That Survives Firmware Upgrades" (*https://www.bleepingcomputer.com/news/security/sonicwall-devices-infected-by-malware-that-survives-firmware-upgrades*), Bleeping Computer, March 9, 2023.

5   Georg T. Becker, Francesco Regazzoni, Christof Paar, and Wayne P. Burleson, "Stealthy Dopant-Level Hardware Trojans: Extended Version" (*https://doi.org/10.1007/s13389-013-0068-0*), *Journal of Cryptographic Engineering* 4, no. 1 (April 2014): 19–31.

6   Eclypsium, *Perilous Peripherals: The Hidden Dangers Inside Windows & Linux Computers* (*https://eclypsium.com/wp-content/uploads/2020/02/Eclypsium-Unsigned-Peripheral-Firmware-Research.pdf*), 2020.

7   "ISO/IEC 11889-1:2015—Trusted Platform Module Library" (*https://www.iso.org/standard/66510.html*), ISO, accessed December 12, 2023.

8   "LoJax UEFI Rootkit Used in Cyberespionage" (*https://www.trendmicro.com/vinfo/us/security/news/cyber-attacks/lojax-uefi-rootkit-used-in-cyberespionage*), Trend Micro, October 1, 2018.

# CHAPTER 11

# People in the Software Supply Chain

There is a saying that security is only as good as its weakest link, and as demonstrated in real-life security breaches, in case after case dating back to the earliest hackers, humans are consistently the weakest link. We are the ones making decisions on how the systems are designed, we select or write the code, and we bring it all together to release it to our customers. Until all code and systems are free of vulnerabilities—which will never happen—we must expect imperfection but strive to improve ourselves in the journey to create more secure applications and products.

Throughout the book, there have been many areas where a person's role in software supply chain security is a factor. Different frameworks such as NIST SSDF, ISA/IEC 62443-4-1 SDL, and NERC CIP provide requirements and controls to lower the risk of compromise. These requirements include training, governance, management, policies, and procedures. Your organization should continuously perform the practices and controls in this chapter—not only once a year or when a new person joins the organization.

According to a 2022 study by ThriveDX, we have seen cybersecurity awareness grow to 97% in companies, but general awareness training is just the start.[1] One way to encourage engagement and adoption of cybersecurity practices is through mandatory cybersecurity training, security champions programs, and internal certifications, as described in this chapter, or external certifications, as shown in Table 11-1.

*Table 11-1. External cybersecurity certifications relevant to software supply chain security*

| Issuing organization | Credential abbreviation | Credential title |
| --- | --- | --- |
| ISACA | CISM[a] | Certified Information Security Manager |
| ISC2 | CCSP[b] | Certified Cloud Security Professional |
| ISC2 | CISSP[c] | Certified Information Systems Security Professional |
| ISC2 | CSSLP[d] | Certified Secure Software Lifecycle Professional |
| CompTIA | PenTest+[e] | CompTIA PenTest+ |
| CompTIA | Security+[f] | CompTIA Security+ |
| EC-Council | CEH[g] | EC-Council Certified Ethical Hacker |

a  "CISM" (*https://www.isaca.org/credentialing/cism*), ISACA, accessed February 27, 2023.
b  "CCSP—Certified Cloud Security Professional" (*https://www.isc2.org/Certifications/CCSP*), ISC2, accessed February 26, 2023.
c  "CISSP—Certified Information Systems Security Professional" (*https://www.isc2.org/Certifications/CISSP*), ISC2, accessed February 26, 2023.
d  "CSSLP—The Industry's Premier Secure Software Development Certification" (*https://www.isc2.org/Certifications/CSSLP*), ISC2, accessed February 26, 2023.
e  "CompTIA PenTest+" (*https://www.comptia.org/certifications/pentest*), CompTIA, accessed February 26, 2023.
f  "CompTIA Security+" (*https://www.comptia.org/certifications/security*), CompTIA, accessed February 26, 2023.
g  "CEH—Certified Ethical Hacker" (*https://www.eccouncil.org/train-certify/certified-ethical-hacker-ceh*), EC-Council, accessed February 26, 2023.

To build a security-minded organization, education using books, videos, courses, and online training for the different roles in the software supply chain security process is extremely valuable and worth the investment. For example, Todd Barnum's book *The Cybersecurity Manager's Guide: The Art of Building Your Security Program* lays the groundwork for a cybersecurity organization, as described in the following section.[2]

# Cybersecurity Organizational Structures

A discussion on people in the software supply chain starts with you and the team you represent. You may be in IT or OT security, application security, product security, audit, or compliance. You may not be a dedicated security practitioner, but if you have the responsibility or accountability for cybersecurity risks or controls in your organization, you are part of the cybersecurity organizational structure.

Typically an established organization has a cybersecurity leader, often titled chief information security officer (CISO) or chief security officer (CSO) if the person also has the security responsibility of the organization's products or services. The security team is accountable and responsible for the cybersecurity risks, policies, procedures, and controls throughout the organization. Often, this team leads the security culture and awareness campaigns within the organization and addresses questions from external parties such as customers and government agencies. The security team often holds external certifications such as CISSP or CISM, and I encourage anyone responsible for application security or secure development to also obtain the CSSLP certification.

---

## People Control 01

Control PPL-01: Establish and maintain a corporate security organization with experienced and well-trained cybersecurity resources. Encourage certification and continuing education of your security staff.

---

# Security Champions

You can extend the reach of your security organization by creating a security champions program. Security champions—people from functional teams who support or lead others to strengthen an organization's security posture—act as liaisons between security and functional teams, encouraging cooperation and communication. Champions can come from R&D, IT, operations, procurement, manufacturing, or anywhere in the organization.

To build a security champions program, first identify people in the organization with a particular interest in cybersecurity, and provide them with the basic cybersecurity training mentioned earlier in this chapter. Then, nurture their interest with advanced cybersecurity training, a security champions community, security working groups, security projects, and communications regarding security initiatives and activities.

Maintaining the security champions' interest is an important way to keep the program thriving. You can design internal certifications or badges for champions in order to recognize their achievements in special topics or skills such as secure design, secure development, secure testing, penetration testing, and manufacturing security, to name a few. Some organizations identify internal certifications or rankings using Olympic levels (e.g., bronze, silver, gold) or martial arts belts (e.g., white, yellow, brown, black). An approach for leveling up would be to present on security topics, create security-related innovations, and take on the responsibility of training others in cybersecurity. A good security champions program will evolve over time and is a major step to increasing and maintaining cybersecurity awareness throughout the entire organization.

---

## People Control 02

Control PPL-02: Establish and maintain a security champions community to engage the organization, raise awareness, expand cybersecurity knowledge, and improve the adoption of cybersecurity principles and policies.

---

# Cybersecurity Awareness and Training

There is no shortage of cybersecurity awareness content and training courses. Free materials are obtainable from many places, such as Amazon's cybersecurity awareness training, which is available in multiple languages.[3] A strong cybersecurity awareness and training program should include training on social engineering attacks (e.g., phishing and all its various forms, email hacking, pretexting, and more, as shown in Table 11-2).[4] The purpose of most attacks is theft or to gain access to accounts, and for some attacks, there is the chance of installing malicious software on devices.

*Table 11-2. Examples of social engineering attacks*

| Attack type | Description |
| --- | --- |
| Phishing | Email mimicking a trusted source but containing malicious links or attachments, and generally sent to a wide audience. |
| Spear phishing | Phishing email specifically targeted to an individual using personal information, for example by mimicking a person's bank. |
| Vishing | Voice phone calls intended to gather confidential information such as credit cards or account passwords. |
| Smishing | SMS texts, often containing malicious links, intended to gather confidential information such as credit cards or account passwords. |
| Email or SMS hacking | By posing as the target, persuades service providers to give control of someone's email or phone number. |
| URL typosquatting | Owning URLs with similar spellings or hidden characters in the URL address to mimic trusted websites and links intended to capture login or personal information. |
| Pretexting | Operating a made-up scenario through email, phone call, or text for the purpose of gathering confidential information such as credit cards or account passwords. |
| Scareware | Pushing pop-ups, windows, or notifications, sometimes in the form of a virus or malware alert, to scare a user into taking action. |
| Access tailgating (physical breach) | An unauthorized person following an authorized person into a restricted area, creating a physical breach. |
| Quid pro quo | Offering something for another thing such as a hacked license in exchange for money. |
| Deepfake[a] | Using a form of artificial intelligence (AI) to create believable, realistic videos, pictures, or audio of events that never happened to simulate an individual. Poses a threat to the public across national security, law enforcement, financial, and societal domains. |
| Disinformation | Releasing intentionally false information with the purpose of deceiving its recipients. This differs from misinformation, which is false information spread without the intention to deceive its recipients. If a decision is based on false information, then the decision may not be in the interest of the individual or company for which they work. |

a   US Department of Homeland Security, *Increasing Threat of Deepfake Identities* (*https://www.dhs.gov/sites/default/files/ publications/increasing_threats_of_deepfake_identities_0.pdf*), 2021.

Continuous awareness and training is critical for highlighting new tactics and techniques performed by malicious actors, and to both improve security and limit liability, many companies require employees to take specific training annually. Your organization can also purchase phishing training tools to test awareness by sending false emails and texts to employees and contractors. These tools can then provide immediate feedback and guidance to anyone falling prey to misleading links or requests. You can even customize the false emails and texts to mimic automated emails from tools your organization owns, such as a GitHub source code management system.

---

### People Control 03

Control PPL-03: Provide a cybersecurity training and awareness program for all roles in the organization. Track completion of mandatory and optional courses.

---

# Development Team

Although some university computer science programs have added cybersecurity to their curricula, those classes are often not mandatory, up to date, or directly associated with the field someone may choose, such as cloud development. Until the educational systems mandate cybersecurity coursework for all technology fields, cybersecurity will be treated as an elective rather than a critical part of the software development lifecycle.

Without cybersecurity education or experience, senior software developers and architects can make the same cybersecurity mistakes as a junior software developer. It is important to require annual development team training and continuing education since tools, security features, and vulnerabilities evolve quickly. Organizations should take responsibility for providing up-to-date education, training, and the events necessary to increase application and product security skills and knowledge, as described in the following sections.

## Secure Development Lifecycle (SDL)

A secure development lifecycle (SDL) is a set of principles that dictate design, coding, build, release, and maintenance techniques that help ensure finished software has a minimum level of security. At the time of this book's publication, two of the most prominent SDL guidelines are from ISA/IEC 62443-4-1 and NIST SSDF, both discussed in Chapter 4.

These SDL systems can be complex, and adoption should be accompanied by training. SDL training is not only for software developers—it should be taken by everyone accountable for products or applications, including management. If your organization does not have application or product security training available through a third-party provider, the Linux Foundation, Microsoft, and SAFECode provide free training materials.[5] You can also purchase training from vendors that specialize in application security.

Secure development is tightly tied to the particular technology platform and software tools being used, and the SDL training should reflect that. The platforms, such as cloud, IoT, OT, and mobile, all have specific and unique security requirements. Therefore, any SDL training must be designed for the software's specific use cases.

A comprehensive training program for development processes and procedures should include thorough training on the software workbench tools used in the development lifecycle. An organization should have role-based training curricula specifically designed for the activities people perform on the project (e.g., developer, tester, build manager), and the organization should monitor the completion of the training curriculum. Ideally, the training should be completed prior to the start of any projects or activities.

Although secure coding and secure testing are part of a comprehensive SDL training program, I mention them here to highlight their importance. Training can be found for secure coding techniques based on their specific programming languages, and also covering topics such as debugging flags, hardcoded objects, and potential security vulnerabilities. Courses can also include the OWASP Top 10, the top CWEs, threat modeling, and the MITRE ATT&CK framework. It is very helpful to augment traditional online or classroom training with hands-on labs where developers have the opportunity to practice secure coding techniques.

After the code is written, a secure development lifecycle requires code reviews, and thus training for those reviews should cover topics such as giving effective feedback, concerns to watch for, and how to identify cybersecurity risk. SDL training should also include the teaching of proper procedures to ensure software integrity throughout the development lifecycle. This training should cover processes such as verifying signatures and authenticity, access controls for operators and administrators of development systems, and code commits; vetting and managing open source code and licenses as well as secure testing techniques; using anonymized data sets; and more.

## Source Code Management

Protecting source code should be among the highest priorities, as described in Chapter 7, for any development and operations team. However, there are some basic approaches involving people that should be observed. First, a tool that allows for logging, tracing, and undoing any activity related to the source code files (e.g., view, download, modifications, deletions, etc.) is essential, and the user information for that tool should be logged. Second, someone should be monitoring the activity of users as it relates to source code. Third, clear policies and procedures for configuration and use of the source code system should be available and well known.

One of the most common mistakes leading to data loss is the accidental storage of source code and private keys on public code repositories. As part of granting access to code repositories, development team members must be trained in the specific policy and procedures for their respective roles in source code management. Procedures and training should, at a minimum, include uploading code (i.e., code commits or check-ins), access control, data classification, intellectual property protection, and open source code management.

## DevSecOps and Cloud

Development and security operations (DevSecOps) is an emerging method for quickly changing, testing, and releasing program features. DevSecOps represents a significant improvement over prior methodologies in adding security as a core software engineering activity and product release requirement. There is no shortage of cloud security and DevSecOps training available, such as the training located on O'Reilly's Learning platform, but detailed training is dependent on the technologies used in the organization.

## Capture-the-Flag Events

Ongoing awareness and training is key for upskilling development teams with regards to ever-evolving threats and vulnerabilities. To put learning into practice in a safe environment, *capture-the-flag* (CTF) events are staged competitions that give developers, testers, security engineers, and other technical experts the opportunity to find hidden, intentionally planted vulnerabilities and weaknesses. Teams or individuals who successfully exploit the vulnerabilities locate the symbolic "flag" that signifies successful completion for each challenge in the competition.[6,7] Challenges are typically sorted by difficulty level (e.g., beginner, intermediate, advanced), and the participants score more points based on the difficulty of the challenge and their speed in solving it.

Organizations can sponsor internal CTFs, or players can join external CTFs sponsored by companies, organizations, and conferences. Development teams can also dedicate time specifically to penetration testing each other's code. The competition and the resulting rewards for effective use of skills can foster camaraderie, a positive security culture, and continued focus on secure development.

# Third-Party Suppliers

As part of a robust software supply chain process, third-party and nth-party suppliers should also have awareness and training as required for their responsibilities. Contracts and agreements with suppliers should include the ability to review the supplier's training program. Suppliers should be able to provide evidence to prove that their people have been trained on administration duties, data classification, and other controls noted throughout this book.

# Manufacturing and Distribution

Within a manufacturing site or distribution center, there is potential for software or firmware compromise, including on the production line itself. All personnel in contact with the systems and processes for creating, building, and assembling products should be trained to recognize and defend against cybersecurity compromise.

One approach to reducing software supply chain risk in the manufacturing and distribution environments is aligning the situations and activities normally seen in these environments. For example, a campaign on phishing emails is not effective for personnel who do not have a corporate email account, but a campaign discussing the importance of not sharing assigned logins and passwords is relevant when there are multiple people working on the same production line.

The following is a list of training topics intended for manufacturing and distribution personnel, systems, and processes:

- Physical security
- Reviewing and confirming the credentials of all personnel on site, especially a vendor's field service representative
- OT and IIoT cybersecurity basics
- Login and password management policies for the systems in manufacturing and distribution, such as HMIs, PLCs, OT, and IIoT
- Malware, ransomware, and viruses
- Data security, intellectual property, and ethics
- Maintaining software and firmware integrity
- Tamper-evident and tamper-proof processes
- Chain-of-custody and logistics security
- Maintenance and patching for cybersecurity vulnerabilities
- Responding to suspected cybersecurity incidents

When designing a training program, recognize there are special conditions that may apply to an organization's manufacturing and distribution staff. These conditions may include technical knowledge, temporary staff, turnover rate of permanent staff, language requirements, and access to the organization's systems, such as manufacturing, test, or lab equipment. When delivering the cybersecurity training, follow the approach and frequency used for safety training. Repetition of cybersecurity training is important to maintain diligence and safeguard against cybersecurity compromise.

In addition to the personnel working the production lines, there are other important roles to train and educate on cybersecurity within the manufacturing and distribution environments. These roles include manufacturing engineers, industrial engineers, managers, network engineers, and IT/OT security resources. Training and certifications on ISA/IEC 62443 provide comprehension of industrial automation and control system (IACS) assessments, design, implementation, operations, and maintenance.[8]

# Customer Projects and Field Services

In the circumstance where people are working on a customer's project, location, or system, you should require personnel to take specialized cybersecurity training for any activities that may introduce risk to the customers or compromise the software supply chain. Training topics can include any of the following:

- Alerting the customer and your organization if any unusual behavior or insecure situation is detected

- Maintaining safe and secure practices when accessing (physically or virtually) a location or system

- Only using equipment, software, or procedures approved by the customer and your organization

- Following procedures, such as scanning or checking the integrity of files, before using or transferring files

# End Users

This chapter would not be complete without mentioning the end user's part in the software supply chain. It is unreasonable to expect end users to have a detailed understanding of security practices, so it is imperative that the product teams make it as easy as possible for them to use software securely.

Education is a great start. Although it is not possible to require end users to take training or read the documentation, your organization can design the products and services to increase cybersecurity awareness and be secure by default. End-user security awareness can be increased through focused documentation, tool tips and help instructions for technical topics, and special videos to describe the security features.

But even with education, people can make mistakes. Therefore, product teams should set built-in features and configurations to assist users in securely operating the product or application.

# Summary

The final link in a strong software supply chain is the cybersecurity posture of the people who take part in it. Detailed training curricula for development teams, suppliers, manufacturing, and services should be available for the tools, technologies, processes, and procedures in use by everyone. The training and awareness plans can be overseen by an experienced cybersecurity organization and promoted by security champions throughout the organization.

Each one of us must be aware of the implications of our actions and strive constantly to observe correct software supply chain practices. With a holistic view of all parts in the software supply chain, organizations around the world can increase their security posture and defend against the malicious actors who threaten our systems, our data, and our lives.

It has been my honor to lead you through software supply chain security. Thank you for investing your time and energy toward this very important topic. This is one of the fastest evolving areas of cybersecurity, with new and changed frameworks, documents, regulations, ideas, and links released daily. I encourage you to stay up to date on software supply chain security by signing up for my newsletter (*https://www.supplychainsecurity.pro/sign-up*). You can also contact me using *cassie@supplychainsecurity.pro* to send updates, feedback, and corrections, schedule a meeting, or request me as a speaker or guest.

# References

1   "Study Shows Increased Maturity in Cybersecurity Awareness Programs and Higher Level of Security at Most Companies" (*https://www.hstoday.us/subject-matter-areas/cybersecurity/study-shows-increased-maturity-in-cybersecurity-awareness-programs-and-higher-level-of-security-at-most-companies*), Homeland Security Today, September 6, 2022.

2   Todd Barnum, *The Cybersecurity Manager's Guide: The Art of Building Your Security Program* (O'Reilly, 2021).

3   Amazon Cybersecurity Awareness Training (*https://learnsecurity.amazon.com/en/index.html*), accessed February 27, 2023.

4   Social engineering is any attempt or method to manipulate someone into providing sensitive or confidential information or access.

5   See "Secure Software Development Fundamentals Courses" (*https://openssf.org/ training/courses*), OpenSSF, accessed December 12, 2023; "Microsoft SDL Core Training Classes" (*https://www.microsoft.com/en-us/download/details.aspx?id=16420*), Microsoft, accessed December 12, 2023; and "SAFECode Training" (*https://safe code.org/training*), SAFECode, accessed December 12, 2023.

6   Flags are typically unique codes, files, source code snippets, or pieces of hardware on a network.

7   Challenges can be of many types, such as web application vulnerabilities, code vulnerabilities, reverse engineering, forensic investigations, and cryptography.

8   "ISA/IEC 62443 Cybersecurity Certificate Program" (*https://www.isa.org/certifica tion/certificate-programs/cybersecurity*), International Society of Automation, accessed March 6, 2023.

# Security Controls

## Infrastructure Security Controls

Control IS-01: Implement policies, processes, and controls required for creating, configuring, updating, and operating environments.

Control IS-02: Log and monitor events such as access control, access elevation, permissions modification, and object execution.

Control IS-03: Limit access to only approved endpoints, require multifactor authentication, and integrate with an identity and access management or single sign-on system. Use least-privilege and need-to-know principles for all accounts (e.g., user, admin, service, application).

Control IS-04: Log and monitor all accounts, whether for users or services, for unusual behavior and unwarranted uploads or downloads. Log and monitor all administration account access and actions through security management tools and security operation centers. Continuously monitor downloads for volume and unusual behavior patterns.

Control IS-05: Maintain an asset inventory for all tools, scripts, and APIs used by the development organization. Using origin and provenance information, validate the authenticity and integrity of the information in the asset inventory.

Control IS-06: Maintain patches and updates, where appropriate, for all applications, systems, and environments.

Control IS-07: Identify threats to applications, systems, and environments. Implement mitigating and compensating controls to prevent threats.

Control IS-08: Prioritize logging, monitoring, and patching of production environments. Integrate with SOC/SOAR/SIEM processes and systems.

Control IS-09: Document all software distribution paths and locations. Monitor distribution locations and deployments for malicious activity.

Control IS-10: Maintain an asset inventory (including tools, applications, services, and APIs) for the manufacturing and supply chain environments. Secure the environments with proper security and compensating controls. Log and monitor all events for devices and systems that have access to software or firmware.

Control IS-11: Contract agreements must clearly state the cybersecurity responsibilities for the infrastructure, access, logging, and monitoring throughout the customer staging process. This includes any customer-specific requirements, personnel access procedures, and change logs.

Control IS-12: Maintain an asset inventory for all applications, systems, tools, and scripts used by the service organization. Monitor all service endpoints and tools for malicious threats.

# Secure Development Lifecycle Controls

Control SDL-01: Maintain a secure development lifecycle (SDL) framework and policy that requires employees, contractors, and third parties to follow SDL practices for applications and products.

Control SDL-02: Document and maintain security requirements for applications and products. Include security requirements that are required by processes, controls, applicable laws, and regulations.

Control SDL-03: Use secure-by-design and privacy-by-design concepts when designing applications and products. Conduct threat modeling on all code, services, systems, infrastructure, APIs, and protocols.

Control SDL-04: Follow secure coding rules, leverage tools, and mitigate known weaknesses to develop secure products and applications.

Control SDL-05: Execute security testing using various tools and techniques on applications and products.

Control SDL-06: Maintain a vulnerability management framework, vulnerability handling policy, and vulnerability disclosure policy for identifying, evaluating, remediating, and disclosing vulnerabilities to external parties.

# Source Code, Build, and Deployment Controls

Control SCBD-01: Use only open source that is well supported and available from legitimate sources. Continuously review all open source code, including updates or patches, for malicious threats and vulnerabilities. Continuously review the source code maintainers and contributors for ownership risk.

Control SCBD-02: Review all open source and commercial licenses for agreement or potential license issues.

Control SCBD-03: Update or patch software, firmware, and code to resolve any remediated vulnerabilities.

Control SCBD-04: Review all generative AI licenses for property rights concerns. Review all generated code for risks, threats, vulnerabilities, and lack of quality.

Control SCBD-05: Maintain a set of secure coding standards specific to the platforms and code languages. Educate developers on secure coding practices.

Control SCBD-06: Use features and plugins for enhancing integrated development environments (IDEs) and Static Application Security Testing (SAST) tools to identify secure coding rules and vulnerable coding patterns. Use Software Composition Analysis (SCA) tools to identify vulnerabilities in open source.

Control SCBD-07: Establish and maintain strict change management policies for code, systems, applications, and environments.

Control SCBD-08: Document the provenance of source code. Review the country of origin and provenance, where possible, for security risks in source code.

Control SCBD-09: Internally host all code packages and library dependencies.

Control SCBD-10: Use ephemeral (short-living) environments for build and CI/CD processes. Perform repeatable and reproducible integrity checks on the build and deployments.

Control SCBD-11: Sign all code, drivers, scripts, and application files using a trusted Certificate Authority private key.

Control SCBD-12: Validate software package integrity through the deployment process by verifying certificates, signatures, and hashes.

# Cloud Controls

Control CLD-01: Document the roles and responsibilities of all parties who manage, administer, and operate cloud environments and applications.

Control CLD-02: Document security controls and requirements for cloud infrastructure and applications. Perform assessments to identify gaps and action plans.

Control CLD-03: Control cloud infrastructure and artifacts in source repositories. Implement change management that only allows changes to be made within repositories.

Control CLD-04: Secure and test all environments, applications, and connections, including APIs, with appropriate technologies and access control. Log and monitor all environments, applications, and connections.

Control CLD-05: Test and scan all aspects of cloud infrastructure, environment, and software.

Control CLD-06: Scan for and prevent changes directly to production environments. Deploy cloud environments using the immutable infrastructure technique.

Control CLD-07: Secure and monitor all connections to, and between, cloud environments, containers, and microservices.

# Intellectual Property and Data Controls

Control IPD-01: Maintain a data classification policy with definitions, criteria, and examples.

Control IPD-02: Maintain an ethics policy that references the data classification policy and the compliance responsibility for employees and contractors. Monitor for compliance with the policies and, when applicable, nondisclosure agreements.

Control IPD-03: Educate all employees and contractors about intellectual property and data loss risks with training on data classifications, ethics, and compliance.

Control IPD-04: Safeguard confidential and sensitive data in all infrastructure, technologies, and systems. Monitor systems and application logs for indicators of data loss.

Control IPD-05: Implement data security techniques to secure data at rest, in transit, and in use.

Control IPD-06: Maintain an artificial intelligence (AI) policy for the usage of public and private large language models (LLMs) in compliance with the data classification policy and data security requirements.

Control IPD-07: Monitor for data loss of code, secrets, certificates, and keys using technologies and services.

Control IPD-08: Implement key management systems to secure secrets, tokens, keys, and other intellectual property.

Control IPD-09: Use secure by design, privacy by design, threat modeling, security testing, and penetration testing to prevent, detect, and remediate design flaws.

Control IPD-10: Secure all infrastructure, system, and application configurations. Regularly review configurations and perform threat modeling to identify risks.

Control IPD-11: Design secure APIs and perform threat modeling, security testing, and penetration testing on APIs.

Control IPD-12: Patch vulnerabilities in infrastructure, systems, and applications to prevent IP and data loss.

# Software Transparency Controls

Control ST-01: Generate a software bill of materials (SBOM) for every production release of software.

Control ST-02: Establish a vulnerability disclosure process and publish vulnerability information based on the organization's disclosure criteria.

Control ST-03: Produce required transparency artifacts such as software attestations.

Control ST-04: Identify and utilize sharing mechanisms for software transparency artifacts.

Control ST-05: Capture provenance information for software, firmware, and hardware.

Control ST-06: Prepare and provide transparency packages for requested software, firmware, and hardware.

# Supplier Controls

Control SP-01: Incorporate cybersecurity into the supplier selection and evaluation processes.

Control SP-02: Research the supplier's cybersecurity posture for risk and transparency.

Control SP-03: Request evidence of a supplier's IT security controls specifically in defense of software development systems, environments, and infrastructure.

Control SP-04: Evaluate technology leadership at the supplier and request evidence of a supplier's application security organizational structure and accountability. Create relationships with cybersecurity leaders at critical suppliers.

Control SP-05: Request evidence of a supplier's secure development practices, frameworks, and controls.

Control SP-06: Request evidence of a supplier's training program for cybersecurity awareness, secure development lifecycle processes, secure coding, and security testing, along with the policy for mandatory training prior to development.

Control SP-07: Request evidence or a demonstration of a supplier's secure development practices that include threat modeling, secure coding practices, static code analysis, and security testing.

Control SP-08: Request evidence or a demonstration of a supplier's build management, DevSecOps, and release management practices, including tools, reports, processes, access controls, approvals, and logs for tools and event management systems.

Control SP-09: Request evidence of a supplier's scanning, vulnerability management, and patching processes, including policies, procedures, reports, logs, and patching service-level agreements.

Control SP-10: Request evidence of a supplier's management practices and reports for cloud infrastructure, access controls, keys, configurations, testing, responsibilities, and service-level agreements.

Control SP-11: Request evidence of a supplier's development services, including code quality reports, test reports, and vulnerabilities. When applicable, request developer information such as locations and evidence of background checks.

Control SP-12: Request evidence of a supplier's access controls and integrity checks for any personnel or process that has access to software or firmware.

Control SP-13: Incorporate cyber agreements into the supplier contracting process that include cyber risk and minimum security standards according to the purchasing organization's policies.

Control SP-14: Incorporate cyber topics and monitoring into the existing supplier management process. Monitoring and reviews should include vulnerabilities, data breaches, and supply chain issues and may require an audit or reassessment.

# Manufacturing and Device Security Controls

Control MDS-01: Validate that manufactured devices were designed, developed, manufactured, tested, and shipped using information security, cybersecurity, and data security best practices.

Control MDS-02: Institute clear policies and procedures for access to secured facilities. Train all personnel on the physical controls and procedures. Maintain and test physical security controls for the organization and locations.

Control MDS-03: Using the information available in the hardware bill of materials (HBOM) and software bill of materials (SBOM), authenticate the components and conduct integrity checks throughout the manufacturing process on any chips, integrated circuits, components, firmware, and embedded software.

Control MDS-04: Verify that chips, components, and products are authentic before using them in the manufacturing process.

Control MDS-05: Trace the physical and digital parts, components, and products through the supply chain to capture the chain of custody for the product.

Control MDS-06: Implement hardware, firmware, and embedded software protection measures within the device.

# People Controls

Control PPL-01: Establish and maintain a corporate security organization with experienced and well-trained cybersecurity resources. Encourage certification and continuing education of your security staff.

Control PPL-02: Establish and maintain a security champions community to engage the organization, raise awareness, expand cybersecurity knowledge, and improve the adoption of cybersecurity principles and policies.

Control PPL-03: Provide a cybersecurity training and awareness program for all roles in the organization. Track completion of mandatory and optional courses.

# Index

## A

access control
  for code repositories, 43
  for labs and test environments, 46
access credentials, stolen, 115
Adobe PDF SBOMs, 135
adversary techniques, curated, 57
Agile, 44
  4-1 SDL standard and, 63
  guidance for practitioners, 67
  management systems for, 44
  Microsoft SDL and, 64
AI (artificial intelligence)
  AI-BOM, 139
  data loss by Microsoft AI research team, 121
  generative AI source code, 79
  source code generated by, no provenance information, 146
  use of intellectual property and private data to train models, security concerns with, 118
  use with SIEM tools, 109
air gapping, 47
Amazon S3 bucket, misconfiguration leading to data breach, 123
American Institute of Certified Public Accountants (AICPA)
  SOC 2 Type 2 report, 160
  suite of system and organization controls (SOC), 100
analysis technologies (software), 81
Apache Log4j, software vulnerabilities in, 5, 48
API gateway, 106
APIs

API-based attestation sharing, 142
  data risks through, 122
  securing in cloud environments, 106
Apple, iOS 15.5 code leak, 115
Apple's Xcode development environment, XcodeGhost malware attack on, 44
application programming interfaces (see APIs)
application security, 55, 57
  ISO/IEC 27034 standard, 65
  metrics on, 68
  testing, 59
  tools and techniques for, 60
application stores, 48
applications
  SDL training for accountable people, 186
  security organization, 156
  standards and certifications for, 56
ASCs (application security controls), 65
assessments (see cyber assessments of suppliers)
asset inventories
  for infrastructure security, 45
  for manufacturing and supply chain environments, 51
  for service systems and tools, 52
ASUS and CCleaner supply chain attacks, 87
attacks
  continual updating of attack paths, 56
  social engineering, examples of, 184
  on supply chains, 1
    impacts of software supply chain security breaches, 3-5
  UEFI as popular attack surface, 179
audits, right to audit suppliers, 166

checksums
    comparing for build reproducibility, 88
    integrity checks with, 174
chief information security officer (see CISO)
chief product security officer (CPSO), 156
chief security officer (CSO), 182
China, software supply chain security regulations and requirements, 6
China-based CNVD, 155, 165
CI/CD (continuous integration/continuous deployment) tools, 44
    ephemeral environments for build processes, 88
    SLSA framework and, 83
CIA (confidentiality, integrity, and availability), 39
CircleCI, loss of keys, 119
"CIS Software Supply Chain Security Guide", 83
CISA (Cybersecurity & Infrastructure Agency), 61
    SBOM uses and practices, 133
    Secure Software Development Attestation Common Form, 141
CISA ICT SCRM Task Force—Small Business template, 153
CISA Known Exploited Vulnerabilities (KEV) Catalog, 155
CISA NRMC—Vendor Supply Chain Risk Management (SCRM) Template, 153
Cisco Trust Portal, cybersecurity information on, 155
CISM certification, 182
CISO (chief information security officer), 154, 156, 182
CISSP certification, 182
cloud, 95-102
    about, 95
    API security, 106
    change management, 103
    cloud container and deployment testing, 59
    cloud management tools, 44
    cloud SDL, 65
    common cloud models, capabilities, and connections, 95
    dependencies in, 86
    deploying immutable infrastructure and applications in, 107

deployment packages or containerized services for software, 48
evaluating cloud applications and environments for potential suppliers, 160
IT security, 155
misconfiguration of cloud data repositories, 121
operating and monitoring, 109
"Practices for Secure Development of Cloud Applications", 67
secure design and development for applications, 105
securing connections, 108
security controls for, 195
security frameworks, controls, and assessments, 97-102
    American Institute of CPAs SOC 2, 100
    Cloud Security Alliance CCM and CAIQ, 98
    Cloud Security Alliance STAR program, 99
    ISO/IEC 27001 information security management systems, 97
    security considerations and requirements, 101-102
    US FedRAMP, 100
shared security responsibilities, 96
sharing SBOMs through private or SaaS clouds, 144
site reliability engineering, 110
testing environments and applications, 107
training in DevSecOps and cloud security, 187
Cloud Security Alliance
    Cloud Controls Matrix (CCM), 97, 98
    Consensus Assessment Initiative Questionnaire (CAIQ), 97, 98
    Security, Trust, Assurance, and Risk (STAR) Registry, 99
Clubhouse, data leak through API, 122
CMMI (Capability Maturity Model Integration), 69
COBIT (see Control Objectives for Information and Related Technologies (COBIT) 2019)
code
    embedded, 78
    integrity of, testing in manufacturing, 175
    reducing code bloat, 130
code development frameworks, 44

code editors, 44
code integrity in manufacturing, 174
code quality, 80-82
    code reviews, 82
    software analysis technologies, 81
code quality tools, 59
code repositories
    accidental release of code to, 119
    cloud, change management in, 104
    public, open source code in, 76
    security controls for, 42
    training development teams on use of, 187
code reviews, 82
    line-by-line review of open source code, 76
    training development teams for, 186
code signing, 88
    firmware public key infrastructure, 178
    signature and certificate validation, 90
    signing software before distribution, 49
code, software, and firmware integrity (in manufacturing), 174-176
Codecov hack, 90
collaboration tools, 44
Colonial Pipeline, ransomware attack on, 2
commercial off-the-shelf (COTS) ICT providers, 33
commercial source code, 78
    software termination and, 164
Common Criteria for Assessing Risk (CCfAR), 31
common security advisory framework (CSAF), 140
    monitoring CSAF files of suppliers, 165
common vulnerabilities and exposures (see CVEs)
Common Vulnerability Scoring System (CVSS), 61
Common Weakness Enumerations (CWEs), 121, 186
compensating controls, 47, 61
Computer Security Resource Center (CSRC), 3
"Concise Guide for Evaluating Open Source Software" (OpenSSF), 77
configuration drifts, 108
configurations
    configuration errors leading to data or intellectual property loss, 121
    security of, 119

consensus assessment initiative questionnaire (CAIQ), 98
containers, 48, 96, 104
    ephemeral build environment, 88
    hermetic (no network access) environment for), 86
    network traffic between, 109
    security considerations for, 101
    security testing, 59
    testing, 107
contract manufacturing (CM), 170
Control Objectives for Information and Related Technologies (COBIT) 2019, 22-24
    controls implementing COBIT IT objectives, 23
    governance principles, 22
counterfeits in manufacturing, 176
CPSO (chief product security officer), 156
CREST OVS (OWASP Verification Standard), 56
critical infrastructure, suppliers to, 35
cryptography
    cryptographic data in secure elements, 179
    data encryption, 117
        encryption techniques, 117
    public/private key, 88
    requirements at the marketing level, 56
    secure cryptoprocessor international standard, 178
    strong encryptions and protocols to secure connections, 109
CSA (see Cloud Security Alliance)
CSAF (common security advisory framework), 140
    monitoring CSAF files of suppliers, 165
CSO (chief security officer), 182
CSPs (cloud service providers)
    authorization for service from US FedRAMP, 100
    requirement to pass SOC 2 audits, 100
CSSLP certification, 183
CSV files, SBOMs in, 135
CTF (capture-the-flag) events, 187
customer projects and field services, cybersecurity education for, 189
customer staging for acceptance tests, 51
customer, company, and supplier relationships, 152

integrity in manufacturing environments, 174

normal boot versus secure boot process, 178

supply chain security for, 2

firmware public key infrastructure (PKI), 178

public key for digital certificates, 120

first party, 151

Forum of Incident Response and Security Teams (FIRST), 61

4-1 SDL (see ISA/IEC 62443 standards)

frameworks and standards (see supply chain frameworks and standards)

frameworks, embedded, 78

free and open source software (FOSS), 3

tools for locating faults in, 59

fuzz testing, 59

## G

generative AI

source code, 79

source code generated by, no provenance information, 146

GitHub, 76

accidental release of code to, 119

GitHub Copilot, 79

litigation against, 146

Google Dependency Management guide, 86

Google SLSA (Supply-Chain Levels for Software Artifacts) framework, 42, 83

Google, confidential code loss, 119

Google, Graph for Understanding Artifact Composition, 144

governments, suppliers to, 35

Graph for Understanding Artifact Composition (GUAC), 144

## H

hardware

supply chain security for, 2

UEFI-supported for secure boot, 179

hardware bill of materials (HBOM), 139, 175

hardware root of trust, 178

hardware trusted platform modules (TPMs), 178

hardware, software, and firmware (cell phone), 3

hash algorithms

decryption in certificate validation, 90

MD5, SHA1, and SHA256, 88

HBOM (see hardware bill of materials)

healthcare suppliers, 35

HTTP Strict Transport Security (HSTS), 109

HTTPS, 109

human error, 115

human machine interfaces (HMIs), 172

human-readable SBOMS, 135

hypervisors, 40

## I

IaC (infrastructure as code), 41

IACS (industrial automation and control system) assessments, 189

ICs (see integrated circuits)

ICS (industrial control systems), 57

use of ISA/IEC 62443-4-1 SDL by developers, 63

ICT (see information and communications technology (ICT) providers)

Idaho National Laboratory—Cyber Security Evaluation Tool (CSET), 153

identity and access management (IAM)

not allowing development teams to self-manage the code repository, 43

IDEs (integrated development environments), 44

feedback from to improve secure coding, 81

IEC (International Electrotechnical Commission), 62

IETF (Internet Engineering Task Force), SCITT working group, 142

IIoT (Industrial IoT), 169

products used by manufacturers, 172

immutable infrastructure, 108

in-toto attestation, 145

industrial automation and control system (IACS) assessments, 189

industrial control systems (ICS), 57

use of ISA/IEC 62443-4-1 SDL by developers, 63

information and communications technology (ICT) providers, 33

standards of interest, 26

Information Security Continuous Monitoring (ISCM) tool, 110

information security management systems (ISMS), 97

Information Systems Audit and Controls Association (ISACA), 22

ISO/IEC 27001 Information Security Management Systems standard, 24, 97
ISO/IEC 27034 Application Security, 65
ISO/IEC 27034 Application Security Control (ASC), 66, 163
ISO/IEC 27036 (Information Security for Supplier Relationships) standard, 34
IT
    connectable, security risks with products, 169
    device authentication, 179
    malware and intrusion detection scanning, 46
    manufacturing and distribution personnel, educating in cybersecurity, 189
    products used by manufacturers, 172
    security in manufacturing environments, 172
    security practices, developer environments and, 41
    security, including environmental security, 155
IT controls framework (COBIT 2019), 22-24

## J

Jenkins, zero-day bugs in plugins, 45
JSON files, SBOMs in, 135
jump server, 41

## K

key management practices, 120
key management tools, 120
keys, 119
    (see also public key infrastructure)
knowledge bases of curated adversary techniques, 57
known exploited vulnerabilities (KEVs)
    beginning with when prioritizing vulnerabilities, 61
    CISA Known Exploited Vulnerabilities Catalog, 155
    in cyber agreements with suppliers, 163
Known Exploited Vulnerability (KEV) catalog, 61

## L

labeling programs for IoT devices, 67
labs and test environments

security controls for, 46-47
large language models (LLMs), disclosing confidential data, 118
lateral movement attacks, 47
laws, regulations, guidance, and directives (software supply chain security), 5-10
licenses
    for generative AI source code, 80
    for open source code, 77
    knowing and complying with, 130
LinkedIn
    data leak through API, 122
Linux Foundation, SDL training, 186
LLMs (large language models), disclosing confidential data, 118
Lockheed Martin, Cyber Kill Chain® framework, 57
Log4j
    remote code execution attacks on, 48
    software vulnerabilities in, 5
logging
    assessing for potential suppliers, 159
    in cloud environments, 109
    exfiltration of data from logging libraries, 123
    for labs and test environments, 46
    for preproduction and production environments, 48
low-code or no-code, 79

## M

Mac operating systems, automatic updates, 79
machine learning (ML)
    ML-BOM, 139
malicious code injections, 42
malware
    attack on 3CX Desktop App, 42
    included in signed live chat software in 2022, 49
    injected during build process, 86
    XcodeGhost malware in 2015, 44
manufacturing (suppliers), 161
manufacturing and supply chain environments, 50
manufacturing execution systems (MES), 172
manufacturing security, 169-177, 188
    chain of custody, 177
    code, software, and firmware integrity, 174-176

over-the-air (OTA) updates, 164
OWASP (Open Worldwide Application Security Project), 59
OWASP A04:2021—Insecure Design, 121
OWASP API Security Top 10, 106, 122
OWASP CycloneDX working group, 134
OWASP Low-Code/No-Code Top 10 list, 79
OWASP SAMM (Software Assurance Maturity Model), 69
OWASP Top 10 CWEs, 121, 186
OWASP Top 10 lists, sources on potential weaknesses, 105
OWASP "Key Management Cheat Sheet", 120

## P

Parler, Clubhouse, and LinkedIn, data leaks through APIs, 122
patch management
    in cyber agreements with suppliers, 164
    for labs and test environments, 46
    in an OT environment, 51
patches
    evaluating patching practices for potential suppliers, 159
    operating systems and frameworks, 78
    patching in cloud environments, 104
    patching systems to prevent data loss from vulnerabilities, 123
    of production environments, 48
    security control for, 57
    SLA for in cyber agreements with suppliers, 163
    in vulnerability management, 61
PbD (privacy by design), 58
penetration testing, 46, 59
    compliance metrics for, 68
people contributing to theft or loss of intellectual property or data, 115
people in the software supply chain, 181-190
    customer projects and field services, cybersecurity education for, 189
    cybersecurity awareness and training, 184
    cybersecurity organizational structures, 182
    development teams, educating in cybersecurity, 185-187
    capture-the-flag events, 187
    DevSecOps and cloud, 187
    secure development lifecycle, 185
    source code management, 186

end users, 189
    manufacturing and distribution, cybersecurity training for personnel, 188
    security champions, 183
    security controls for, 199
    third-party suppliers, 188
permissions, 51
    in build management processes, 87
    for DevSecOps pipeline, 104
    excessive, 121
    modification of, 42
personal health information (PHI), 114
personal identifiable information (PII), 114
phishing training tools, 185
physical products or components for labs or testing environments, 46
physical security, 174
PKI (see public key infrastructure)
PLCs (see programmable logic controls)
PowerShell, 52
practices and technology, information about, 147
prebuild SBOM tools, 134
preconfigured environments, 41
preproduction (or staging) environments
    security controls for, 48
printed circuit board assembly (PCBA), 169
privacy by design (PbD), 58
privacy protection standards, 171
privacy regulations, identifying violations of, 118
private data, use in training AI models, concerns with, 118
privileges, 43
    (see also permissions)
    elevating access privileges, 41
    least-privilege controls for preproduction and production environments, 48
product and application security metrics, 68
product security, 58
    (see also application security)
product/application security organization, 156
production environments
    alerts and, 41
    security controls for, 48
products
    SDL training for accountable people, 186
    security processes and secure development lifecycle, 157

## About the Author

**Cassie Crossley** is an experienced cybersecurity technology executive in information technology and product development. She has many years of business and technical leadership experience in secure software supply chain, cybersecurity, product/application security, software/firmware development, program management, and data privacy. Cassie has designed frameworks and operating models for end-to-end security in software development lifecycles, third-party risk management, cybersecurity governance, and cybersecurity initiatives. She is a member of the CISA/NTIA SBOM working groups and presents frequently on the topic of SBOMs and software supply chain security.

Cassie has held positions at Schneider Electric, Ceridian, Hewlett-Packard, McAfee, Lotus, and IBM. She has an MBA from California State University, Fresno, and a bachelor of science degree in technical and professional communication with a specialization in computer science from Southern Polytechnic State University (now consolidated into Kennesaw State University).

## Colophon

The animal on the cover of *Software Supply Chain Security* is an Indochinese roller (*Coracias affinis*), also known as a Burmese roller. The Indochinese roller is stocky and brightly colored. Its wings, tail, and belly are covered in various shades of blue, from sky blue to deep indigo. The bird's brilliant colors are best observed while it is in flight with its wings spread wide. It has a long, compressed bill with a hooked tip.

The Indochinese roller can be found across eastern India and Southeast Asia. It prefers open areas, such as grasslands and agricultural land, and it can also be found in scrub forests. This bird enjoys perching on trees and wires along roadsides.

Fortunately, Indochinese rollers are considered to be of least concern on endangered species lists. However, many of the animals on O'Reilly covers are endangered; all of them are important to the world.

The cover illustration is by Karen Montgomery, based on an antique line engraving from Lydekker's *Royal Natural History*. The series design is by Edie Freedman, Ellie Volckhausen, and Karen Montgomery. The cover fonts are Gilroy Semibold and Guardian Sans. The text font is Adobe Minion Pro; the heading font is Adobe Myriad Condensed; and the code font is Dalton Maag's Ubuntu Mono.

Printed in the USA
CPSIA information can be obtained
at www.ICGtesting.com
JSHW050026090724
66058JS00007B/102

9 781098 133702